W9-BIW-899

INSTRUCTOR'S MANUAL

to accompany

THE LONGMAN READER
Seventh Edition

Judith Nadell

John Langan
Atlantic Cape Community College

Eliza A. Comodromos
Rutgers, The State University of New Jersey

PEARSON
Longman

New York Boston San Francisco
London Toronto Sydney Tokyo Singapore Madrid
Mexico City Munich Paris Cape Town Hong Kong Montreal

> **⚠ This work is protected by United States copyright laws and is provided solely for the use of instructors in teaching their courses and assessing student learning. Dissemination or sale of any part of this work (including on the World Wide Web) will destroy the integrity of the work and is not permitted. The work and materials from it should never be made available to students except by instructors using the accompanying text in their classes. All recipients of this work are expected to abide by these restrictions and to honor the intended pedagogical purposes and the needs of other instructors who rely on these materials.**

Instructor's Manual to accompany Nadell/Langan/Comodromos, *The Longman Reader, Seventh Edition*

Copyright ©2005 Pearson Education, Inc.

All rights reserved. Printed in the United States of America. Instructors may reproduce portions of this book for classroom use only. All other reproductions are strictly prohibited without prior permission of the publisher, except in the case of brief quotations embodied in critical articles and reviews.

ISBN: 0-321-25935-1

5 6 7 8 9 10–DPC–07 06 05

CONTENTS

EXEMPLIFICATION 44

DIVISION-CLASSIFICATION   58

PROCESS ANALYSIS   74

COMPARISON-CONTRAST   88

CAUSE-EFFECT   102

DEFINITION   118

ARGUMENTATION-PERSUASION   132

COMBINING THE PATTERNS   163

TEACHING COMPOSITION
WITH THE
LONGMAN READER

Teaching offers many pleasures. Among the foremost, for us, is the chance to get together with colleagues for some shoptalk. Trading ideas, airing problems, sharing light moments, speculating about why some assignments set off fireworks and some fizzle—all this helps us in our day-to-day teaching.

In this Instructor's Manual, we would like to share with you some thoughts about teaching freshman composition and about using **THE LONGMAN READER.** We'll explain our approach for introducing each pattern of development and indicate what we emphasize when discussing the professional essays in each section. Also, we'll offer possible answers to the "Questions for Close Reading" and "Questions About the Writer's Craft" that follow each professional essay. These responses aren't meant to be definitive. Although we purposely avoided open-ended, anything-goes questions, we understand that the responses represent *our* view only. You may not agree with all our interpretations. That's fine. If nothing else, our answers may suggest another way of viewing an essay.

AT THE START OF THE COURSE

Frankly, many students dread freshman composition—a bitter pill to swallow for those of us who have made the teaching of writing our life's work. But it's important to understand that many students' past experiences with writing have not been positive. Rather than trying to pretend that all our students are pleased about being in a writing class, we work to get out in the open any unhappiness they may have about writing and writing teachers.

Here's how we go about airing any negative feelings that may exist. On the first day of class, we acknowledge students' feelings by saying something like this: "I guess some of you wish you didn't have to take this course. In fact, you may feel that the only thing worse would be having to take a course in public speaking." Our remark elicits smiles of self-recognition from many students, and the whole class seems to relax a bit. Then we ask students to explain why they approach the writing course with such uneasy feelings. Many have sad tales to tell about writing courses and writing teachers. Here are summaries of some of the comments we've heard over the years:

- In the past, my papers were returned so covered with red ink that I could barely make out my own writing. I felt discouraged to see how much I had done wrong and angry to see my work covered over with comments.
- I could never figure out what my teachers wanted. Different teachers seemed to look for different things. Since there were no clear standards, I've never understood the qualities that make up good writing.
- Writing papers always took me too much time and felt like an endless chore. Getting the first draft done was hard enough, but revising was even worse. And the payoff for writing several drafts didn't seem worth the effort.

- I knew in my head what I wanted to say but didn't know how to get my thoughts down on paper. My ideas never came out quite right. I had writer's block whenever I sat down to put pen to paper. I stared at the desk, daydreamed, fidgeted, and had real trouble getting started. Finally, just before an assignment was due, I dashed off something to hand in, just to get it over with.

As such sentiments are aired, students discover that their experience has not been unique; they learn that others in class have had similarly frustrating experiences. We also confirm students' impressions by telling them that each semester many students recount comparable sagas of woe. We reassure the class that we understand the obstacles, both inner and outer, they have to face when writing. And we tell them that we will work to make the freshman writing course as positive an experience as possible. But we also say that we'd be dishonest if we led them to believe that writing is easy. It isn't. We have no magic formula for turning them into A-plus writers. On the other hand, because we are writers and because we work with writers, we know that the composing process can be satisfying and rewarding. We tell the class that we hope they'll come to share our feelings as the semester progresses.

From here, we move to an activity that continues to break the ice while familiarizing the class with the workshop format we use at various points in the semester. Students form groups of two and then four, chatting with each other for about five minutes each time. To get them moving, we put some questions on the board: what are their names, where are they from, where are they living while attending college, what other courses are they taking, what is their intended major, and so on. After a few seconds of nervous silence, the class begins to buzz with friendly energy.

When ten minutes or so have passed, we stop the activity and explain why we "wasted" precious class time just socializing. During the semester, we explain, they will learn a good deal about writing from other classmates as they meet in small groups and respond to each other's work. So it makes sense for them to get to know each other a bit right at the outset. Also, we tell the class that we hope they will find sharing their writing as interesting and fun as chatting together. As a final step in building a spirit of community, we circulate a piece of paper on which each student writes his or her name and e-mail address. Before the next class, we have the sheet typed and reproduced so that everyone can have a copy of the class directory.

ASSIGNING THE FIRST TWO CHAPTERS IN THE BOOK

During the first or second class, we emphasize to students that the course should help them become sharper readers as well as stronger writers. With that in mind, we assign the chapter on "The Reading Process" as well as the chapter on "The Writing Process," up to the section titled "Organize the Evidence" (page 39). While the writing chapter may be assigned all at once, we've found that it works more effectively when broken into two assignments. Since the writing process *is* at the heart of the course, we want to make sure students read the chapter carefully enough to understand the process fully.

When students return to class having read the reading chapter and the first part of the writing chapter, we answer any questions they may have and go over the answers for the activities in the writing chapter (see page 12 of this manual). Then we move into a discussion of prewriting. We tell the class that prewriting loosens a writer up. Exploratory and tentative, prewriting helps reduce the anxiety many people feel when facing the blank page. With prewriting, a writer doesn't have to worry, "This better be good." After all, no one except the writer is going to read the prewritten material.

The best way for students to discover what prewriting is like is for them to try it for themselves. So, we say, "Let's suppose you had to write an essay on why students dislike English classes or what teachers could do to make English courses more interesting." Then we ask them to select one prewriting technique discussed in the book (questioning the subject, brainstorming, freewriting, or mapping) to generate the raw material for such an essay. Often, we distribute scrap paper or yellow lined paper for them to use, reinforcing the message that prewriting is tentative and vastly different from finished work.

At the end of the class, we ask students to use the prewriting just prepared in class as the basis for the first draft of an essay. And we assign the rest of the writing chapter, telling students to pay special attention to the guidelines in the chapter, especially those in the sections "Organize the Evidence" and "Writing the First Draft."

At the start of the next class, we review the rest of the writing chapter and discuss the answers to the chapter's activities. We've found that many students do not understand that writing is a process. Having them go through the sequence described in the chapter introduces them to the concept of a writing process and shows them what one such process might be like. Now that they have had a taste of the writing process, it is time to explain (as the book does on pages 13, 20, 29–30, 36–37, and 46–47) that each writer customizes the steps in the sequence to suit his or her needs and style. Not everyone writes the same way, we emphasize, and we urge students to choose the approach that works best for them.

Students then take out the first draft of their papers. But we do not have them hand in the essays. Instead, we have them get back into the same groups of two they were in the previous class and spend about ten minutes giving each other feedback on the effectiveness of the drafts. To focus their observations, they are asked to use the checklist on the book's inside front cover. After hearing their partner's response to their work, students get busy revising their essay right there in class. We then collect the papers, promising only to read—not grade—them. Reviewing the papers, we explain, will give us a good sense of what each writer does well and what needs to be worked on. Finally, we end the class by telling students that we don't expect them to have mastered all the material in the book's first two chapters. But now that they have read the chapters carefully and have worked through the reading and writing processes, they should have a clear sense of how to proceed during the rest of the semester. We assure them that throughout the course we will refer to the opening two chapters as need arises.

WAYS TO USE THE BOOK

THE LONGMAN READER is arranged according to nine patterns of development: description, narration, exemplification, division-classification, process analysis, comparison-contrast, cause-effect, definition, and argumentation-persuasion. Introductions to the patterns are designed to help students understand the distinctive features of specific rhetorical strategies. The more accessible experiential patterns are presented first, before moving on to the more demanding analytic patterns.

If you adopt a rhetorical approach in the course, you need not feel confined by the order of patterns in the book; each chapter is self-contained, making it possible for you to sequence the modes however you wish. And, of course, there's no need to cover all the essays in a chapter or even all the rhetorical patterns. It is more realistic to assign two or three selections per pattern, perhaps concentrating on one of the selections for class discussion. A word of warning: If you tell a class which of several assigned selections will be discussed, some students will skip the other selections. You'll probably want to explain to students that there are many ways to use a rhetorical pattern and that reading *all* the assigned essays will give them an understanding of the options available.

For rhetorically organized courses, we suggest that you emphasize early in the semester that professional writers don't set out to write an essay in a particular mode. The patterns emerge as the writers prewrite and organize their ideas; they come to see that their points can best be made through a particular rhetorical strategy or combination of strategies.

It's helpful, we've learned, to assign selections before *and* after students write an essay. For example, if students are going to write a causal analysis, you might have them read "Our Schedules, Our Selves." Then, after reviewing their drafts and seeing the problems they have had with, let's say, causal chains, you might have them examine the way Darley and Latané trace complex causal relationships in "Why People Don't Help in a Crisis."

Some instructors using a rhetorical approach in their courses place a special emphasis on exposition. If this is your orientation, you might want to begin with the exemplification chapter. That section stresses the importance of establishing a clear thesis and providing solid support for the essay's central point. Then you might move to the description and narration chapters; these underscore the importance of, respectively, a dominant impression and a narrative point, both developed through specific supporting details.

If you prefer to design the course around themes rather than rhetorical patterns, the thematic table of contents (at the front of the textbook) will help you select essays on timely issues. For such a course, we recommend that you have students read a number of essays on a given theme. The fact that several essays on the same theme use different rhetorical strategies helps students see that the patterns are not ends in themselves, but techniques that writers use to make their points.

CREATING A PROCESS-ORIENTED CLASS ENVIRONMENT

We've found that creating a workshop atmosphere in the classroom helps students view writing as a process. When a new paper is assigned, we try to give students several minutes to start their prewriting in class. In other classes, time may be set aside for students to rework parts of their first draft. We may, for instance, ask them to sharpen their introductions, conclusions, sentence structure, or transitions.

In our experience, it's been especially productive to use class time for peer evaluations of first drafts. For these peer review sessions, students may be paired with one other classmate or they may meet with three or four other classmates. (We've found groups of more than five unwieldy.) Feedback from someone other than the course instructor motivates students to put in more time on a draft. Otherwise, some of them will skip the revision stage altogether; as soon as they've got a draft down on paper, they'll want to hand it in. Hearing from other classmates that a point is not clear or that a paragraph is weakly developed encourages students to see that revision involves more than mechanical tinkering. They start to understand that revision often requires wholesale rethinking and reworking of parts of the essay. And, after a few feedback sessions, students begin to identify for themselves the problem areas in their writing.

You'll find that many students squirm at the thought of reacting to their classmates' work. So it's not surprising that they tend to respond to each other's papers with either indiscriminate praise or unhelpful neutrality. To guide students, we prepare a brief checklist of points to consider when responding to each other's work. (You might, for example, adapt the checklist on the inside front cover or those in each of the pattern chapters to fit a particular assignment.) With such a checklist in front of them, students are able to focus their impressions and provide constructive feedback.

There are a number of ways to set up peer review sessions. Here are a few possibilities:

- After pairing students or placing them in small groups, have each essay read aloud by someone other than the author. Students tell us that hearing another person read what they've written is invaluable. Awkward or unclear passages in a paper become more obvious when someone who has never before seen the essay reads it aloud.
- Place students in small groups and ask them to circulate their papers (in hard-copy or via e-mail) so that everyone has a chance to read all the essays. Then have each group select one especially effective paper to read aloud to the rest of the class. Alternately, you may ask each group to select a strong essay that needs work in a few spots. These essays are then read aloud to the rest of the class. Everyone discusses each paper's strengths and what might be done to sharpen the sections that miss the mark.
- Ask one or two students to photocopy their drafts of an assignment, making copies so that everyone can look at the papers. In class, the other students—either as a whole or in groups—react to the papers up for scrutiny that day.

A quick aside: At the start of the course, students are reluctant to "offer their papers up for sacrifice"—as one student put it. But once they're accustomed to the process, they are not at all skittish and even volunteer to be "put on the chopping block"—another student's words. They know that the feedback received will be invaluable when the time comes to revise.

As you no doubt can tell, we have a special liking for group work. Since it gives students the chance to see how others approach the same assignment, they come to appreciate the personal dimension of writing and develop an awareness of rhetorical options. The peer process also multiplies the feedback students get for their work, letting them see that their instructor is just one among many readers. Group activities thus help students gain a clearer sense of purpose and audience. Finally, we have found that peer review encourages students to be more active in the classroom. When students assume some of the tasks traditionally associated with the instructor, the whole class becomes more animated.

SOME CAUTIONS ABOUT GROUP WORK

If you are new to group work, you may have the uneasy feeling that the group process can deteriorate into enjoyable but unproductive rap sessions. That *can* happen if the instructor does not guide the process carefully.

Here are several suggestions to steer you clear of some traps that can ensnare group activities. First, we recommend you give very clear instructions about how students are to proceed. Providing a checklist, for example, directs students to specific issues you want them to address. Second, we believe in establishing a clear time schedule for each group activity. We might say, "Take five minutes to read to yourself the paper written by the person on your left," or "Now that all the papers in your group have been read, you should vote to determine which is the strongest paper. Then take five minutes to identify one section of the essay that needs additional attention." Third, although we try to be as inconspicuous as possible during group work, we let students know that we are available for help when needed. Sometimes we circulate among the groups, listening to comments, asking a question or two. But more often we stay at the desk and encourage students to consult with us when they think our reaction would be helpful.

RESPONDING TO STUDENT WORK

Beyond the informal, in-class consultations just described, we also meet during the course with each student for several one-on-one conferences of about fifteen to thirty minutes. Depending on our purpose, student needs, class size, and availability of time, a number of things may occur during the individual conferences. We may review a paper that has already been graded and commented on, highlighting the paper's strengths and underscoring what needs to be done to sharpen the essay. Or we may use the conference to return and discuss a recent essay that has or has not been graded. In the last few years, we have tended not to grade or write comments on papers we're going to review in conference. Instead, we take informal notes about the papers and refer to them when meeting with students. We've found that this approach encourages students to interact with us more freely since their attention isn't riveted to the comments and grade already recorded on the paper. Finally, we end each conference by jotting down a brief list of what the student needs to concentrate on when revising or writing the next assignment. Students tell us this individualized checklist lets them know exactly what they should pay attention to in their work.

When students hand in the final draft of a paper, we ask them to include their individualized checklist. Having a checklist for each student enables us to focus on the elements that typically give the student trouble. And, candidly, having the checklist in front of us tames our not-so-noble impulse to pounce on every problem in an essay.

In our oral and written comments, we try to emphasize what's strong in the essay and limit discussion of problems to the most critical points. Like everyone else, students are apt to overlook what they've done well and latch on to things that haven't been so successful. If every error a student makes is singled out for criticism, the student—again, like everyone else—often feels overwhelmed and defeated. So unless a student is obviously lackadaisical and would profit from some hard-hitting, teacherly rebukes, we try to make our comments as positive and encouraging as possible. And rather than filling the paper with reworked versions of, let's say, specific sentences and paragraphs, we make liberal use of such remarks as these: "Read these last three sentences aloud. Do you hear the awkwardness? How could you streamline these sentences?" Or "Doesn't this paragraph contradict what you say at the beginning of the preceding paragraph? What could you do to eliminate the confusion?"

When responding to a paper, we often suggest that the student review or reread a professional essay, the introduction to a rhetorical pattern, or sections of the writing chapter. And we always end our comments with a brief list of points to be added to the student's personalized checklist.

USING PORTFOLIOS TO ASSESS
STUDENT PROGRESS

You may wish to have your students present a portfolio of their work for grading at the conclusion of the course, instead of giving grades for each paper in succession. Using such a portfolio system alters somewhat the way you respond to individual student papers as they are submitted, because you assign no grades to them. The written and oral feedback on a paper is geared solely to making the essay a more effective piece of communication rather than to justifying a particular low or high grade. This forces all concerned—instructors and students—to stay focused on how to improve writing rather than on what might pull a paper down or on what score a paper should get. If students balk at "floating free" of grades for the whole course, you might occasionally supply a tentative grade or give students grades on one or two essays so they get a feel for the standards. As the course progresses, however, the issue of what constitutes a strong paper should be resolved. The students will be reading the successful papers in the text, examining and commenting on the essays of other students, and hearing a plenitude of helpful comments about writing.

You should indicate clearly at the start of the course that students must complete each essay as well as all other practices, journal entries, and so forth that you assign, but that the writing component of their final grade will be based upon a portfolio of polished work. Clearly establish the minimum number of essays to be included in a completed portfolio. Typically, a course might be represented by four final-draft essays, plus some late-in-the-term in-class writing. In addition, you may wish to examine the successive drafts for one of the revised papers. In order to receive a grade, each student meets with the instructor for a conference about the writing progress demonstrated in the portfolio. After discussing the writing's strengths and areas needing improvement, the instructor and student agree on a grade.

Such a portfolio system has several advantages. It stresses to students that writing well is an ongoing process and encourages them to make subsequent revisions of their essays as they acquire new insights into writing. It forces them to take responsibility for their progress beyond the achievement they reach in the first submitted version of an essay. It instills the notion of a writing community, for once they have gotten beyond the initial series of structured feedback sessions which you have built into the course, students must initiate feedback from their peers and from the instructor on any revisions they do. Finally, such a system dramatizes the reality that writers write for other people, and that reaching the audience, not jumping hurdles to get a grade, is the goal of writing.

AT THE END OF THE COURSE

Even if you don't use formal portfolios for grading, we suggest you ask students to present their best revised work to you at the end of the semester. Our students keep all their papers in a folder, and so have no trouble retrieving essays written weeks or months earlier. Near the end of the course, we ask students to select—for one more round of revision—three or four essays, with each paper illustrating a different rhetorical pattern. We use these reworked versions of the essays to assign a final grade to each student. If you structure your course around themes and issues, you'll probably want to require that each paper deal with a different theme.

As the semester draws to a close, we also ask students to complete the questionnaire at the back of the book. Their responses let us know which selections worked well and which did not, helping us make adjustments in future semesters. So that you too can find out how the class reacted to the assigned selections, you might ask students to give the completed forms to you rather than having students mail their questionnaires to the publisher. If you do collect the forms, we hope that you'll forward them to us at Longman after you've had a chance to look them over. This kind of student feedback will be crucial when we revise the book.

An especially rewarding way to end the semester is to have the class publish a booklet of student writing. Students revise and then submit two of their strongest papers to a class-elected editorial board. This board selects one essay from each student in the class, making an effort to choose essays that represent a mix of styles and rhetorical approaches. After a table of contents and a cover have been prepared, the essays are gathered, duplicated, and stapled into booklet form. Depending on the equipment and funds available, the booklet may be photocopied or designed on a computer.

Students respond enthusiastically to this project. After all, who can resist the prospect of being published? And knowing that their writing is going public encourages students to revise in earnest. The booklets yield significant benefits for us, too. They help build a bank of student writing to draw on in subsequent semesters. As a bonus, the booklets allow us to reconnect with the experiences, thoughts, and feelings of the students passing through our classes year after year. Such booklets have been an ongoing source of pleasure.

A SUGGESTED SYLLABUS

On the following pages we present a syllabus that will give you some further ideas on how to use **THE LONGMAN READER** (LR). Note that the syllabus assumes the course meets once a week, for three hours, over a fifteen-week period. The syllabus can, of course, be easily adjusted to fit a variety of course formats.

Week 1

- Provide an introduction to the course and handle necessary business matters.
- Direct a "getting to know each other" activity (see page 2 of this manual).
- Have students prepare an in-class writing sample to get an initial sense of their writing needs.
- Assignments—ask students to:
  a. Read "The Reading Process" in the LR.
  b. Read "The Writing Process" in the LR through page 39.

Week 2

- Discuss assignments, including the writing process activities.
- Return the in-class papers. Review common sentence skills problems.
- Read and work through the rest of the writing process chapter.
- Introduce students to "Description," covering selected material on pages 71–83.
- Assignments—ask students to:
  a. Read the introduction to "Description" in the LR (pages 71–83).
  b. Read two (teacher-designated) description selections. (We suggest that the first selection be "Flavio's Home.") Before doing so, complete the Pre-Reading Journal Entry for each.
  c. Answer the close reading and craft questions following the selections.

Week 3

- Answer questions about the description chapter and discuss the two assigned description selections.
- Have students do prewriting (brainstorming, freewriting, group work, etc.) for one of the writing assignments at the end of the assigned description selections. (If they

8

select the "Writing Assignment Using a Journal Entry as a Starting Point," they should have already done prewriting—through the journal entry—before reading.)
- Assignments—ask students to:
  a. Complete the description essay.
  b. Review grammar, punctuation, and usage as needed.

Week 4

- Initiate peer review of students' description essays (see pages 4–6 of this manual). Give students the option of handing in their papers in present form or revising them by the next class.
- Introduce students to "Narration," covering selected material on pages 120–33 of the LR.
- Read and discuss in class a narrative selection: "The Fourth of July" or "Salvation."
- Assignments—ask students to:
  a. Read the introduction to "Narration" (page 120–33) in the LR.
  b. Read two more (teacher-designated) narrative selections, first completing each Pre-Reading Journal Entry.
  c. Answer the close reading and craft questions following the selections.

Week 5

- Pass back and discuss students' description essays.
- Answer questions about the narration chapter and discuss the two assigned narrative selections.
- Have students do prewriting (brainstorming, freewriting, group work, etc.) for one of the writing assignments at the end of the two assigned narrative selections.
- Assignments—ask students to:
  a. Complete the narrative essay.
  b. Review grammar, punctuation, and usage as needed.

Week 6

- Initiate peer review of students' narrative essays (see pages 4–6 of this manual). Give students the option of handing in their papers in present form or revising them by the next class.
- Introduce students to "Exemplification," covering selected material on pages 168–82 of the LR.
- Read and discuss in class the exemplification selection "The 'Values' Wasteland" or "Sexism and Language."
- Assignments—ask students to:
  a. Read the introduction to "Exemplification" (pages 168–82) in the LR.
  b. Read two more (teacher-designated) exemplification selections, first completing each Pre-Reading Journal Entry.
  c. Answer the close reading and craft questions following the selections.

Week 7

- Pass back and discuss students' narrative essays. Answer questions about the exemplification chapter and discuss the two assigned exemplification essays.
- Have students do prewriting (brainstorming, freewriting, group work, etc.) for one of the writing assignments at the end of the two assigned exemplification selections.
- Assignments—ask students to:
  a. Complete the exemplification essay.
  b. Review grammar, punctuation, and usage as needed.

Week 8

- Initiate peer review of students' exemplification essays (see pages 4–6 of this manual). Give students the option of handing in their papers in present form or revising them by the next class.
- Introduce students to "Division-Classification" or "Process Analysis," covering selected material on pages 221–36 or 281–96 of the LR.
- Read and discuss in class the division-classification selection "The Ways We Lie" or the process selection "Your New Computer."
- Assignments—ask students to:
  a. Read the introduction to "Division-Classification" (pages 221–36) or "Process Analysis" (pages 281–96) in the LR.
  b. Read two more (teacher-designated) division-classification or process analysis selections, first completing each Pre-Reading Journal Entry.
  c. Answer the close reading and craft questions following the selections.

Week 9

- Pass back students' exemplification essays. Answer questions about division-classification or process analysis chapters and discuss the two assigned selections.
- Provide prewriting (brainstorming, freewriting, group work, etc.) for one of the writing assignments at the end of the two assigned selections.
- Assignments—ask students to:
  a. Complete the division-classification or process analysis essay.
  b. Review grammar, punctuation, and usage as needed.

Week 10

- Initiate peer review of students' division-classification or process analysis essays (see pages 4–6 of this manual). Give students the option of handing in their papers in present form or revising them by the next class.
- Introduce students to "Comparison-Contrast," covering selected material on pages 337–50.
- Read and discuss in class the comparison-contrast selection "A Fable for Tomorrow" or "And Then I Went to School."
- Assignments—ask students to:
  a. Read the introduction to "Comparison-Contrast" (pages 337–50) in the LR.
  b. Read two more (teacher-designated) comparison-contrast selections, first completing each Pre-Reading Journal Entry.

c. Answer the close reading and craft questions following the selections.

d. Write a comparison-contrast essay.

e. Review grammar, punctuation, and usage as needed.

Week 11

- Pass back and discuss students' division-classification or process analysis essays.
- Answer questions about the comparison-contrast chapter and discuss the two assigned selections.
- Initiate peer review of students' comparison-contrast essays (see pages 4–6 of this manual). Give students the option of handing in their papers in present form or revising them by the next class.
- Introduce students to "Cause-Effect" or "Definition," covering selected material on pages 381–96 or 432–44. If appropriate, introduce cause-effect activity described on page 102 of this manual.
- Read and discuss in class a cause-effect or definition selection: "Why We Crave Horror Movies" or "Entropy."
- Assignments—ask students to:
  a. Read the introduction to "Cause-Effect" (pages 381–96) or "Definition" (pages 432–44) in the LR.
  b. Read two more (teacher-designated) cause-effect or definition selections, first completing each Pre-Reading Journal Entry.
  c. Answer the close reading and craft questions following the selections.
  d. Write a cause-effect or definition essay.
  e. Review grammar, punctuation, and usage as needed.

Week 12

- Pass back and discuss students' comparison-contrast essays.
- Answer questions on the cause-effect or definition chapter and discuss the two assigned selections.
- Initiate peer review of students' cause-effect or definition essays (see pages 4–6 of this manual). Give students the option of handing in their papers in present form or revising them by the next class.
- Introduce students to "Argumentation-Persuasion," covering selected material on pages 476–509 of the LR.
- Read and discuss in class one pro-con set of essays: "Time to Think About Torture" and "Now the Talk Is About Bringing Back Torture."
- Assignments—ask students to:
  a. Read the introduction to "Argumentation-Persuasion" (pages 476–509) in the LR.
  b. Read three more (teacher-designated) argumentation-persuasion selections, first completing each Pre-Reading Journal Entry. (At least one of these selections should focus on a controversial social issue—see pages 132–33 of this manual.)
  c. Answer the close reading and craft questions following the selections.

Week 13

- Pass back and discuss students' cause-effect or definition essays.

- Answer questions about the argumentation-persuasion chapter and discuss the three assigned argumentation-persuasion selections.
- Discuss the three argumentation-persuasion essays.
- Initiate prewriting (brainstorming, freewriting, group work, etc.; see pages 3–4 of this manual) for one of the writing assignments at the end of the three assigned argumentation-persuasion selections. The writing assignment should require the student to focus on a controversial social issue.
- Assignments—ask students to:
  a. Complete the argumentation-persuasion essay.
  b. Review grammar, punctuation, and usage as needed.

Week 14

- Answer questions about the argumentation-persuasion chapter and discuss the three assigned argumentation-persuasion selections.
- Provide peer review of students' argumentation-persuasion essays (see pages 4–6 of this manual). Give students the option of handing in their papers in present form or revising them by the next class.
- Ask students to revise several essays written earlier in the course. These essays should be submitted in the final class (see pages 7–8 of this manual).
- If appropriate, have students organize a forum on controversial issues. (See page 133 of this manual for our comments on the activity.)
- Assignment—ask students to prepare their oral presentations for delivery during the in-class forum on controversial social issues.

Week 15

- Have students submit their folder of revised work.
- Have students deliver their oral presentations on controversial social issues.
- Provide group feedback on the forum.
- Conclude the course.

ANSWERS FOR "THE WRITING PROCESS" CHAPTER

Activities: Prewrite (pages 26–27)

1. **Set A**
   3 Abortion
   2 Controversial social issues
   5 Cutting off state abortion funds
   4 Federal funding for abortions
   1 Social issues

   Set B
   4 Business majors
   3 Students divided by major
   1 College students
   2 Kinds of students on campus
   5 Why many students major in business

2. "Day-care," "male and female relationships," and "international terrorism" are clearly too broad to be used as topics for a 2- to 5-page essay.

Activities: Identify the Thesis (pages 30–31)

1. **Limited Subject**: The ethics of treating severely handicapped infants

   FS Some babies born with severe handicaps have been allowed to die.
   TB There are many serious issues involved in the treatment of handicapped newborns.
   OK The government should pass legislation requiring medical treatment for handicapped newborns.
   A This essay will analyze the controversy surrounding the treatment of severely handicapped babies who would die without medical care.

   Limited Subject: Privacy and computerized records

   TB Computers raise some significant and crucial questions for all of us.
   FS Computerized records keep track of consumer spending habits, credit records, travel patterns, and other personal information.
   OK Computerized records have turned our private lives into public property.
   A In this paper, the relationship between computerized records and the right to privacy will be discussed.

2. Below are possible thesis statements for each set of points.

   Set A
   Possible Thesis: Students in college today are showing signs of increasing conservatism.

   Set B
   Possible Thesis: If not closely monitored, experiments in genetic engineering could yield disastrous results.

3. Below are possible thesis statements for each set of general and limited subjects.

General Subject	Limited Subject	Possible Thesis
Psychology	The power struggles in a classroom	The classroom is often a battlefield, with struggles for power going on among students and between students and teacher.
Health	Doctors' attitudes toward patients	In hospitals, doctors often treat patients like robots rather than human beings.
American Politics	Television's coverage of presidential campaigns	Television coverage of political campaigns emphasizes the visual at the expense of issues.

| Work | Minimum-wage jobs for young people | The minimum wage is too low to inspire young people to work hard and advance themselves. |

Activities: Support the Thesis with Evidence (pages 38–39)

1. In each set below, the irrelevant point is preceded by an "X."

   Set A
   Thesis: Colleges should put less emphasis on sports.
   Encourages grade fixing
   X Creates a strong following among former graduates
   Distracts from real goals of education
   Causes extensive and expensive injuries

   Set B
   Thesis: America is becoming a homogenized country.
   Regional accents vanishing
   Chain stores blanket country
   X Americans proud of their ethnic heritage
   Metropolitan areas almost indistinguishable from one another

2. Below are possible points of support for each thesis statement.

   Thesis: The trend toward disposable, throw-away products has gone too far.
   1. Fast-food chains generate huge amounts of non-biodegradable refuse.
   2. Parks and recreational areas are strewn with non-recyclable beer cans.
   3. Roadways are littered with non-returnable soda bottles.

   Thesis: The local library fails to meet the needs of those it is supposed to serve.
   1. The hours are limited and inconvenient.
   2. The part-time, inexperienced staff provide insufficient assistance.
   3. The collection is outdated and incomplete.

   Thesis: Television portrays men as incompetent creatures.
   1. College male washing colors and whites together, to horror of older women in laundromat.
   2. Father caring for child but unable to cope with emergency.
   3. Men concerned only with taste of product, while wives are knowledgeable about healthfulness.

Activities: Organize the Evidence (pages 45–46)

1. **Thesis:** Our schools, now in crisis, could be improved in several ways.
   I. Teachers
      A. Certification requirements for teachers
      B. Merit pay for outstanding teachers
   II. Schedules
      A. Longer school days
      B. Longer school year

III. Curriculum
   A. Better textbooks for classroom use
   B. More challenging content in courses

2. **Thesis:** Friends of the opposite sex fall into one of several categories: the pal, the confidante, or the pest.

Overall Pattern of Development: *Division-Classification*

- Frequently, an opposite-sex friend is simply a "pal."—develop with *definition*
- Sometimes, though, a pal turns, step by step, into a confidante.—develop with *process analysis*
- If a confidante begins to have romantic thoughts, he or she may become a pest, thus disrupting the friendship.—develop with *cause-effect*

DESCRIPTION

OPENING COMMENTS

Some colleagues tell us they prefer to omit description when they teach freshman writing. Emphasizing the analytic side of exposition, they consider descriptive writing a digression, a luxury that they don't have time for in an already crowded syllabus. To them, descriptive writing belongs in a creative writing course, not in freshman composition. On the other hand, some instructors *do* include description, but they discuss it after narration.

We feel that descriptive writing should be included in freshman composition. And we've found that description can be covered before narration with excellent results. In other words, we recommend that description be the first pattern studied in the course.

Why do we feel this way? For one thing, when students begin by writing descriptive essays, they learn the importance of specific details, and they start to develop the habit of observation. (The sensory chart described on page 75 is one way to encourage such attention to detail.) Also, since descriptive writing depends on creating a dominant impression, description helps students understand the concept of focus early in the semester.

Descriptive writing also teaches students to select details that enhance an essay's central point. Finally—and most importantly—students can discover real pleasure in writing descriptive pieces. They are challenged by the possibility they can make readers feel as they do about a subject. They enjoy using words to share a place, person, or object that has personal significance to them. Every semester, we have several students who admit that descriptive writing changed their attitude toward composition. For the first time, they see that writing, though difficult, can be rewarding and fun.

The selections in this chapter represent the wide range of techniques found in descriptive writing. We suggest you start with Parks's essay because its imagistic power dramatizes the way vivid sensory details support a dominant impression. Similarly, Angelou's essay "Sister Flowers" captures the way our sensory perceptions affect our emotional responses. This piece is particularly useful in showing students how to use metaphor and simile to convey abstract concepts and shape concrete images. We think that students will find Soto's "The Jacket" a compelling and emulable reflection on childhood experience; the author recollects complex childhood emotions by means of ambivalently remembering an artifact of his youth. And White's justly celebrated "Once More to the Lake" serves as a poignant rendering of personal experience. To create his effect, White uses flashbacks, a technique usually associated with narration. Finally, using a restrained tone and carefully chosen details, Judith Ortiz Cofer evokes the mood of precious childhood memories.

ANSWERS FOR PREWRITING ACTIVITIES

Below we provide suggested responses to selected prewriting activities at the end of Chapter 3. Of course, other approaches are possible. (p. 82)

1. There are many ways to use description in these two essays; below we've listed some of the possibilities. In classroom use of this activity, we suggest you have students share their responses. They'll be surprised and often delighted to discover their neighbors have devised quite different uses for description in the essays. Sharing and comparing such prewriting conveys the invaluable point that writers are individual and their writing is unique.

   Topic: How students get burned out
   Describe ineffective studying methods: cramming, skimming
   Describe student with 6 courses struggling with homework
   Draw portrait of aloof professor assigning too-difficult work
   Describe student working and carrying full load

   Topic: Being a spendthrift is better than being frugal
   Describe allure of some purchase: dress, sneakers, etc.
   Describe appeal of shopping center or mall
   Describe gourmet meal at expensive restaurant

   Topic: Being a spendthrift is worse than being frugal
   Describe shocked clerk ringing up your large purchase
   Describe empty pockets and meager lunches after a spree
   Describe sleepless night after charging a lot

ANSWERS FOR REVISING ACTIVITIES

Below we provide suggested responses to selected revising activities at the end of Chapter 3. Of course, other approaches are possible. (p. X82

3. Here are some possible ways to revise the sentences to create distinct, contrasting moods. Other versions are, of course, possible.

   a. Around the filthy, lopsided table slouched four grubby, droopy-eyed old men.

      Alert and eagle-eyed, the four natty old poker players sat tensely around the felt-topped table.

   b. Enticed by media attention to the movie's special effects, hordes of boisterous teenagers thronged the street outside the theater showing "Race to Doom."

      Snaking down the alley beside the theater, a line of silent, slouch-hatted customers waited to see the notorious film.

   c. The skinny twelve-year-old girl teetered, wobbled, and finally tripped as she walked into church in her first pair of high heels.

      With head held high, hips swaying, and her eyes roving to see if anyone noticed, Mary Beth strolled down Main Street in her first pair of high heels.

4. We suggest that you offer your students the chance to read each other's revisions of this paragraph. Such exposure to the versions of others helps them see a variety of possibilities in improving a piece of writing.

17

Here are the main problems in the paragraph:

— Details about driving on Route 334 are irrelevant and should be eliminated.
— Statement that car has been "washed and waxed" detracts attention from arrival at farm.
— Short, choppy sentences could be combined with others nearby: "Its paint must have worn off decades ago"; "They were dented and windowless." For example, such combined sentences might read: "Then I headed for the dirt-colored barn, its roof full of huge, rotted holes"; "As I rounded the bushes, I saw the dirt-colored house, its paint worn off decades ago"; "A couple of dented, windowless, dead-looking old cars were sprawled in front of the barn."
— Spatial order is broken by placing description of house in between details about what is near the barn.

FLAVIO'S HOME

Gordon Parks

Questions for Close Reading (p. 90)

1. The dominant impression is implied. While Parks is explicit about his overall attitude to poverty in paragraph 1, this material is not the thesis. Rather, the dominant impression pertains more specifically to Flavio. It might be stated as, "Even in the midst of the worst afflictions of poverty, the human spirit survives in certain optimistic, energetic, caring individuals such as the twelve-year-old boy Flavio."
2. In Flavio's family, there's no sense of understanding or emotional nurturing of children; rather, all the family's focus is on survival. At twelve, Flavio is the oldest child of eight, ranging down to infancy. His parents work, leaving him with the care of the household and the other children. His mother is a laundress who washes clothes in the river, and the father sells bleach and kerosene at a small stand. The parents seem too fatigued to be interested in their children; the father relates to them primarily by giving commands and demanding instant obedience.
3. The neighborhood is on a steep, difficult-to-climb mountainside. Paragraphs 2–3, 14, and 21 describe the sights and sounds Parks encounters on this arduous climb. He reports encountering "mud trails, jutting rock, slime-filled holes and shack after shack propped against the slopes on shaky pilings." The trail is also crowded with people going up and down; "bare feet and legs with open sores climbed above us," Parks writes (21). While the mountainside is "a maze of shacks," from it one can see the beaches with the "gleaming white homes of the rich" (2). Flavio's home is described in paragraph 6. It is a one-room shack, six by ten feet, constructed of miscellaneous boards with numerous gaps in the walls. The wooden floor is rotten and spotted with light leaking in through the holes in the roof. One corner has a hole dug for a toilet; it lets out onto the side of the mountain.
4. Flavio seems well aware that hosts should not eat in front of guests, but he is probably afraid that his domineering and skeptical father would be angered by an offer to join them. He may also be reluctant to be a good host because there isn't enough food to go around; his family lives on the brink of starvation, and he knows the guests do not need the food as much as his family. Parks and Gallo understand that Flavio really can't or shouldn't offer food, and so they refuse.
5. *barrios* (1): Latin-American term for districts

jacaranda (2): tropical tree having clusters of pale purple flowers
jaundiced (3): yellow-toned, ill with a disorder of the bile (liver)
spigot (14): faucet

Questions About the Writer's Craft (p. 90)

1. The dominant impression we receive of Flavio is of a child ravaged by poverty yet who possesses an open and persevering soul. Throughout the essay, Parks reveals Flavio's character by describing what Flavio says and does rather than what the boy is like as a person. He gives us numerous details of Flavio's physical appearance (3, 11, 23), pointing out the boy's thinness, stick-like limbs, sunken eyes, jaundiced coloring, wrenching coughs, and filthy, skimpy clothing. Parks also notices one other thing—the brilliant smile that instantly crosses Flavio's face as he sees the strangers. Parks details each time the smile reoccurs—when the boy opens the door (4), offers food (10), carries Parks's camera (22), recovers from a coughing spell (23), and enters the doctor's office (29). The nobility of the boy's spirit also comes through in other details: his competence in household tasks and care of his siblings (5, 7, 9, 23–26) and his refusal to let Parks carry wood for him (22).
2. Parks describes how household tasks are made difficult by the need to conserve water. In paragraph 7, we see the process by which Flavio gets the rice washed, the children bathed, and the floor scrubbed, with only one pan of water. In paragraph 10, the boy serves dinner, a task complicated by the existence of only three plates and two spoons. He prepares breakfast in paragraph 23, making a fire and reheating the dinner. These processes add to the dominant impression of Flavio by showing us his discipline, ingenuity, and steadiness.
3. Parks conveys strong sensory images in such phrases as "a rusted, bent top of an old gas range," "a piece of tin," "grimy walls," "a patchwork of misshapen boards," "other shacks below stilted against the slopes," "rotting," "layers of grease and dirt," "shafts of light slanting down," "spaces in the roof," and "large hole." We are able to flow from image to image because Parks uses numerous transitions of spatial organization: "beneath it," "between them," "under layers," slanting down through," "in the far corner," and "beneath that hole." Parks also uses a clear organizational pattern in the description; he begins describing the room with one important object, the stove. Then he moves from the walls to the floor; he ingeniously indicates the roof's condition by pointing out the sunlight dappling the floor from the holes above. He concludes by describing a hole in the "far corner" which serves as a toilet and which empties out on to the slope of the mountain. This detail, that the latrine empties essentially into thin air, conveys the precariousness and primitiveness of the home.
4. The effect of this scene is to dramatize the huge disparity between the rich and poor in Rio, between not only their dress, but their emotional lives, the one basic and elemental, the other extravagant and romantic. The hotel lobby is filled with people dressed up for the evening in formal attire; Parks finds himself hoping the elevator will be empty since he has just been in the slums and is not very presentable. But a couple in evening clothes enter the elevator and embrace romantically, totally ignoring him. This action symbolizes the way in which the moneyed classes so easily ignore the "stink of the favela," even when it is right in the elevator with them.

THE JACKET

Gary Soto

Questions for Close Reading (p. 95)

1. Initially, Soto contends that an ugly, ill-fitting jacket caused him academic, social, and emotional harm. He conveys the gist of this idea at the very beginning of his essay ("My clothes have failed me. I remember the green coat that I wore. . . .") and states it more explicitly in paragraph 10: "I blame that jacket for those bad years." But what is less explicitly stated is that despite the jacket's ugliness and the alienation it caused him, Soto came to feel he truly "owned" the jacket, assuming something like kinship to it and what it represented. This is implied in the final sentence of paragraph 12. So students might express the overarching idea of the essay as: "In spite of the embarrassment and alienation it caused the narrator, the ugly green jacket ultimately came to be a somewhat comforting old companion to him."

2. Soto's family seems to have been poor. The mother's comment in paragraph 10 that "there were children in Mexico who would love that jacket" suggests that their family may have come to the U.S. from a poor place where anything new—ugly or not—would be appreciated. Soto speaks with mild contempt of his mother's "cheap ways" (10). The children drank powdered milk (12), which is less expensive than ready-to-drink milk. Also, Soto shared a bedroom with his brother (4) and wore oversized (3), undersized (3, 9), and ragged (10) clothes—most notably, the green jacket.

3. As a child, Soto apparently was fond, yet somewhat disrespectful, of his mother. Although he loathed the jacket, he gave her a smile of thanks after receiving it (4)—perhaps to spare her feelings. But later he "yelled" at her about the jacket (10). The statement that his mother "always seemed to be at the stove" (10) suggests condescension from Soto as both a boy and a man. So does his remark that he had thought his mother "understood" the kind of jacket he wanted because she had "listened so long" (2). As an adult, Soto affectionately refers to his mother as "my mom" (4), yet he harshly blames her for her "bad taste" and "cheap ways" (10). His childhood ambivalence toward his mother seems to have continued into adulthood.

4. When he first receives the jacket from his mother, he seems disappointed though curious about it. The jacket is nothing like the black biker jacket he wanted, and he says, "I wanted to cry because it was so ugly and so big" (3). But in paragraph 4, he describes how he tried on the jacket and struck several poses in it to see how it looked. Unfortunately, he concludes, the jacket is every bit as ugly as he first suspected. Soon after, the narrator comes to equate the jacket with embarrassment and failure. He describes his first day of school wearing the jacket, during which he got a D on a math quiz, was targeted by "the playground terrorist" (6), and was what he perceived as the object of teachers' and students' ridicule (6–7). The narrator then comes to blow out of proportion the jacket's effects, saying "I blame that jacket for those bad years" (10) and holding it responsible for any and all difficulties he experienced, including poor academic performance and rejection by girls (8–9). At this point, we may begin to suspect that Soto intends the jacket to symbolize a generally awkward period of more than an actual cause of his problems. This is confirmed at the end of the essay, when the narrator's contempt for the jacket—and, by extension, for himself and his situation in life—turns to reluctant acceptance. He cares enough about the jacket to Scotch tape it when it rips and to continue wearing

it despite its "camouflage" appearance. And though he flings it away in a rage, the narrator later "swipe[s] the jacket off the ground" and "drape[s] it across" his lap. At this point, the ugly jacket has become a security blanket of sorts, something familiar and strangely comforting to the narrator. This feeling is expressed in his calling the jacket "that green ugly brother" who remained with him, in spirit if not in fact, "that day and ever since" (12). In other words, the narrator has come to accept and even embrace the jacket and the ugliness it represents because they are a part of the complex person he is.

5. *guacamole* (2): mashed avocado
   braille (7): a writing system of raised dots that can be read by touch
   palsied (10): afflicted with palsy, a disease that causes trembling and paralysis
   camouflage (11): clothing that has green, brown, tan, and black splotches and tends to blend into natural surroundings
   tortilla (12): flat bread made from cornmeal or wheat flour

Questions About the Writer's Craft (p. 95)

1. Although the brief description of the jacket itself in paragraph 2 is spatial ("I touched the vinyl sleeve, the collar, and peeked at the mustard-colored lining"), Soto in general organizes his description chronologically. As he grew bigger and stronger, the jacket became smaller and sicklier in appearance. Transitional terms and phrases that help to establish chronological order include "the next day" (2, 6), "during the morning recess" (6), "during lunch" (7), "when I returned to class" (7), "a few minutes later" (7), "during that time" (9), "at lunchtime" (9), "about that time" (10), "that winter" (10), "later" (11), and "ever since" (12).

2. Soto personifies the jacket as a "stranger" (2), then an "enemy" (3), and finally an "ugly brother" who "tagged along wherever I went" (10) and "breathed over my shoulder that day and ever since" (12). This personification implies that the narrator initially saw the jacket as foreign and threatening, then adopted a stance of overt hostility toward it, then came to live with it as something annoying and embarrassing but unavoidable. He also personifies the jacket as injured and sick. When the jacket first was torn, the narrator examined the tear as he would "a cut on my arm" (5). Later the rip was a "wound" patched with Scotch tape that "peeled off like a scab" (10). Eventually the torn sleeve "shriveled into a palsied arm" (10). This personification reflects how the narrator felt when he wore the jacket: wounded and debilitated. But ultimately, he came to accept and "own" the jacket's ugliness.

3. Similes such as "flapped the jacket like a bird's wings" (4), "my arms feeling like braille from goose bumps" (7), "my teeth chattered like a cup of crooked dice" (7), and "my forearms stuck out like the necks of turtles" (9) imply that the narrator felt vulnerable, exposed, and ridiculous.

4. In paragraph 2, the narrator contrasts the jacket he asked for—"black leather and silver studs, with enough belts to hold down a small town"—with the jacket he received—"the color of day-old guacamole" with a "vinyl sleeve" and "mustard-colored lining." This extreme disparity between what was desired and what was received introduces the humor of the piece, which revolves around the narrator's disappointment with the jacket. In paragraph 9, he contrasts his desire for female companionship with his lonely reality of leaning against chainlink fences with other lonely boys, "propellers of grass spinning in our mouths." This contrast of desire and reality reinforce the narrator's frustration with his situation, which he blames on the ugly jacket.

SISTER FLOWERS

Maya Angelou

Questions for Close Reading (p. 101)

1. The dominant impression is implied and can be stated as, "The care and attention of a loving mentor is crucial to a child's healthy development, particularly in times of crisis." In addition, Angelou seeks to draw a portrait of beloved Mrs. Flowers, the essence of whom Angelou expresses when she writes, "[Mrs. Flowers] was one of the few gentlewomen I have ever known, and has remained throughout my life the measure of what a human being can be" (paragraph 5).

2. Mrs. Flowers represents for Angelou the gentility and sophistication as well as the benevolence that she has read about in novels and seen in films, but has never encountered first-hand, especially not among her fellow townspeople. She says, "She appealed to me because she was like people I had never met personally" (11) and calls her "the aristocrat of Black Stamps" (2). Flowers's stunning beauty and impeccable grooming (2–4) powerfully impress Angelou, who lives in a community of relatively poor and minimally-educated people. Still more fascinating is Flowers's refined grace (12), dazzling intellect, and stirring eloquence (22), all of which inspire Angelou to strive for a standard she previously thought accessible only to privileged whites. Angelou reflects, "She made me proud to be Negro, just by being herself" (11). Most of all, Angelou is profoundly honored and grateful that Flowers would not only spend time with her but also impart to her the "lessons for living" that would form the foundation of Angelou's subsequent existence.

3. Angelou humorously describes her frustration and embarrassment when witnessing her unrefined Momma speaking to the highly-educated and proper Mrs. Flowers. In particular, Angelou is ashamed of Momma's calling Mrs. Flowers "*Sister* Flowers." To the young Angelou, such an informal appellation is inconsistent with what she considers the obvious superiority of her elegant neighbor. In Angelou's opinion, "Mrs. Flowers deserved better than to be called Sister" (7). Worse still is Momma's flawed grammar as she speaks to Flowers; Angelou agonizes over Momma's incorrect and missing verbs and says that she "hated [Momma] for showing her ignorance to Mrs. Flowers" (7). Despite Angelou's intense embarrassment over Momma, Momma and Flowers share an amicable and mutually respectful friendship—a fact which perplexes Angelou, who calls their relationship "strange" (6). Flowers does not object to Momma's calling her "Sister" and in fact might be pleased to be included in the community of women; similarly, Momma feels enough kinship with Flowers to call her "Sister." The two women often engage in "intimate conversation" with each other (10), and it is implied that Momma has asked Flowers's assistance in mentoring the withdrawn young Angelou. Years later, Angelou finally realizes that Momma and Flowers were indeed "as alike as sisters, separated only by formal education" (7), a notion reinforced by Flowers's insistence that Angelou appreciate the wisdom of "mother wit," such as that of Momma (35).

4. The first significant lesson Mrs. Flowers teaches Angelou is about the beauty and power of language. In the process of convincing young Angelou that she needs to participate verbally in class, Flowers explains that "it is language alone which separates [man] from the lower animals," a notion that was "a totally new idea" to Angelou (23). Soon after, in a statement that Angelou remembers as "valid and poetic," Flowers says, "It takes the human voice to infuse [words] with the shades of deeper meaning" (24). Flowers's melodic, invigorating reading of *A Tale of Two*

Cities convincingly illustrates to Angelou the vast power of words. (Clearly, this lesson had a tremendous impact on Angelou, presently a renowned writer not only of novels but also of poetry.) The next important lesson concerns the nature of wisdom and intelligence. Probably perceiving Angelou's embarrassment at Momma's lack of refinement, Flowers informs her that many unschooled people are more knowledgeable and intelligent than some highly educated scholars. "Mother wit," she asserts, is every bit as valuable (if not more so) as book knowledge, for it contains "the collective wisdom of generations" (35). Flowers's lesson on knowledge is summed up when she advises Angelou to "always be intolerant of ignorance but understanding of illiteracy" (35). Following this advice, it seems likely that young Angelou would think twice before judging Momma harshly again. Beyond these explicitly-stated lessons, Angelou also receives the invaluable understanding that she is a unique and likable individual worthy of the attention of an exemplary woman, a realization that will help rebuild her wounded self-confidence.

5. *taut* (2): tightly pulled or strained
    voile (2): a light, sheer fabric
    benign (4): kind and gentle
    unceremonious (8): informal
    gait (8): particular way of walking
    moors (11): broad area of open land, often containing patches of wetness
    incessantly (11): continuing without interruption
    scones (11): small biscuit-like pastries
    crumpets (11): small, round, cake-like breads
    heath (11): large area of land containing low-growing shrubs
    chifforobe (17): tall piece of furniture containing drawers and space for hanging clothes
    sacrilegious (17): disrespectful of something held sacred
    infuse (24): to introduce into as if by pouring
    couched (35): expressed
    aura (42): an invisible atmosphere seeming to surround something or someone

Questions About the Writer's Craft (p. 102)

1. Angelou relies primarily on visual and occasionally on both tactile and auditory impressions to convey Flowers's "aristocratic" appearance. In paragraph 2, Angelou describes her graceful bearing that never evidences extremes of weather and her thin frame which lacks the "taut look of wiry people." Flowers's attire is the next object of Angelou's attention as she observes the elegant woman's airy "printed voile dresses," "flowered hats," and gloves (2). Angelou then describes Flowers's "rich black" complexion, comparing it to the visual and tactile image of an easily peeled plum (3). Angelou also details Flowers's "slow dragging" smile (15), thin black lips, "even, small white teeth" (4) and "soft yet carrying voice" (6). Later, she mentions Flowers's "easy gait" (8). In general, Angelou organizes these details of Flowers' appearance spatially, moving first from her physical carriage and attire up to her face and zeroing in on her smile (although she returns to Flowers's "easy gait" later in the essay.)

    To describe her reaction when she first arrived at Flowers's home, Angelou invokes the sense of smell when, for example, she cites the "sweet scent of vanilla" (29). She then draws upon the visual sense to describe what she observes: "browned photographs" and "white, freshly done curtains" (32). The next part of the visit calls upon the visual as well as the taste faculty as Angelou describes eating Flowers's delectable cookies ("flat round wafers, slightly browned on the edges and butter-yellow in the center") and drinking the refreshing, cold lemonade (34). The tactile sense is appealed to when she mentions the "rough crumbs" of the cookies scratching against her jaw (34). And the sense of sound is evoked as Angelou remembers Flowers's reading voice, "cascading" and "nearly singing" (37). Overall, Angelou organizes this last set of richly-textured sensory impressions spatially as well as chronologically; that is, she presents the details as she moves through the house and as the afternoon progresses.

2. The first figure of speech is the simile Angelou uses in comparing herself to an old biscuit (1). This image establishes young Angelou's shame and withdrawal following the rape; indeed, her depression is what prompts Flowers to find time to talk with the child. Angelou then employs a series of striking figures of speech to describe Flowers's character and demeanor. The most powerful appear in paragraph 11. There Angelou provides a series of similes using "like" to compare Flowers with the gentle, elegant "women in English novels who walked the moors . . . with their loyal dogs racing at a respectful distance" and "the women who sat in front of roaring fireplaces, drinking tea incessantly from silver trays full of scones and crumpets." The final simile of the paragraph is an implied one; although it lacks "like," it deliberately mirrors the structure of the previous two similes: "Women who walked over the 'heath' and read morocco-bound books and had two last names divided by a hyphen." The function of these similes comparing Flowers to female British gentility is to reinforce the notion of Flowers as "the aristocrat of Black Stamps" (2). The basis of Flowers's allure for Angelou is her otherworldly elegance and sophistication, particularly when juxtaposed with the ordinary citizens of Black Stamps. That this elegant and gracious woman actually seeks out the young Angelou is enough to transform the child from an "old biscuit" into one who excitedly runs down the road, flush with the pleasure of being liked.

3. The technique of imagined conversation injects humor into Angelou's portrait of herself as a child, while also allowing readers greater insight into her character by giving them access to her mental processes. The young Angelou's imagined scoldings of Momma resoundingly illustrate her embarrassment with "uncouth" Momma. Here, Angelou seems caught between two worlds: that of "backwards" Momma and Black Stamps and that of education and opportunity seemingly offered by the outside world. As Mrs. Flowers instructs, however, much wisdom resides in "mother wit" like Momma's, and given this lesson, young Angelou would probably be led to re-evaluate her embarrassed attitude toward Momma.

4. From Angelou's very first statement about Mrs. Flowers, it is apparent that race is a significant facet of life in Angelou's town. Flowers is said to be "the aristocrat of Black Stamps," a statement that draws its power from the notion that aristocrats have traditionally been white. This depiction of Flowers as being uniquely regal is heightened by Angelou's comparing her to English female gentry (11) and by her observation that Flowers behaves differently from the average "Negro woman" (14) in town. Most significantly, Angelou states that Flowers made her "proud to be a Negro, just by being herself" (11), a difficult feat given the racist climate of the day. The town's appellation "Black Stamps" (12) implies the existence of a "White Stamps," a fact later confirmed when Angelou mentions "powhitefolks" (13). Angelou indicates that no Negro, not even the elegant Flowers, is immune to the disrespect of the town's self-aggrandizing poor whites. Indeed, even Angelou's reverence for Flowers "would have been shattered like the unmendable Humpty-Dumpty" (13) if the "powhitefolks" had called this revered idol by her first name, Bertha. Angelou lives in a world that would sanction such racially-inspired disrespect and insult. In paragraph 42, Angelou refers to "Southern bitter wormwood," a subtle reference to racism. In such a world, it is difficult for a black

child—especially one so traumatized and wounded—to develop a strong sense of self. But that is just what the encounter with Mrs. Flowers achieves; it makes young Angelou "feel proud" to be a Negro, and with that comes the loosening of trauma's hold on her.

ONCE MORE TO THE LAKE

E. B. White

Questions for Close Reading (p. 109)

1. White's thesis is implied. One way of stating it is as follows: "In taking his son to revisit the lake where he experienced so many significant childhood events, White learns that he can only partly recapture the feelings and atmosphere of days long past. Instead, he gets in touch with a premonition of his own death."
2. White suggests that his return to the lake was rather casual and impulsive (1). While he normally preferred the ocean, he says, sometimes the turbulence of the sea made him long for the calm of a placid lake in the woods. In addition, he could take his son along and introduce him to fresh water fishing. On a deeper level, he seems to have longed to revisit a place of significance from his youth and to share its pleasures with a son.
3. In paragraph 4, the author lies in his bed, hearing his son sneak out in the dawn light to take a motorboat out on the lake, just as White had himself done as a boy. His son's behavior is so similar to his own as a youth that he suddenly feels as if "he was I, and therefore . . . that I was my own father." Another significant transposition occurs when they are fishing (5). A dragonfly, an unchanging element of nature, alights on his rod and gives him the dizzying feeling that he has moved back in time, until he "didn't know which rod [he] was at the end of." Finally, in paragraph 10, he identifies deeply with his son's attempts to gain mastery over the motorboat; he feels again all the same feelings he had in his youth as he grew to have a "spiritual" relationship with the motor.
4. The visit shows that things have remained much the same through the years. Nature has not changed much, nor has the town or the accommodations. In fact, White feels that the visit reveals the "pattern of life indelible" (8). Some details have changed, however, in keeping with the times. For example, the road has only two tracks, from the tires of automobiles, not three, from horse-drawn carriages (7); also, the boat is a modern outboard, not the one- and two-cylinder inboard motors of his youth. The waitresses are still country girls, but they have been impressed by the actresses in the movies and keep their hair cleaner than the waitresses of the past (7). Finally, the store serves Coke rather than old-fashioned sodas like Moxie and sarsaparilla (11).
5. *incessant* (1): continuous, not stopping
   placidity (1): peacefulness, calmness
   primeval (3): primitive
   transposition (4): a reversal or switching of place
   undulating (6): rippling, moving in wave-like fashion
   indelible (8): permanent, unerasable
   petulant (10): irritable, grouchy
   languidly (13): lifelessly, spiritlessly, without energy

1. White presents the descriptions of the present-day lake very objectively. "There was a choice of pie for dessert, and one was blueberry and one was apple, and the waitresses were the same country girls . . . the waitresses were still fifteen; their hair had been washed, that was the only difference—they had been to the movies and seen the pretty girls with clean hair." But White's descriptions of the past are sensuous and evocative, full of imagery that suggests they are more powerful than the present images. The memories of the past overtake and dominate the present experiences.

2. In paragraph 2, White calls the lake a "holy spot" and recalls a memory of the lake at dawn, when the woods along the shore seemed to form a "cathedral." Later, in paragraph 10, he describes the experience of learning to operate a motorboat as getting "really close to it spiritually." His description of the summer at the lake in paragraph 8 uses prayer-like language: "pattern of life indelible," "summer without end." These images convey White's almost religious reverence for nature: its beauty, peace, and permanence.

3. This passage uses the metaphor of a melodrama for the storm. This comparison points out that the storm is full of noise and turbulence but, in reality, is not dangerous. The storm's "audience," the children, in particular, get all excited about it, but to White, an old hand at the lake, the storm's "drama of electrical disturbance" is familiar. The storm is a joyfully scary event; the "gods grinning" suggests a pagan image of nature gods playing with the elements just for fun. The campers celebrate by running about and swimming in the rain. There is a serious undercurrent to the storm, however. While a harmless imitation of danger, it nevertheless sets the stage for White's premonition of death in the next paragraph.

4. The feeling grows out of a complex of events. The mock-danger of the storm has intensified everyone's reactions. White has enjoyed the storm as a piece of theatre; he remains on the sidelines wittily analyzing the scene. But the storm arouses the vitality of his son, who joins the frolicking campers. This action is the final example of how the son is growing up and away from his parent. (The boy takes the boat out by himself, for example.) When White feels a "sympathetic" iciness in his groin as his son dons his cold wet swimsuit, he is on one level identifying sensuously (again) with the boy's experience. In "biblical" terms, a child is the fruit of its father's "groin," and so the iciness also represents White's sudden awareness that his vitality is decreasing; to use the image of the melodrama, his scene is ending, while his son is center-stage. The many transpositions of identity between father and son have hinted at this final thought; White feels more and more like his own father, who, we can assume, has died.

A PARTIAL REMEMBRANCE OF A
PUERTO RICAN CHILDHOOD

Judith Ortiz Cofer

Questions for Close Reading (p. 115)

1. Cofer states her thesis in the second paragraph, partly in the first sentence and partly in the last: "It was on these rockers that my mother, her sisters, and my grandmother sat on these afternoons of my childhood to tell their stories, teaching each other, and

my cousin and me, what it was like to be a woman, more specifically, a Puerto Rican woman. . . . And they told *cuentos*, the morality and cautionary tales told by the women in our family for generations: stories that became a part of my subconscious as I grew up in two worlds, the tropical island and the cold city, and that would later surface in my dreams and in my poetry." The rest of the essay describes one of these story-telling sessions, and includes a recounting of one of the family *cuentos*.

2. The participating women include her grandmother, her mother. and her aunts, all members of older generations. At the time of the essay, the author is aged eleven or twelve, no longer a child who can be told to leave the room or "go and play." Yet, she is not a woman who can freely participate in the sessions. Rather, she sits quietly, occupied in some childish pursuit such as reading a comic book, and is allowed to "overhear" the stories. As she writes, she sat "pretending to be in another world, while absorbing it all in a sort of unspoken agreement of my status as silent auditor" (3). These sessions occur in the late afternoon, when the men are still at work, and the boys of the family have gone off to a park to play baseball.

3. The story about Maria la Loca is designed to warn women against trusting men too much. Being left at the altar is equated with going crazy, becoming ugly and ridiculous (3, 6, 8, 11), and of course, with never having another chance to marry. It is a tale that suggests that women's fates are tied up with how they are treated by men, and that therefore, they should be extremely sensible and careful so that they too are not victimized. Mama's views are based on the treachery of men in Mama's time. She described how, when she was young, a man could leave a girl at the altar and never be found, never be held accountable. Married men, she says, sometimes had several families all over the island of Puerto Rico. "Hombres with the devil in their flesh, . . . [would] take a job at one of the haciendas, only to have a good time and to seduce the women" (4). As Cofer puts it, "in Mama's eyes, a man set free without a legal contract was a man lost" (5). She believes that men marry because that is the only way they can have legitimate children and also obtain sex, which Mama euphemistically explains as "what no decent (synonymous with 'smart') woman would give away for free" (5). Her negative opinion of men is also conveyed in her "little swipe at men," the use of the word "*macho*" to describe the man who abandoned Maria, at a time when *macho* meant "stud" in the reproductive sense, rather than a dominating, womanizing male (8).

4. Throughout the telling of the *cuento*, Cofer shines a spotlight on Mama's daughters, in each instance describing the woman's relationship to men and her reaction to the story. In this way, the personalities and personal histories of the women become like refractions of the story, each woman's life measured to the standard of her husband's treatment of her.

   In paragraph 5, the youngest and yet-unmarried aunt, Aunt Laura, is pictured. She is embarrassed by the story because she is the same age as Maria had been—seventeen—and she is also engaged to be married. Her fiancé has gone to New York to "make his fortune" and will return in a year for the marriage. According to Cofer, Mama was doubtful about the marriage occurring, because to her, "a man set free without a legal contract was a man lost" (5). Cofer returns to Laura in paragraph 11, where she describes her as "on the verge of tears" and nervously rocking in her chair.

   Aunt Nena, the oldest daughter, is described in paragraph 9. She is married, but not happily. Her husband had lost his first wife, and so she cares for two stepchildren in addition to her own three, while her husband lived on the mainland in order to earn money. His "main interest in life was accumulating wealth." Cofer notes that the future held sorrow for this aunt, as she later left her children with

Mama to "slave" in a factory to help her husband with his dream. She apparently suffered greatly from the separation from her family. Finally, she was different from the other women in the family, in that she read all the time, but she "came alive to Mama's words, rocking gently" in her chair (9).

Also in paragraph 9, Cofer describes her mother, a daughter happily married who could view the La Loca story peacefully and "conspiratorially." She had married young, "an unspotted lamb," into a well respected although not wealthy family. Her husband, we learn in paragraph 7, is in the U.S. Navy, and the family shuttles between Paterson, New Jersey, and Puerto Rico. Like Aunt Nena, she endures separations having to do with her husband's military position, during which she is terrified. However, she can relax when her husband returns, suggesting that their marriage is strong and that he is a protective man. Overall, she does not seem to be as sad as Aunt Nena.

5. *intricately* (1): using many interrelated parts or facets
    embellishing (2): enhancing (a tale) with fictitious additions
    cautionary (2): giving warning
    histrionic (3): affected in behavior or speech
    conclave (3): a private or secret meeting
    auditor (3): listener; person who overhears
    impassively (3): without showing any sign of emotion or feeling
    ministrations (3): attentions
    matriarchal (3): like a woman who runs a family or tribe
    quest (7): search in order to find something
    chameleons (7): lizards with the ability to change the color of their skin
    surveillance (7): watch kept over a person, group, etc.
    conspiratorially (9): acting secretly together towards the same goal
    aberration (9): deviation from what is common, normal, or right
    mesmerizing (10): fascinating, hypnotizing
    denouement (11): the final resolution of a plot
    ravished (11): raped
    impromptu (13): without previous preparation

Questions About the Writer's Craft (p. 116)

1. Cofer provides numerous details about Maria. First, she describes her physically (paragraph 6). She is "a town character," who combines the body and face of a fat old woman with the movements of a young girl. "She would swing her hips in an exaggerated, clownish way, and sometimes even hop and skip up to someone's house" (6). She avoids speaking, but grins an ugly smile when questioned, much as a shy or awkward child might do. People taunted her, but she seemed not to notice. She was also reputed to hum to herself all the time. Later in the essay, we are given a description of her as the abandoned young bride-to-be: "a princess in her lace as she waited at the altar" (11). In between, we are provided the details of her tragedy; she "was once a beautiful girl. . . . 'but this *macho* made a fool out of her and ruined her life'" (8). Her illness is called a "honeymoon with death" that left her "ravished, no longer young or sane" (11). At the end, we are told the final detail, that the song Maria hums incessantly is the wedding march (13). Maria's decline after her abandonment represents, according to Mama, the fate of any woman who fails to be vigilant and careful in her choice of a man. The focus on her physical appearance makes Maria a visible, ever-present reminder of how low a woman can fall if she makes a poor choice. She is an object of mockery whose degradation is visible to all.

28

2. The details about the young Cofer reflect off the haunting power of the story of Maria La Loca. During her childhood, Cofer felt that she was an "odd-ball," like Maria, because she led a dual existence. Part of her time was spent in New Jersey, where she was treated like an immigrant, and part was spent in Puerto Rico, where her English-accented Spanish made her seem American. In neither place did she truly fit in. She and her brother became "cultural chameleons," who could "blend into a crowd," quietly adjust to apartment life during stormy weeks in New Jersey, or fly free during summers in Puerto Rico. She was, she says in paragraph 7, on a "serious quest for a definition of normal." The cautionary tale of the weird Maria echoes all the more strongly in the mind of a child ill at ease everywhere.

3. Cofer "braids" the story with descriptive material about the listeners, her aunts and mother because she wishes to show the effects of the story on the women. She also wants to convey the power of storytelling and the values it embodies in the culture of Puerto Rico. Mama's narrative is essentially a story within a story. The encasing story is a simple one, just the tale of how the women gathered, Cofer had her hair braided, and the grandmother danced Cofer around to the wedding march at the end of her story.

   The grandmother's narrative is told in paragraphs 4, 6, 8, 11–13, and is handled as direct quotations from Mama. The reader can recognize when the story resumes because it comes as dialogue. After each of these narrative paragraphs, Cofer clearly signals the reader that she is switching topics. At the start of paragraph 5, the phrase, "The whole time she was speaking" helps the reader switch out of the narrative into the storytelling scene. In paragraph 6, the second sentence of the paragraph indicates that Cofer is leaving the story to provide her own description of Maria La Loca (6) and of her (Cofer's) position as an outsider to the pueblo (7). In paragraph 9, Cofer moves from providing a bit of linguistic background to Mama's story to a description of her mother. She handles this by describing her own action of peeking at her mother. After this long interlude, Cofer returns to the story of Maria by using a transition indicating the time, "That day, Mama told   . . ." (11). In paragraph 13, the two stories merge, as Mama indicates that the tune Maria always hums is "The Wedding March," and pulls Cofer into "an impromptu waltz."

4. The braiding serves two purposes; it displays the grandmother's values and also parallels her storytelling. Mama begins to braid the author's hair near the start of the story without being asked, with the goal of taming Cofer's messy mop. She is clearly a person with a great deal of personal strength, who likes things disciplined and clear rather than all in a mess. That the braiding displays the grandmother's character comes through in Cofer's first description of the braiding in paragraph 3: "Mama had taken my long, tangled mane of hair into her ever-busy hands. Without looking down and with no interruption of her flow of words, she began braiding my hair, working at it with the quickness and determination that characterized all her actions." Cofer returns to the braiding several times in the essay, each time providing more clues about the grandmother. In paragraph 5, Cofer reports that the braiding was painful: "Mama would be weaving my hair into a flat plait that required pulling apart the two sections of hair with little jerks that made my eyes water; but knowing how grandmother detested whining and *boba* (sissy) tears, as she called them, I just sat up . . . straight and stiff.   . . ." We learn here that a kind of stoicism and bravery is admired in this family. Later, in paragraph 11, the author mentions that the story was making her Aunt Laura very uncomfortable, but that Mama "ignored Laura's obvious discomfort, digging out a ribbon from the sewing basket she kept by her rocker while describing Maria's long illness." She demands of Laura the same bravery in response to pain that she expects of the young girl whose hair she is braiding.

29

Also throughout the essay, Cofer suggests the parallel between the braiding and the grandmother's story. In paragraph 8, Cofer comments that Mama was "knitting my hair with the same intensity she was putting into her story . . ." In a sentence which is itself a marvel of braided images, Cofer explicitly discusses this parallel in paragraph 10: "The aroma of coffee perking in the kitchen, the mesmerizing creaks and groans of the rockers, and the women telling their lives in *cuentos* are forever woven into the fabric of my imagination, braided like my hair that day I felt my grandmother's hands teaching me about strength, her voice convincing me of the power of storytelling." Finally, Cofer notes the story ends just as the grandmother finishes the braid: "Mama lamented while tying the ribbon to the ends of my hair, pulling it back with such force that I just knew I would never be able to close my eyes completely again" (11).

NARRATION

OPENING COMMENTS

In our classes, we introduce narrative writing *after* description because we have found that descriptive writing helps students acquire many of the skills needed to write engaging narratives. For example, through descriptive writing, students discover the need to generate evocative details, use varied sentence structure, and establish a clear point of view.

Also, we often encounter students who are reluctant to write a narrative at the very start of the course. Schooled in the belief that a lightning bolt will strike them if they use "I" in an essay, they are more comfortable starting with description because it lends itself more easily to the objective third person point of view. (Obviously, both narration and description can be written in either the first or third person, but beginning writers tend to associate narration with the first and description with the third person.)

Even if it is not the first pattern covered, we suggest that narration be introduced near the beginning of the course. Everyone, after all, likes a good story, and most students have written narratives in high school and so feel comfortable tackling them in college.

Despite some students' familiarity and seeming ease with the narrative pattern, it's a good idea to keep in mind that narration requires a sophisticated repertoire of skills. Pacing, choice of details, telescoping of time, point of view: all offer a real challenge.

Students seem to have particular trouble understanding point of view. Because they tend to be more familiar with the first rather than the third person, we've found it useful to ask them to write two versions of the same narrative—one in the first and one in the third person. Such an assignment shows students how point of view changes a story and makes them aware of the advantages and limitations of each perspective.

Although each narrative in this chapter is filled with drama and tension, students find special power in the conflicts underlying Orwell's "Shooting an Elephant" and Hughes's "Salvation." While Lorde's piece reminds students of the value of sensory details, it also illustrates careful pacing and strong characterization. The play-by-play action of Dillard's essay "The Chase" is especially useful in showing students how to create suspense. And Mayblum's powerful account of his harrowing escape from the World Trade Center on 9/11 demonstrates the raw force and immediacy inherent in the narrative form.

ANSWERS FOR PREWRITING ACTIVITIES

Below we provide suggested responses to selected prewriting activities at the end of Chapter 4. Of course, your students are bound to come up with their own inventive approaches. (p. 132)

1. There are numerous ways to use narration to open these two essays. Below we've listed some of the possibilities. In going over this activity in class, we suggest you have students trade responses or read them aloud to each other, so that they are all aware of the diversity of responses to the assignment.

31

Topic: The effect of insensitive teachers on young children
   Teacher being sarcastic to student making a mistake
   Teacher joking about student's clothes choices
   Child's reading mistakes increasing as teacher corrects
   Child crying after a teacher's cruel remark
   Teacher punishing harshly for small transgression
   Name-calling or labeling of a child for being different

Topic: The importance of family traditions
   Family seated at Sunday dinner
   Sugary donuts for all at breakfast for a family birthday
   Generations gathered at a holiday for a yearly reunion
   Fourth of July kite-flying with all the cousins
   Gathering at year's end to view selected family videos

2. Below are possible conflicts for each situation. Dialog for each conflict will vary according to each student's experiences.

   a. Friend criticizes your food choices as unhealthy

      Friend embarrasses you by snacking on food throughout store

   b. College choice is on the other side of the country

      College choice does not offer the major your parents wish you to take

   c. Counter-demonstrators accost your group

      Some protesters break the law by trespassing and are arrested

   d. Fighting the desire to go to the gym instead of studying

      Telling friends to be quiet or go away

ANSWERS FOR REVISING ACTIVITIES

Below we provide suggested responses to selected revising activities at the end of Chapter 4. Of course, your students are bound to come up with their own inventive approaches. (p. 132)

3. Here are some ways to revise the sentence sets to create first a negative connotation and then a positive connotation. Other versions are possible, of course.

   a. The raucous clanging of the bell signaled that the last day of lectures and homework was finally over.

      With a gentle dinging sound from the school bell, the last day of high school quietly ended.

   b. We strode over to admonish our neighbors for polluting the air with burning leaves.

      We had a neighborly chat with the Joneses, while the autumn leaves burned fragrantly in their yard.

c. The sun slicing through my window jolted me upright in bed, and I was forced to admit that daylight had come.

The lemony-yellow sunshine poured across my bed, and I sat up, grateful the new day was finally here.

4. It's a good idea to set aside some time for students to exchange their versions of the paragraph with others. Seeing how others handled the assignment can open their eyes to techniques they haven't thought of.

Students should keep in mind as they revise that this is an introductory anecdote. It needs to be brief and pointed. Here are the main problems in the paragraph:

— The reference to the type of car the writer was driving is irrelevant and should be deleted.
— The speeding car should be described.
— The description, "The car didn't slow down . . ." is slow-paced and indirect; rewrite to state that the car "sped. . . ."
— Description of car coming, light changing, couple crossing, is too slow; condense and make more dramatic.
— "Dressed like models" is irrelevant, unless other details are added later in the paragraph to indicate how rumpled and bloody their clothes now are.
— The sentence about the man "jump[ing] to the shoulder" is short and choppy.
— Describe man's and woman's locations and injuries more visually, instead of saying he "wasn't hurt" but "it was clear she was."
— Narrator's calling police is a digression; condense events to get to the point: she died.
— Give more visual details of speeding car stopping, driver getting out, instead of saying he "looked terrible"; give us a picture of him drunk.
— Use his repeated offenses as a lead-in or stronger transition to the final sentence, the thesis.

THE FOURTH OF JULY

Audre Lorde

Questions for Close Reading (p. 137)

1. Here is one possible way of stating the essay's implied thesis: "Lorde's eighth grade graduation was supposed to mark the end of her childhood. But it was her Fourth of July graduation-present trip to Washington, D.C., that truly marked the end of her innocence, because there she encountered the harsh reality of racism."
2. This picnic is Lorde's mother's idea of what it means to take care of her family, even to the extent that she provides different pickles (one type for the father, another type for the kids), wraps peaches separately so they won't bruise, and puts in a tin of rosewater for messy hands. Being a good mother also means packing the things your family enjoys, like "'marigolds' . . . from Cushman's Bakery . . . and rock-cakes from Newton's" (paragraph 4). All these domestic details of a caring mother underscore the injustice, the horrific irony of the way the family is treated at the ice cream counter. Although Lorde's mother probably believed in her heart that packing

the picnic was a way to keep her family safe from food touched by the hands of strangers, more importantly, it was also a way to keep her children away from the racist situation they would most likely encounter in the railroad dining car. In short, these elaborate picnic preparations were evidence of the mother's avoidance of unpleasantness at all costs.

3. There are two reasons Lorde gives us for her inability to comprehend her parents' admonitions against white people. First of all, Lorde's parents never gave her any reasons; they just expected her "to know without being told" (7) the logic behind their warnings and the source of their feelings regarding white people. In addition, she has difficulty accepting such a dictate when her mother, as she tells us, "looked so much like one of those people we were never supposed to trust" (7). The fuzziness of the dictate leaves Lorde doubly vulnerable to the experience she encounters at the ice cream counter.

4. In paragraphs 5 and 6, Lorde illustrates her mother's attempt to sidestep racism and her father's attempt to make up for it. By packing an elaborate picnic for the trip, Lorde's mother successfully avoids subjecting her family to the racism they would surely have encountered had they attempted to eat in the dining car. And when Lorde's sister is denied access to her own senior class trip because, truth be told, they would be staying in a hotel that "did not rent rooms to Negroes," Lorde's father tries to offset Phyllis's disappointment by planning a family trip instead. In paragraph 7, Lorde explains her parents' behavior more fully. She writes: "They handled it as a private woe. My mother and father believed that they could best protect their children from the realities of race in america and the fact of american racism by never giving them name, much less discussing their nature."

   In the picture Lorde draws for us in paragraph 18, her family does not so much deal with the situation as ignore it. After the waitress delivered her message, Lorde tells us, "Straight-backed and indignant, one by one, my family got down from the counter stools and turned around and marched out of the store, quiet and outraged, as if we had never been Black before." But when she questions her parents about this obvious injustice, they don't answer her. In fact, they never address the incident, "not because they had contributed to it, but because they felt they should have anticipated it and avoided it" (19). Lorde gets increasingly angry not only because her parents do not share her heated emotions, but also because they seem to accept responsibility for what happened. Also, her sisters mimic her parents' pretense of denial, and this invalidation of her response from all members of the family heightens Lorde's fury and anger. Moreover, while she is given the freedom to articulate her fury in a letter to the President of the United States, because her father insists upon reviewing the letter before she sends it off, we wonder whether she will be permitted to fully express her righteous rage.

5. *fabled* (1): famous; legendary
   injunction (7): order or demand
   progressive (8): favoring progress or reform
   dilated (9): enlarged
   vulnerable (9): unprotected
   travesty (10): a ridiculous representation of something
   decreed (13): ordered
   pretense (19): false appearance

Questions About the Writer's Craft (p. 137)

1. Lorde uses transitions of time and place to let us know when and where events occur. In the first sentence of the essay, Lorde establishes a general time frame when

she writes that events occurred "on the edge of . . . summer." The final sentence of paragraph 1 narrows that time frame down to the Fourth of July. In paragraph 2, we learn that Lorde's family took the trip "during the day" and that it was made by train. We know that the train leaves New York City and passes through Philadelphia; Lorde writes, "I remember it was Philadelphia because I was disappointed not to have passed by the Liberty Bell" (3). In paragraphs 8 and 12, she signals the family's arrival at their destination ("In Washington, D.C., we had one large room with two double beds and an extra cot for me") as well as the family's movement out of the hotel to see the sites ("I spent the whole next day after Mass squinting up at the Lincoln Memorial"). Paragraph 13 reveals the passage of time ("Later that Washington afternoon my family and I walked back down Pennsylvania Avenue"), while paragraphs 15 and 16 set the scene at the ice cream parlor ("Two blocks away from our hotel, the family . . . stopped . . . at a . . . soda fountain . . . Corded and crisped and pinafored, the five of us seated ourselves one by one at the counter") and indicate Lorde's place in the scene ("There was I between my mother and father"). Paragraph 18 reveals the family's response to the waitress's refusal to serve them (". . . one by one, my family . . . got down from the counter . . . and marched out of the store"). That day ends with Lorde's writing a letter to the President of the United States, which her father promises she can type out on the "office typewriter next week" (19). The "whole rest of that trip," Lorde writes, she felt sick to her stomach (20).

2. In paragraphs 5–7, 9–11, and 19–20, Lorde moves from the events of the day to other discussions. Nevertheless, the information she provides in these instances is critical. The last sentence of paragraph 5 and the whole of paragraphs 6 and 7 are used to convey the way her parents handle racism and how their behavior affects her. Although the information in these paragraphs does not advance the narrative itself, what she reveals here has much to do with the experience she is describing. Her parents' failure to explain "the realities of race in america and the fact of american racism" leaves her open to the confusion and pain she feels while in Washington.

In paragraphs 9–11, we learn that Lorde has trouble seeing clearly every summer; her eyes are unable to adjust to the "dazzling whiteness" of July. At first, this little aside about squinting seems arbitrary and unnecessary, but later we find that it is actually a metaphor for being blinded to racism: Just as her parents "did not approve of sunglasses, nor of their expense" (thus forcing her to squint her way through each summer, never seeing clearly), they also did not approve of racism discussions, nor of the cost of exposing their children to the reality of racism (thus forcing Lorde into a sort of blindness that made the day of clarity all the more painful).

In paragraph 19, Lorde tells us that her sisters, like her parents, behaved as though nothing was wrong with what happened in the ice cream parlor. In fact, her whole family seemed to have a tacit agreement that denial was the best way to handle—or not handle—racism. Lorde feels alone in her inability to accept injustice. As a result, Washington, D.C., becomes a solid block of whiteness that makes her sick to her stomach, and the trip itself proves to be "[not] much of a graduation present after all" (20).

3. Lorde's use of the lower case is appropriate. Given the soul-searing incident she experiences in Washington, D.C., the nation's capital, on the holiday commemorating that nation's declaration of independence and its promise of freedom and justice for all, the use of lower-case letters conveys her lack of respect for a country and a leader that fail to uphold those promises implied in the celebration of the Fourth of July.

4.   In paragraph 20, Lorde repeats the word "white" over and over again: "The waitress was white, and the counter was white, and the ice cream I never ate in Washington, D.C., that summer I left childhood was white, and the white heat and the white pavement and the white stone monuments of my first Washington summer made me sick to my stomach for the whole rest of that trip and it wasn't much of a graduation present after all." Like Lorde, who feels overcome by the prevalence of racism, we too are overcome by the word "white" and can understand Lorde's experience: Racism is constant and exists everywhere.

SHOOTING AN ELEPHANT

George Orwell

Questions for Close Reading (p. 146)

1.   Orwell's thesis is implied. One possible way of stating it is: "Members of a ruling imperialistic class feel compelled to behave so as not to lose face or power over the populace, even if it means doing something against their better judgment."
2.   Orwell felt pressured by the people, almost overwhelmed by their power over him through their mere presence. In theory, he explains at the start of the selection, he "was all for the Burmese and all against their oppressors, the British" (2). But, in reality, he felt the common people of the country were "evil-spirited little beasts who tried to make my job impossible" (2). During the shooting incident the people were "happy and excited," he says, and they watched him "as they would a conjurer about to perform a trick." He resentfully saw himself as having to spend his life "trying to impress the 'natives'" (7). He reports later that, as he fired a shot, the crowd emitted a "devilish roar of glee" (11). His choice of words shows that he resented and disliked the Burmese.
3.   Orwell shoots the elephant because the two thousand native people standing behind him expect him to. They want vengeance for the man it killed, the meat the carcass will provide, and the entertainment of watching the shooting. "The people expected it of me and I had got to do it" (7), he writes. There is an implication that if he decided not to shoot the elephant, both he and the empire would suffer a loss of prestige, but the main concern in Orwell's mind is the "long struggle not to be laughed at" (7). He is even afraid to "test" the animal's mood by going closer for fear it might attack and kill him before he could shoot, thus giving the crowd a sight it would enjoy as much as the slaughter of the beast.
4.   Despotic governments result from the need to maintain power over subtly resistant people; such a government can rule only by fulfilling the people's expectations and responding to every crisis with the expected force. Orwell points to the irony that he stood armed in front of an unarmed crowd, yet he was powerless to do as he wished or as his judgment told him. Instead, he felt himself "an absurd puppet pushed to and fro by the will of those yellow faces behind" (7).
5.   *imperialism* (2): a country's policy of gaining power by acquiring and ruling territories
     prostrate (2): lying face down, as in submission or adoration
     despotic (3): tyrannical, all-powerful
     mahout (3): the keeper and driver of an elephant
     miry (5): swampy, muddy
     conjurer (7): magician

futility (7): uselessness, ineffectiveness

sahib (7): "Master"; Indian title of respect when addressing Europeans

Questions About the Writer's Craft (p. 146)

1. What Orwell calls a "tiny incident" lasted only a short time, perhaps only an hour at most. Orwell uses clear transitions of time to keep us oriented as to what is happening, but he provides no specific clock time. "Early one morning," the narrative begins (3); after the death of the coolie, the action steps up and the transitions indicate things are happening at a rapid pace: ". . . he could not have been dead many minutes . . ." (4); "As soon as I saw the dead man . . ." (4); "the orderly came back in a few minutes . . ." (5); "meanwhile some Burmans had arrived . . ." (5); "As soon as I saw . . ." (6); "I thought then . . ." (6); "But at that moment . . ." (7); "I perceived in this moment . . ." (7); "But I had got to act quickly . . ." (8); "For at that moment . . ." (9); "When I pulled the trigger . . ." (11); "In that instant, in too short a time . . ." (11); "He looked suddenly stricken . . ." (11); "At last, after what seemed a long time—it might have been five seconds . . ." (11); "And then down he came . . ." (11). In paragraphs 12 and 13, Orwell describes the refusal of the animal to die: "I waited a long time . . ." "Finally I fired . . ." ". . . but still he did not die" (12). The incident ends with Orwell leaving the scene but learning later that the animal took half an hour to die.

2. The first two paragraphs introduce us to the alien, far-off world where the narrative took place. In addition to setting the scene, Orwell explains what he was doing in Burma and, more importantly, gives us an emotional perspective from which to view the event. We learn in a general way about the bitterness between the colonialists and the native inhabitants and about the psychological effect his job as a policeman had on him. His confession that he was "young and ill-educated" and not even aware the British Empire was collapsing helps us feel empathy for him in the incident that follows. Without this information, we might not be willing to forgive him the shooting of the elephant or its horrible death, or comprehend the sense of victimization he felt despite his position as an "authority."

3. Orwell uses analogies in three important places. Two of the analogies are from the theater and relate to the sense of falseness that Orwell feels about his role in the colony. With the crowd watching him, he compares himself to "a conjurer about to perform a trick" with "the magic rifle." Then he helps us to understand his own psychological state at that moment by using another theater image: "Here was I . . . seemingly the lead actor of the piece; but in reality I was only an absurd puppet pushed to and fro by the will of those yellow faces . . ."; in the East, he says, the white man "becomes a sort of hollow, posing dummy . . . . He wears a mask, and his face grows to fit it" (7). Paragraph 10 continues this analogy, as Orwell describes the crowd breathing "a deep, low, happy sigh, as of people who see the theatre curtain go up at last." The third analogy compares the elephant to an elderly person; as Orwell watches the beast in the rice paddy, he feels it has a "preoccupied grandmotherly air." After he fires the first shot, he says the elephant "looked suddenly stricken, shrunken, immensely old. . . . His mouth slobbered. An enormous senility seemed to have settled upon him. One could have imagined him thousands of years old" (11).

4. Orwell vividly evokes the suffering of the elephant by carefully observing the animal's movements after the shot. He notices the subtle but "terrible change" that came over it, in which "every line of his body had altered." The analogy with an old man helps structure his observations that the elephant seemed paralyzed, then sagged to his knees and slobbered. Other trenchant details include the image of the animal

standing "weakly upright" again and the image of him toppling "like a huge rock," "his trunk reaching skywards like a tree," and trumpeting once (11). In paragraph 12, Orwell provides a graphic description of the beast's death agony. He reports firing over and over; into a picture that has so far been in black-and-white, he interjects colors. He remembers that the elephant's "mouth was wide open" so that he "could see far down into caverns of pink pale throat," and that "the thick blood welled out of him like red velvet." In this paragraph, too, we hear sounds: the "tortured breathing," the "dreadful noise," and the "tortured gasps" that continued "steadily as the ticking of a clock."

THE CHASE

Annie Dillard

Questions for Close Reading (p. 151)

1. Dillard states her thesis in the second paragraph. "I got in trouble throwing snowballs, and have seldom been happier since." The rest of the essay describes this event, elaborating on what made this moment so monumental.
2. According to Dillard, football was a "fine sport" because it required creativity and secrecy. She writes, "You thought up a new strategy for every play and whispered it to the others. You went out for a pass, fooling everyone." And yet the best part of football was the full body-and-soul participation it required. It was all or nothing: "If you hesitated in fear, you would miss and get hurt. But if you flung yourself wholeheartedly at the back of . . . [your opponents'] knees—if you gathered and joined body and soul and pointed them diving fearlessly—then you likely wouldn't get hurt, and you'd stop the ball." This complete involvement and focus was the most important aspect of the game, not only because the team's score depended on the players' concentration and courage, but because the players' own fate was at stake. To succeed at the game, to secure their fate, they had to give it their all, without hesitation, without fear.
3. Dillard's decision to trail Mikey Fahey increases both their odds of being caught. Not only will traveling together slow their pace, as they must focus both on where they are going and on each other, but it will hamper their chances of eluding the driver. He need keep only one in his line of vision to have them both in his sight. Hence, the driver behaves sensibly when he chooses to follow the pair of snowball culprits rather than trying to run down a lone escapee—that is, he has a greater chance of actually catching someone. Moreover, his eventual diatribe will hardly be worth the run if he has only one person to whom he can deliver it.
4. A businessman, probably on his way to work, this man is certainly not dressed for a trek through the snow. Nevertheless, he embarks on one and refuses to stop until his mission is accomplished. He is a man who will not give up. In paragraph 10, Dillard describes both his appearance and persistence: "He was in city clothes: a suit and tie, street shoes. Any normal adult would have quit, having sprung us into flight and made his point." Apparently, this man's "point" cannot be made simply by scaring the children away from the scene of the crime. His point requires more, and he is ready to give his all to make it. Thus, even though Dillard expects him to quit, he keeps on coming.

He chases the children silently, intent on his task, dedicating his whole self to the present moment, to the job at hand. His behavior indicates to Dillard something that greatly surprises her and, as a result, the driver is transformed from man to hero to saint. She thought only children who played football knew what this man, this adult, also knows: To truly succeed, "you have to fling yourself at what you're doing, you have to point yourself, forget yourself, aim, dive" (13). As the driver does this, Mikey and Dillard are pushed to do the same. Together they experience the exhilaration of full body-and-soul involvement, of sheer abandon to a purpose.

5. *crenellated* (5): furnished with battlements, indented
   spherical (6): rounded
   translucent (6): letting light pass through but not transparent
   embarked (7): started
   simultaneously (14): occurring or done at the same time
   dismayed (14): astonished, dumbfounded
   labyrinths (15): puzzles, mazes
   prow (16): front
   perfunctorily (18): mechanically, routinely
   redundant (19): excessive and unnecessary repetition in expressing ideas

Questions About the Writer's Craft (p. 151)

1. In paragraph 3, Dillard begins presenting rich sensory details. She tells us that "six inches of new snow had just fallen." While this detail helps us imagine the way the neighborhood looks, blanketed in a whiteness not yet marred by footprints or snow plows, it also indicates to us the way the day sounds—quiet, muffled, almost silent. These sensory details help Dillard establish the day's atmosphere—one of anticipation—for this clean, snow-covered world seems to be waiting for something to happen. She highlights the sense of expectancy when she details where the children are, what type of place it is, and what they are doing: They are standing "in snow on a front yard on trafficked Reynolds Street, waiting for cars."

   The sensory details in paragraph 5 reinforce the way the day felt ("it was cloudy and cold"). The paragraph also describes, through simile, the trails that cars left on the snowy street: "a complex trail of beige chunks like crenellated castle walls." These tiremarks, she tells us, even have a sound ("they squeaked"). Still, the tiremarks belie the fact that the street is not terribly busy; the children "wished for more traffic." As a matter of fact, there is so little traffic the children have time in between cars to retreat into solitude, a solitude so complete Dillard can make "a perfect iceball, from perfectly white snow, perfectly spherical, and squeezed perfectly translucent."

   Dillard's sensory details not only reinforce the snowy silence of the world surrounding the key players, but also suspend the action. And to heighten the drama, to create nail-biting tension, Dillard uses play-by-play action (7–9), virtually forcing us to wait for what happens next. Her paragraph-breaks intensify the suspense. For example, she ends paragraph 7 just as the snowballs are being thrown. She then withholds the outcome of this action by breaking for the next paragraph. Only when we move on to paragraph 8 do we learn that a snowball met the intended target, hitting "the driver's windshield right before the driver's face," making "a smashed star with a hump in the middle." We are forced to wait once again as Dillard breaks for paragraph 9, where we learn the consequence of this direct hit.

   To add further to the drama and suspense, Dillard varies sentence length within paragraphs—some short and choppy (10–12), others lengthy and multi-layered (13, 14, 16). The short, simple sentences, as well as the choppy, multi-layered sentences, propel us forward, like the runners. However, as the runners tire from the distance they cover (ten blocks) and from the time it takes for the driver to actually catch them, the pace of the writing slows down. The longer compound and complex sentences work to draw out the chase, bringing it slowly around to a climactic close.

Finally, to emphasize the single-mindedness of both the escapees and the driver, Dillard repeats, in close succession, certain words and phrases. Look, for instance, at the repetition of words and phrases in paragraphs 12 ("we ran"), 13 ("He chased us silently"), and 15 ("he caught us"). Notice how the repetition works to stress only what is happening at that time, drawing our focus to that action alone. We cannot project ourselves forward; the repeated words and phrases hold us where we are, caught up in what is happening at that moment.

2. Dillard repeats the word "perfect" in paragraph 6. A form of the word appears four times in one sentence. "I started making an iceball—a perfect iceball, from perfectly white snow, perfectly spherical, and squeezed perfectly translucent so no snow remained all the way through." The repetition helps establish how delicate a process creating an iceball is; achieving perfection is tough work. It takes time and concentration to render something precisely. By using the word "perfect" to describe all aspects of the iceball, Dillard raises the object to a piece of hard-won art—something so valuable, so coveted, so dangerous, she tells us, that "the Fahey boys and I considered it unfair actually to throw an iceball at somebody, but it had been known to happen." And, of course, the word "perfect" captures the quintessential nature of the whole experience of the chase.

3. Spatial organization is used to structure the descriptive passages in paragraphs 12 and 13. Dillard uses clear movements through space to keep us oriented. The words "around," "up," "under," "through," "down," "across," "between," and "over" help us follow the runners' movement: "He chased Mikey and me around the yellow house and up a backyard path, . . . under a low tree, up a bank, through a hedge, down some snowy steps, and across the grocery store's delivery driveway. We smashed through a gap in another hedge, entered a scruffy backyard and ran around its back porch and tight between houses to Edgerton Avenue; we ran across Edgerton to an alley and up our own sliding woodpile to the Halls' front yard; . . . We ran up Lloyd Street and wound through mazy backyards . . ."(12).

These spatial signals not only help readers follow the trail; they also emphasize two important points: how meandering the path was that Dillard and Mikey traversed and how determined the man was. He was willing to follow them regardless of how lost he became or how treacherous the terrain.

4. Narrative immediacy is often achieved through dialogue; yet Dillard uses dialogue but once in her essay—when the driver finally addresses the children: "'You stupid kids,' he began perfunctorily." The essay's lack of dialogue does not, however, work as a disadvantage. On the contrary, the central characters' silence, matching the snowy silence outside, speaks volumes. Through their silence, we come to understand much about these people. Mikey and Dillard need not communicate to find their way through the neighborhood; the driver doesn't need to yell and scream to make his purpose known. Words simply aren't necessary. Paradoxically, the silence gives voice to their excitement, their fear, their thrill in the moment, their equal determination. The silence cancels out the need for spoken language. Indeed, when the driver *does* speak, his words can't carry the weight that his silence shouldered. "You stupid kids"—the only words we actually hear spoken—seem lame in comparison to all that was implied by his previous absence of utterance. Perhaps for this reason, Dillard does not record the rest of the driver's speech—it was, after all, "a mere formality, and beside the point" (19).

SALVATION

Langston Hughes

Questions for Close Reading (p. 156)

1. The thesis in this selection is implied. You could state it this way: "As a boy, Langston Hughes pretended to be saved and lost his faith at the same time." Another way of expressing it is: "Religious fervor sometimes leads to religious hypocrisy and disillusionment."
2. There are many pressures on the young Hughes. He is the last child left on the "mourner's bench," the only one left unsaved, and he suffers shame (11) and guilt. His aunt, the minister, and the whole congregation pray for him "in a mighty wail" (7) and beg him to be saved. He feels the pressure of time passing (11) and that of the heat as well (6). Finally, Wesley invites him to join in a deception and gives him an example of a person who pretends to be saved without suffering any vengeance from God; Langston comes to understand that perhaps the only way to be saved is to pretend.
3. Wesley does not seem to be a believer, for he chooses deception without any qualms. On the other hand, Langston believes what his aunt has told him about salvation: you see a light, and Jesus comes into your life. Langston is patient and trusting, while Wesley is cocky and profane.
4. Auntie Reed sees only what she wants to see; hearing him crying in his bed the night of the revival, she believes he is emotionally overwhelmed by his religious conversion. She fully accepts the values of her church and takes the external event of walking from the mourners' bench to the altar as proof of salvation. She does not seem to have any understanding of psychology at all. If her nephew told her the truth of his experience in the church, one of two things would probably happen: he would convince her that he is a sinner because he had lied in church, or he would cause her to lose her faith as he has lost his.
5. *revival* (1): a meeting for the purpose of reawakening religious faith
    knickerbockered (11): dressed in knickerbockers, full pants gathered below the knee
    punctuated (14): emphasized, accentuated
    ecstatic (14): rapturously joyful and excited

Questions About the Writer's Craft (p. 156)

1. Hughes creates suspense by drawing out the description of his turmoil as the lone unsaved sinner for almost one-third of the essay (6–11). By this point, we already know the expectations his aunt and the preacher have for him, and he begins the portrayal of his shame by introducing the possibility of deception: Wesley's false salvation (6). We wonder throughout the next five paragraphs whether Langston will hold his ground, be saved, or lie. Another technique that increases the suspense is the use of very specific details about how he was pressured. He tells us the imagery of the songs sung the night of the children's meeting (3, 4). Also, he uses dialogue to show Wesley's irreverent invitation and to present the scene of the minister passionately calling him to the altar.
2. Because he has the role model of Wesley's sacrilege, the narrator understands that lying is a safe option for him to choose. Wesley, in a sense, is his "salvation" from the shame of not being saved. Wesley also serves as a foil to Langston; by contrast, Langston's honest and trusting nature is all the more apparent. Learning that Wesley

41

is proud about his deception, we can feel more strongly the poignancy of Langston's bitter tears.

3. "The whole room broke into a *sea* of shouting," Hughes writes, and "*waves* of rejoicing" filled the church. Through this metaphor, he portrays the unified and overwhelming force of the congregation as it engulfs the last converted sinner. The image also suggests Langston is helpless and even drowning in the religious ecstasy around him.

4. The hymns sung at the children's revival meeting take on a personal meaning for the young Langston. We are told, for example, that one song is about a hundred lambs, of which ninety-nine are saved and one is left out in the cold (2). A second hymn provides an image of hell ("the lower lights are a burning") to motivate "poor sinners" to be saved. The songs thus threaten the boy with the torments of cold and fire unless he comes to Jesus.

THE PRICE WE PAY

Adam Mayblum

Questions for Close Reading (p. 163)

1. Mayblum's narrative point is that democracy is stronger than terrorism: "If you want to make us stronger, attack and we unite. This is the ultimate failure of terrorism against the United States" (paragraph 12). Alternatively, some students might rephrase the narrative point along these lines: "Despite the chaos and horror wreaked by the September 11 terrorist attacks, people in the Towers united in their attempt to help each other survive."

2. The main conflict is between people and a life-or-death crisis: getting out of a building that has been struck by an airplane.

3. Mayblum says he is writing so that he and others never will forget what happened (1). His expressions of grief, anger, and guilt suggest that he also is writing to help himself cope with these feelings. In addition, he might be writing to clear up his own confusion about the events of that day.

4. Mayblum refers to the destruction, injuries, and deaths at the World Trade Center as the "price we pay to be free" (12). In other words, the freedoms that Americans enjoy—and, presumably, the dominant international role the U.S. has assumed as a result of those freedoms—put the U.S. at risk of evoking opposition epitomized by the terrorist attack on September 11th.

   Answers to the second question may vary. Some students may agree with Mayblum's analysis, which is optimistic and resilient in nature. Others might disagree, arguing that terrorists wish to kill Americans not because Americans enjoy many individual liberties but because they feel U.S. foreign policy is imperialistic, exploitative, and supportive of oppressive governments.

5. *aka* (2): an abbreviation for "also known as"
   lurched (2): moved suddenly and roughly
   reams (2): large amount
   ticker-tape (2): including paper strips released into the air in celebration
   succumbed (3): fallen victim to
   junction (3): place of connection
   ushered (3): led
   retrospect (3): hindsight

nuclear winter (9): life-destroying environmental darkening and cooling caused by nuclear explosion

fallout (9): descending radioactive particles caused by nuclear explosion

debris (9): scattered pieces of something that has been destroyed

engulfed (10): swallowed up

commotion (11): disturbance, confusion

gypsy cab (11): a taxi that cruises the streets for customers

Questions About the Writer's Craft (p. 163)

1. While answers may vary regarding the effect of present tense in the essay, here are some possibilities. Mayblum's present-tense frame (1, 12) makes the opening and the conclusion more immediate and helps readers to identify with the author and his harrowing experiences. Throughout the essay, present tense adds impact where it breaks chronological order to indicate that a particular person may have died, as in "I do not know what happened to her" (8) and "Pray for him and all those like him" (11). However, where present tense halts the action for an insignificant statement, it can be seen as diffusing tension and slowing the pace. For example, the statement "Seventy-eight is the main junction to switch to the upper floors" (3) lacks importance and therefore could have been de-emphasized. Similarly, instead of removing readers from the time of the attack by stating "In retrospect, I recall seeing Harry" (3), Mayblum could have written simply "I saw Harry." The sentences "I am only thirty-five. I have known him for over fourteen years" (3) would have been less distracting and more effective later in the essay, where Mayblum makes the important statement "I fear that Harry is lost" (11).

2. Sentence fragments and short sentences help to convey the situation's urgency, fragmentation, and sharp impact. Like sentence fragments, the absence of quotation marks also contributes a sense of urgency—as if no time or thought can be wasted on formal correctness.

3. *We* and *our* highlight the unity and cooperation that prevailed at the World Trade Center, underscoring Mayblum's theme that Americans will unite if attacked.

4. Answers will vary. Some students may say these examples represent the comforts and pleasures of life in America. Others, in contrast, may find them problematic since all three examples apply only to privileged Americans. Many Americans cannot find work, let alone decide where they want to work. Many lack adequate food, let alone the option of eating whatever they want. And many either do not take vacations or must take their vacations when their employers permit them to. One might argue that more universal and significant examples—such as freedom of speech, freedom from torture, and freedom from imprisonment without due process—would have conveyed Mayblum's point more effectively.

EXEMPLIFICATION

OPENING COMMENTS

When we first started teaching, we were caught off guard by students' seeming inability to provide detailed, specific examples in their papers. But we soon uncovered one reason for the vagueness of their writing. Many of them arrived in college with the notion that good writing is abstract and full of highfalutin language. Warned by dutiful high school English teachers not to pad their papers, many students had come to regard specific details and "for instances" as fluff.

We've found an almost sure-fire way to help students appreciate how powerfully examples can affect a reader. We have them react (see page 170) to two versions of some student writing, one flat, lifeless, and sorely in need of supporting details, the other enlivened with specifics. When we question students about their reactions ("Which version is more interesting?" "Which gives you more of a sense of the writer?"), we actually see them coming to grasp the full importance of vigorous supporting detail.

Next, we spend some class time on prewriting activities. These help students learn how to generate examples for their essays.

That skill mastered, some of our eager-to-please students then give us too much of a good thing. Heaping their papers high with examples, they force readers to wade through a mass of specifics that don't lead anywhere. When this happens, we emphasize that writers need to be selective and choose the most striking examples to support a point.

Varied in subject and mood, the professional selections in this chapter illustrate the power that writing derives from rich supporting detail. Beginning with a dramatic opening illustration, Sykes then uses a variety of example types to reveal a generation headed for trouble. Nilsen tackles the uses and abuses of language by citing numerous examples. By piling on instances of how preteens are encouraged to mature too soon, Hymowitz provides a convincing case that the "tween" phenomenon has come to dominate youth culture. Johnson, through a series of poignant personal experience examples, illustrates the precarious nature of the human condition. Finally, Ehrenreich's comical discussion of men's interpersonal talents dramatizes the value of selectivity, of finding just the right specifics.

ANSWERS FOR PREWRITING ACTIVITIES

On the next page, we provide possible responses to selected prewriting activities at the end of Chapter 5. Of course, your students are bound to come up with their own approaches. (p. 181)

1.   There are many ways to use exemplification in these two essays; the lists below only begin to name the possibilities. We suggest that you have students share their ideas for examples, perhaps with a partner or in small groups. Seeing what others have come up with makes the point clearly that writing involves invention and individuality.

Topic: Why public school teachers quit
    Teacher who has to work a second job to support family
    Ex-teacher now a mail carrier, better paid
    Science teacher recruited by industry
    Teacher resenting blame and criticism of education today
    Teacher toiling late at night over tests and lesson plans

Topic: Defining a preppie
    Female wearing pearls with baggy shorts on a chilly day
    Male wearing rugby striped shirt with a crest and loafers
    Preppies' conversation centering on grades and careers
    Preppie male going out for crew or tennis
    Preppie female playing intramural lacrosse or field hockey

ANSWERS FOR REVISING ACTIVITIES

Below we provide possible responses to selected revising activities at the end of Chapter 5. Of course, your students are bound to come up with their own approaches. (p. 181)

We suggest you offer students the chance to read each other's reworked versions of the paragraphs in activities 3 and 4. Such exposure to others' work helps them to see new ways of handling the revision and can encourage them to be more creative.

3. Here are the main problems with the paragraph:

    — Needs examples of how stores might be modernized: new signs, more professional window display, interior renovation.
    — Nature of the improvements to streets should be shown by examples: potted plants, outdoor sculptures, decorative benches, outdoor cafes.
    — Examples needed of how town could be made more "fun to walk."
    — Examples of the "attention-getting events" should be provided.

4. Here are the main problems with the paragraph:

    — Vague descriptions ("trendy," "fine") need replacement by vigorous images. A strong example or two is needed here.
    — Point about trendy clothes should be tied in to the idea of the costliness.
    — Singling out women is sexist; at the very least such a charge needs supporting examples. Indeed, more thought may well show that men are similarly vulnerable.
    — Shampoo example should occur at the end of the paragraph, because the movement of the paragraph is from things that don't wear out to things that do wear out. Change the opening words of the sentence to fit it into its new location.
    — "Slight changes" is vague; an example is necessary.
    — Statement that men are "naive" and are "hoodwinked" is sexist and irrelevant; this point also needs to be more clearly tied in to the point that the desire for the new is costly to the consumer.

THE "VALUES" WASTELAND

Charles Sykes

Questions for Close Reading (p. 190)

1. Sykes's thesis is that the American educational system is not providing students with firm guidelines to help them make moral choices. This thesis is stated directly in paragraph 3 ("A 1992 survey by the Josephson Institute for Ethics of nearly 7,000 high school and college students, most of them from middle-and-upper middle-class backgrounds, found the equivalent of 'a hole in the moral ozone' among America's youth") and reiterated elsewhere in the essay: "'I think it is very easy to get through high school and college these days and hardly ever hear, *That's wrong.*'" (paragraph 4); "'Their IDI-ology is exceptionally and dangerously self-centered, preoccupied with personal needs, wants, don't-wants and rights.'" (4); "In pursuit of success, or comfort, or self-gratification, the IDI's are blithely willing to jettison traditional ethical restraints, and as a result IDIs are more likely to lie, cheat and engage in irresponsible behavior when it suits their purposes" (4); and "In its place [of moral role models], we provide children a jumbled smorgasbord of moral choices" (5).

2. "At one time," Sykes writes in paragraph 5, "American students used to study historical role models like Benjamin Franklin, Florence Nightingale, Thomas Edison, Madame Curie, Abraham Lincoln, and George Washington—whose stories were used to provide object lessons in inventiveness, character, compassion, curiosity, and truthfulness." Modern education, however, allows students to choose their own values and refuses to teach them that some values are more important, or moral, than others. Sykes maintains that in a misguided fear of "moralizing" and in an attempt to allow students freedom to work out their own value systems, modern educators have failed to give students the ability to distinguish right from wrong and serious moral questions from trivial ones.

3. Sykes feels that educational theorists are responsible for the imposition of this ineffective and amoral system. Specifically, he singles out "developers of Values Clarification and other nonjudgmental approaches to moral decision making" (9) who have imposed upon schools an educational philosophy dedicated to promoting the concept of "individual identity." Central to the development of this identity, such theorists argue, is students' freedom to choose what sort of morality they wish to adopt. To teach that honesty, charity, or patriotism are *a priori* virtues would, according to these theorists, deprive students of the essential opportunity to work out their values for themselves.

4. The object of each exercise is to encourage students to develop their own value systems by examining a situation requiring them to make a moral choice. In both cases, students are presented with a narrative involving a life-and-death situation in which they are required to make a decision about the value of human life, and in both they are asked to recognize the importance of certain human virtues in preserving life. But in the case of the survivors in the cave (15), students are invited to assert the value of their own lives as opposed to—or at the expense of—other people's. Significantly, the exercise does not suggest that opting to be last in line may be the most moral choice. In the exercise positing moral choice in a lifeboat (18), students are asked to judge the value of human vs. animal life, regardless of how cherished that animal life may be.

Theoretically, there is no "right" answer in the cave situation, and coming to a "successful" result hinges on each student's ability to describe his or her worthiness to classmates. In the lifeboat excuse, however, there clearly is a "right" choice, although instructors may or may not choose to emphasize it, and students are not inclined to condemn classmates who choose "wrongly."

Sykes faults both exercises. They fail to emphasize that "there might be universal and objective moral principles at stake" (18), and they invite children to make moral choices without ultimately indicating which of those choices are morally superior. Interestingly, both situations, although theoretically possible, are essentially artificial—far removed from and not realistic for most students. Asking students what they would do if trapped in a cave or in a lifeboat may not produce more realistic responses than asking children what they would do if they found a genie trapped in a bottle.

5. *unrepentant* (1): feeling no regret for what one has done (or failed to do)
    self-actualization (4): to develop or achieve one's full potential
    precept (5): a rule or principle prescribing a particular course of action or conduct
    emulate (5): to strive to equal or excel, especially through imitation
    perseverance (5): steady persistence in adhering to a course of action
    smorgasbord (5): a varied collection
    bête noir (9): one that is particularly disliked
    moralizing (9): expressing moral judgments or reflections
    cognitive (10): related to the faculty of knowing
    rationalization (14): devising self-satisfying but incorrect reasons for (one's behavior)
    fraught (17): filled or loaded with something (usually something bad)

Questions About the Writer's Craft (p. 190)

1. The opening example of the unrepentant rapist is effective for several reasons. It is vivid, shocking, and graphic—important qualities in any introductory paragraph for drawing readers into the essay. Further, it provides a dramatic personalization of the issues discussed in the essay. Like a "dolly-in" in cinematography, the essay focuses on the Spur Posse member and lets him speak for himself: "'They pass out condoms, teach sex education and pregnancy this and pregnancy that. . . . But they don't teach us any rules.'"

    This opening example is the only one in the essay that establishes a link between student misbehavior and an educational philosophy that fails to teach morality. The examples in the second and third paragraphs (the Rhode Island study reporting on young people's high tolerance for sexual aggression and the write-in survey and Josephson Institute survey indicating that a high percentage of adolescents cheat, steal, shoplift, and so on) simply raise disturbing questions about the morality of America's youth. Unlike the first example, these examples don't posit a connection between schooling and behavior. However, Sykes obviously intends these examples of immoral behavior to shock readers. As such, they pave the way to his argument that values-free education is a poor way to direct young people toward moral behavior.

2. For some classes it may be sufficient to discuss the ironic and dramatic effect of yoking together two apparently contradictory terms. We notice that the word 'Values' in the title is in quotation marks, a standard way of indicating that a word is being used in a special sense, often sarcastically, as it is here. The word "value" implies an exalted absolute, but this "values clarification," according to Sykes, has produced students with no values at all, or none worthwhile—that is, a wasteland.

The dramatic juxtaposition of the two concepts catches our attention, as it does in terms like "Christian soldiers" or "tough love." More advanced classes might benefit from mention of the importance to modern literature of T.S. Eliot's "Wasteland." Such a comment would throw further light on the modern concept of "The Wasteland" as a symbolic burial ground of absolute values.

3. Sykes peppers his essay with statistics in paragraph 2 and 3 and makes little use of them thereafter. These statistics, like the strong opening description of the Spur Posse rapist, provide a powerful introductory statement on which the author—and the reader—can chew for the rest of the essay. Moreover, statistics generally seem impressive, particularly to readers concerned about "scientific method" and the supposedly objective nature of truth. By citing numbers—2,000 Rhode Island students, 126,000 teenagers, "more than 60 percent of high school students," etc.—Sykes gives his essay a tone of factuality and objectivity. However, students should not be too willing to accept Sykes's statistics just because they represent numbers rather than words; neither should we dismiss them for the same reason. Much educational theory is framed in vague abstractions and lofty theorizing without much fact (or statistics) to back them up. It is refreshing to find an educational commentator who—instead of offering generalities like "Student morality is on the decline"—reports survey results indicating that a third of high school students shoplift or sixty percent cheat on exams.

4. This is a serious essay on a serious subject. "Youth is going to hell and denying the virtues of its parents and ancestors" has been a common theme in prophetic literature since Biblical times. Sykes's commentary shares in this tradition of gloom with an almost prophetic tone of warning and despair. The darkness of Sykes's tone serves to underscore the severity of the problem.

SEXISM AND LANGUAGE

Alleen Pace Nilsen

Questions for Close Reading (p. 197)

1. Nilsen states her thesis very broadly at the end of paragraph 2: "Anyone living in the United States who listens with a keen ear or reads with a perceptive eye can come up with startling new insights about the way American English reflects our values." Students may wish to refine this statement; here is one possibility: "American English is sexist, for it contains many words with negative connotations for females and just as many words with positive connotations for males."

2. In English, animal terms commonly applied to women usually imply negative qualities, such as undesirability, ugliness, aggressiveness, or meanness. On the other hand, similar animal-derived terms applied to men tend to be neutral or to emphasize positive qualities such as physical strength, intelligence, or competence. Nilsen supplies complementary instances of this phenomenon in paragraphs 3 and 4. For example, a shrew is a nagging woman, but *shrewd* means an astute and clever person, as in a "shrewd businessman" (3).

3. Different job names serve to glorify men's work and minimize the significance of women's work, even when the tasks performed are the same. Serving food, for example, is a waitress's job in most restaurants, but in the armed forces, food is served by orderlies, who are really just male waitresses under a different name. Likewise, Nilsen points out, the armed services have men assigned to be clerk-typists, medics and adjutants, positions called "secretary," "nurse," and "assistant" in

48

civilian life and normally performed by women. Outside the armed forces, men become chefs and tailors, while women performing the same duties are called cooks and seamstresses. The different sets of terms tell us that men do not want to be identified with any typically female activities, and they will do certain jobs only when they are retitled with a masculine-sounding, "higher-status" term (13).

4. Positive terms for women emphasize youth, beauty, and sweetness. Nilsen gives as examples terms derived from words for baby animals (8), food (20), and flowers (21). Such terms suggest that women are sexually seductive, passive and fragile, or like nonhuman pets or objects. The many masculine associations with words for violence seem to be a result of the reality of our culture—most violence is committed by men (17–18). As Nilsen says, "We have very negative feelings toward someone who is hurting us or threatening us or in some way making our lives miserable. To be able to do this, the person has to have power over us and this power usually belongs to males" (18).

5. *unscrupulous* (5): immoral, unprincipled
enticing (7): alluring, attractive, seductive
connotation (8): implied (suggested) meaning
virile (11): masculine, manly; having the strength and energy of a man
lexical (15): relating to words
maudlin (15): overly sentimental; weepy
vigilante (16): a citizen without authority who pursues and punishes criminals

Questions About the Writer's Craft (p. 197)

1. Each point Nilsen makes is bolstered by myriads of examples. Since we may never have noticed these patterns of positive and negative connotations in our language, we might be surprised and doubtful about the validity of her ideas. But Nilsen overwhelms any such objections by supplying so many specific instances of what she means. She clearly recognizes that our tendency to ignore the characteristics of our own language may make us resist the notion that language itself can be sexist. With so many examples at hand, Nilsen can take on the most suspicious anti-feminist and convince him (or her) that our language contains many negative judgments about women.

2. Nilsen examines the use of negative animal terms for women and positive ones for men (3–6, 8–10), the positive connotations of descriptive terms for male characteristics (11, 16), and the application of object-nouns to women (20–21). These three motifs are introduced to us in the headings that divide the essay. These headings serve as transitions; they also outline the organization and tell us the next main idea we are going to encounter.

3. Beginning with animal terms for humans allows Nilsen to start the essay dramatically. These animal terms are the most blatant, shocking, and—in the case of terms applied to women—degrading examples of sexism in language. We are likely to be intrigued and shocked by the contrasts between "shrew" and "shrewd" and "lucky dog" and "bitch"; we feel eager to read on. The section lets us know that the essay is not going to be a dry analysis of English semantics, but a presentation of ideas that affect us on a gut level.

4. Throughout the essay, Nilsen maintains a neutral, analytic tone. She establishes this tone of seriousness at the outset, by putting her ideas in the perspective of cultural anthropology, and she continues it by using objective terminology, avoiding loaded words, and qualifying her statements: ". . . not only a mixed metaphor, but also *probably* the most insulting animal metaphor we have" (4); "Other animal metaphors *do not have definitely* derogatory connotations for the female, but they *do seem to*

indicate frivolity . . ." (6); "*Probably* the most striking examples . . ." (9). Also, her use of headings contributes to the sense that we are reading a formal report on research. Nilsen avoids a stuffy or impersonal tone, however. She often refers to her audience through the use of the first-person plural: "Most of us feel . . ." (4); "We see it in our animal metaphors . . . (8); "The names we give to young children . . ." (14). She also occasionally speaks directly to her readers: "Look at the differences between . . ." (6); "Now, how can the Marines ask someone who has signed up for a *man-sized job* to do *women's work*?" (13).

Despite this tone of objectivity, Nilsen is very open about her own point of view on sexism in our language; she says, for example, ". . . I was shocked to discover that we have remnants of this same attitude in America" (8). In large part, Nilsen conveys her point of view implicitly; in paragraph 3, for example, she says quite neutrally that "we can uncover some *interesting* insights into how our culture views males and females," yet the examples she offers shock us into understanding her view that English debases women.

TWEENS: TEN GOING ON SIXTEEN

Kay S. Hymowitz

Questions for Close Reading (p. 204)

1. Hymowitz doesn't directly state her thesis. Instead she quotes others stating it: "There is no such thing as preadolescence anymore. Kids are teenagers at ten" (paragraph 3); "There's a deep trend . . . toward kids getting older younger" (6); "The 12- to 14-year-olds of yesterday are the ten to 12s of today" (6).
2. Tweens like to think of themselves as sophisticated: "flirtatious, sexy, trendy, athletic, cool" (7). Girls project this image by wearing body adornment such as makeup or earrings, attention-getting hairdos, and trendy, often sexually suggestive clothes. Comparably, boys exemplify tweendom in an increased concern with fashion, especially pricey designer wear, as well as in other aspects of personal appearance, such as piercings and ultra-modern hairstyles.
3. A growing number of children under the age of fifteen are committing violent crimes (12); engaging in sexual activity (13–14); using alcohol and drugs, especially marijuana (15); and developing eating disorders (16).
4. She attributes the tween phenomenon primarily to parental absence and "a sexualized and glitzy" marketplace (18). These two factors, in turn, elevate the authority and influence of tweens' peer group, resulting in a vicious circle of negative influences. Another cause that Hymowitz addresses but seems to regard as secondary is the earlier physical maturation of kids today than in the past (17).
5. *glowering* (1): staring with an angry look
Talmudic (1): relating to a particular collection of ancient Jewish religious writings
rites (1): religious ceremonial acts
demographic (3): relating to population trends
pragmatic (5): practical
ideological (5): relating to a body of beliefs
regalia (8): finery
donning (8): putting on
ply (8): participate in
emblazoned (10): prominently marked
de rigueur (10): required

eschewing (11): rejecting
tentative (14): hesitant
proclivities (14): inclinations
connotations (14): suggested meanings
stigma (15): mark of disgrace
pernicious (16): harmful
correlation (17): co-occurrence, correspondence
augment (18): increase

Questions About the Writer's Craft (p. 205)

1. The personal nature of this example draws the reader's interest, as do the variety of specific examples Hymowitz presents to illustrate her point. In addition, this anecdote gains Hymowitz credibility in discussing the topic of tweens because it establishes her own personal experience with the phenomenon.
2. Hymowitz draws from a broad spectrum of examples in her essay. She cites specific names, such as of celebrities and retail stores (1, 8), in presenting the kinds of tween preoccupations. Personal anecdotes play an important role; the essay opens with the vivid example of Hymowitz's own daughter (1) and goes on to cite anecdotes from others, such as the fifth-grade Ohio teacher who caught two students in the bushes (14). These anecdotes reinforce the pervasive nature of the tween phenomenon while also demonstrating the author's personal experience with it. Another category of examples that Hymowitz marshals is that of expert opinion. She cites numerous educators and psychologists about the alarming behaviors of tweens (3, 6–9, 13, 15–16)—her thesis is even conveyed in the words of these experts. These citations compellingly establish and explain the tween problem. In the same vein, she cites studies and statistics (4, 6, 7, 12, 13, 15, 17) to help define tweendom and, more significantly, to demonstrate the alarming ramifications of tween behaviors.
3. Hymowitz's tone is concerned and disapproving, somewhat bitter, and sometimes mocking or sarcastic. For example, she dismissively states that her daughter reads movie ads "with all the intensity of a Talmudic scholar" (1). Hymowitz renders the word "empowered" ironical by placing it in quotation marks (5) and sarcastically says that students "showed their respect" by dressing like prostitutes (8). Strongly negative terms such as *vulgar* (5), *crass* (5), *hooker* (9), *painted* (9), and *pernicious* (16) clearly convey Hymowitz's disapproval.
4. In these paragraphs, Hymowitz use female clothing as a way of contrasting the preteens of earlier generations with today's tweens. She demonstrates the gap between the childish, modest clothing such as "little-girl flowers, ruffles, white socks, and Mary Janes" (8) worn in the past and the less-modest or sexually provocative clothing such as tank tops (discussed in paragraph 9), black mini-dresses (8), platform shoes (8), "midriff-revealing shirts" (8), and mini-skirts (8) worn by comparably aged girls today.

BOMBS BURSTING IN AIR

Beth Johnson

Questions for Close Reading (p. 210)

1. The thesis is stated through a metaphor at the very end of the essay: "[Bombs] can blind us, like fireworks at the moment of explosion. . . . But if we have the courage

to keep our eyes open and welcoming, even bombs finally fade against the vastness of the starry sky" (15). In other words, life's unexpected tragedies can seem devastating and insurmountable when they occur; but we must courageously live on, recognizing that even these misfortunes are part of life's greater mystery and beauty.

2. Johnson states directly, "News that reached me today makes me need to feel her [Maddie] near" (2), referring to the revelation that Maddie's five-year-old playmate, Shannon, was unexpectedly diagnosed with a brain tumor. This jarring discovery reminds Johnson of the fragility of life and the randomness of misfortune, for Maddie could just as easily have been the one stricken with the tumor. Compelled by the maternal impulse to protect her child from impending harm, Johnson draws Maddie near. Though Johnson knows she has no power over the bombs that might explode in life, she feels slightly more secure having her daughter nearby.

3. The reactions of Maddie, Sam, and Johnson to the news of Shannon's illness provide a snapshot of the process of evolving maturity. Only five years old, Maddie fails to understand the gravity of Shannon's condition, and she is too young to be "faze[d]" by bombs in general (8). Johnson sees her younger self in Maddie, recalling her own "childhood . . . feeling of being cocooned within reassuring walls of security and order" (8). Maddie declares her certainty that Shannon "will be okay," having learned in school about a boy who recovered from an illness (5, 7). Maddie's confidence in Shannon's recovery and her willingness to change the subject—"Can we go to Dairy Queen?" (7)—contrast with the response of thirteen-year-old Sam, who is "not so easily distracted" (6). Perched between childhood and adulthood, Sam is aware of how serious Shannon's condition is, yet he still seeks his mother's guarantee that the child will recover: "She'll be okay, though, right?" (6). Just like his mother in her adolescence, Sam struggles as "the protective curtain between us and the bombs" (10) is slowly being drawn away from him. Finally, Johnson represents the adult stage of awareness, for she is most shaken by the news and is least confident that a happy ending is in sight. This essay itself serves as a testament to how much the news has affected her, for Shannon's "bomb" has inspired Johnson to reflect on life's bombs in general. Having lived through numerous occasions when very bad things have happened to very good people, Johnson lacks any illusions about life's fairness. During Johnson's adolescence, the sudden death of her best friend taught Johnson the life-changing lesson that "there was no magic barrier separating me and my loved ones from the bombs. We were as vulnerable as everyone else" (11). Because the friend died in her sleep without contributing to her own demise in any way, Johnson as a teenager was forced to realize that no rules of logic or fairness govern the bursting of bombs. Nevertheless, as an adult, she demonstrates the need for comfort that characterizes children; she draws her child close to her and takes solace in the conclusion that despite the bombs that potentially may burst, life must be lived and people must be loved.

4. Given the knowledge that "the greater our investment in life, the larger the target we create" for life-bombs, individuals may respond in one of two ways. One option is to withdraw from life and scale back commitments to others, reducing the potential for pain and loss. In Johnson's words, people may "refuse friendship, shrink from love, live in isolation, and thus create for ourselves a nearly impenetrable bomb shelter" (13). The other option is to immerse oneself in life, willing to brave potential bombs in order to experience life's joys and beauties, "to truly live, to love and be loved" (13). Johnson advocates the latter path, and she marvels at the resilience of the human spirit, which inspires people to live on: "I am moved by the courage with which most of us, ordinary folks, continue soldiering on. We fall in love, we bring our children into the world, we forge our friendships, we give our hearts, knowing with increasing certainty that we do so at our own risk" (13). Those

who isolate themselves from life, she implies, lose far more in the end than those who say "yes, yes to life" and only periodically suffer.

5. *ferrying* (4): transporting
   shrapnel (6): fragments from exploded artillery
   faze (8): disturb; disconcert
   cocooned (8): sheltered; protected
   tremors (9): vibrations
   incantations (10): charms or spells ritually recited
   vulnerable (11): susceptible to harm or injury
   intertwining (12): joined together; interrelated
   impenetrable (13): unable to be entered or understood
   soldiering on (13): bravely moving forward
   prognosis (14): predicted outcome of a disease
   fragility (14): state of being breakable

Questions About the Writer's Craft (p. 211)

1. The first example that Johnson emphasizes—and the one that frames her essay—is the anecdote about Shannon. (Johnson ponders the sad news about Shannon's illness, then delivers the news to her children.) This incident receives so much attention for several reasons. It reminds Johnson of how fragile life is, how randomly calamity strikes, and, therefore, how easily one of her own children could have been the target of a "bomb" like the one that hit Shannon. This news then triggers a series of memories about tragedies that Johnson witnessed in the past and jars her into meditating on the occurrence of misfortune in general.

   These memories are ordered chronologically, beginning with incidents in Johnson's youth that affected her least and progressing to events in her adolescence and adulthood that impacted her most. In paragraph 9, she briefly catalogues "tiny shockwaves"—incidents that were peripheral to her life. She does not describe these memories in great detail because, as she admits, she was unaware of the gravity of these incidents as a child and young adolescent. In paragraph 10, however, she says, "As we got older, the bombs dropped closer." She goes on to catalogue more harrowing events, ones that were closer to her life, such as a peer's suicide and the deaths of a carful of acquaintances. Yet, she says, "we still had some sense of a protective curtain between us and the bombs." But in paragraph 11, Johnson describes the single most destructive bomb, the one that changed her life. Here she develops at great length the example of her best friend's sudden death at the age of sixteen. She focuses on this crisis because of her degree of intimacy with this friend (as opposed to earlier acquaintances) and because this tragedy marked a turning point for Johnson, a rite of passage from innocent childhood into knowing maturity. After this event, she "found [herself] shaken to the core of [her] being" (11), more worldly-wise and less secure in the world around her. Johnson then quickly catalogues bombs that dropped in her late-adolescent and adult life. She does not focus special attention on them because, as an adult, she was more equipped to handle the barrage of misfortune that she witnessed—secondhand, in one instance (her professor's loss of two children), and firsthand, in others (the pain of love, the failure of her marriage, and the death of her father). She says, "I became more aware of the intertwining threads of joy, pain, and occasional tragedy that weave through all our lives" (12); as a result, she came to regard misfortune as part of life's cycle and was not as rattled when it ran its course.

2. In paragraph 6, Johnson contrasts how she wishes life could be with how life actually is. She begins by describing a more ideal world, signaled by a series of

53

sentences beginning "I want." She wishes she could, in all honesty, assure her son that Shannon will be fine; that her children could "inhabit a world where five-year-olds do not develop silent, mysterious growths in their brains" to begin with; that the medical terms being applied to Shannon were "words for *New York Times* crossword puzzles, not for little girls" (6). However, this fantasy is cut short by the blunt, bleak admission, "But I can't," followed by her reason for abandoning illusions: "the bomb that exploded in Shannon's home has sent splinters of shrapnel into ours as well, and they cannot be ignored or lied away" (6). This stark contrast between wish and reality supports Johnson's main idea that in life, we have no control over when and where bombs will drop; all we can do is live fully and love each other in order to weather life's inevitable misfortunes.

3.   Johnson uses repetition in these two paragraphs, usually to emphasize magnitude and/or quantity. In paragraph 9, the similarly-structured "*There was the* little girl who . . . ," "*There was the* big girl who . . . ," and then "*A* playful friendly custodian . . . ," and "*A* teacher's husband . . ." appear consecutively as Johnson itemizes the different people affected by bombs in her youth. The repetitive syntax emphasizes the number of bomb victims while also demonstrating how a wide range of people were equally vulnerable. Johnson employs repetition for the same reason at the beginning of paragraph 10, where she again itemizes bomb victims: "*A* friend's sister . . . ," "*A* boy I thought I knew . . . ," "*A* car full of senior boys . . . ." Later in the same paragraph, she reiterates "if only" four times to illustrate how she and her peers were powerless in the face of such tragedy, left only to repeat the same futile phrase over and over again.

4.   The title, "Bombs Bursting in Air," introduces the central image of bombs, an image that reverberates throughout the essay. The title is derived from the line in "The Star-Spangled Banner" sung expressively by Johnson's daughter, Maddie, at the athletic event that opens the essay (2). Maddie's lively emphasis on the "b's" triggers a series of painful reflections for the author, who is still reeling from the devastating news about young Shannon's brain tumor. Johnson comes to refer to such unanticipated tragedies in life as "bombs," which burst in air—and in life—without warning and with lasting effect. She goes on in the essay to delineate the impact and aftermath of bombs in her own past, using terms like "exploded" (3), "shrapnel" (6), "shockwaves", and "tremors" (9), in showing how she grew out of youthful naiveté and into painful awareness of life's dark realities. The more one opens oneself up to life and love, she observes, "the larger the target" one becomes for devastation and loss (13). Despite her dark awareness, Johnson emerges with a renewed faith in the human spirit that inspires "ordinary folks [to] continue soldiering on" (13). At the end of the essay, she says that humans are faced with a choice: we may either withdraw from life in order to avoid potential bombs, or we may courageously "keep our eyes open and welcoming," realizing that "even bombs finally fade against the vastness of the starry sky" (15).

Overall, the metaphor of bombs is effective not only because it captures the explosive impact that life's calamities may have, but also because it is a highly accessible image for readers.

WHAT I'VE LEARNED FROM MEN

Barbara Ehrenreich

Questions for Close Reading (p. 216)

1. Ehrenreich states her thesis directly in the beginning of the second paragraph: "But now, at mid-life, I am willing to admit that there are some real and useful things to learn from men." In paragraph 2, she explains that a main useful thing is "how to get *tough.*" The rest of the essay goes about explaining the "real and useful things" in more depth. Another important statement for the reader seeking orientation to the essay's progress occurs in paragraph 4: "In conversations with men, we do almost all the work. . . . Wherever we go, we're perpetually smiling. . . . We're trained to feel embarrassed if we're praised, but if we seek a criticism coming at us from miles down the road, we rush to acknowledge it. And when we're feeling aggressive or angry or resentful, we just tighten up our smiles or turn then into rueful little moues." The essay then discusses in this order the problems with women's taking too much social responsibility and smiling too much (5–9); their dismissal of praise and embracing of criticism (10); and their weak anger (11).
2. Ehrenreich responded to his inappropriate behavior in the way she had been trained to after "30-odd years of programming in ladylikeness" (3). Although "disgusted," she remained polite and pretended not to notice his advances. Even when he put his hand on her knee, she genteelly moved it away, rather than confront him directly. Finally, he apparently made an attempt to embrace or grab her, "there was a minor scuffle," and she left. She chastises herself for this wimpy, "ladylike" behavior. At the end of the essay (12), she describes her current view of how she should have handled him. She begins by moving her chair away from his side to opposite him so that she can see his face. He chatters, but she does not respond. Instead she stares at him with arms crossed, leaning back, letting him know she feels her time is being wasted. She avoids the typical female responses of "apologetic shrugs and blushes." And then, "at the first flicker of lechery," she says, she stands and coolly rebukes him: "All right, I've had enough of this crap." Then, "slowly, deliberately, confidently," she walks out. This manner of handling him would have been confrontational and impolite, but also "tough"—a sign that she had learned an important skill from men.
3. At the end of paragraph 3, Ehrenreich equates behaving "like a lady" with behaving "like a ninny." In the next paragraph, she elaborates on this negative view of "ladylikeness." Its essence is a "persistent servility masked as 'niceness,'" she says. In other words, women play "nice," but what they are really doing is subjugating themselves to the needs and plans of others.
4. "Macho stars" appeal to women because they contrast with women's typical behavior. The male stars Ehrenreich describes are in control; they have power and use it to take care of themselves. They face down punks, they swagger, they shrug off the law. And they never use the strategies adopted by women to smooth over human relations; they do not "simper," "chatter aimlessly," or "get all clutched up." "Therein . . . lies their fascination for us," Ehrenreich concludes. She goes on to suggest ways in which women can "toughen up," citing the Jean Baker Miller article (6). She advises us to stop smiling (7), gushing and chattering (8–9), and learn to show our anger (11).
5. *euthanasia* (1): mercifully causing the death of an incurably ill person
    guttural (1): harsh or throaty

lecherous (3): inappropriately and insistently seductive
distractingly (3): in order to divert the attention of another
unconscionable (3): excessive or unreasonable
ninny (3): a fool or simpleton
servility (4): slavish obedience
veneer (4): deceptive outward appearance
moues (4): pouts
marauders (5): raiders, plunderers
aura (6): a pervading quality surrounding a person or thing
brazenly (6): boldly, impudently
deference (9): respectfulness
taciturn (9): silent and impassive
purveyors (10): providers or sellers
emulating (11): imitating in an attempt to equal
basso profundo (11): a deep, low vocal pitch
blandishments (12): statements intended to cajole or coax

Questions About the Writer's Craft (p. 217)

1. Ehrenreich presents this personal example early in order to explain what she means by women needing to learn some new types of behavior and to persuade us that this is so. Many of the later examples in the essay are generalizations about women's behavior, so that including a personal example at the start establishes credibility for Ehrenreich's point of view. We are likely to agree that if she, a mature, convinced feminist, can lapse into this ineffective, self-destructive, incompetent behavior, then the behavior must be epidemic among women. She returns to this personal example at the end in order to show a revised version of her behavior, a version in which she is powerful and effective. This reevaluation of the experience helps us to understand what type of behavior she is recommending.

2. There are numerous contrasting examples in the essay. The introduction humorously posits Ehrenreich's own lifelong failure to get the attention of waiters with how men "can summon a maitre d' just by thinking the word 'coffee.'" The rest of the essay gives more serious contrasts between women's and men's behaviors. Paragraph 4 presents the contrast of how males and females act in conversations; paragraph 5 contrasts typical macho film-star behavior with the coping strategies women typically use. Paragraph 6 implicitly contrasts women's failure to accept and acknowledge their powerfulness with men's power; the next paragraph contrasts women's tendency to smile all the time with Clint Eastwood's two dour expressions. Paragraph 8 contrasts men's and women's conversational styles. In paragraphs 9 and 10, Ehrenreich contrasts two types of female behavior, one actual, the other possible. In 9, she contrasts women's usual perkiness and smiles with the absence of these qualities, noting that serious women's faces cause men to wonder if the women are out-of-sorts or even hostile. Then she contrasts two women's styles of taking credit (10). Paragraph 11 returns to the contrast of male and female styles, this time styles of anger. Finally the conclusion presents Ehrenreich's fantasy of the ideal response to the lecherous professor, in contrast to her description in paragraph 4 of her actual ineptitude in that situation.

3. Ehrenreich appears to consider her audience to be primarily female. She uses "we" throughout the essay, assuming an identification by the reader. In addition, her frequent jibes at various quirks of male behavior show she isn't writing for men or even a mixed audience. Such remarks convey that she expects her readers to be at least partially sympathetic to her position. She also describes herself as "a full-grown

feminist" (3), and most likely she feels her readers will respect or even share this identity.

4.	Ehrenreich's tone is definitely not "ladylike" or "nice." She frequently exaggerates in order to achieve a harsh satiric tone; she uses a blunt or smart-alecky "tough guy" tone in some places, and she clearly does not care, like the macho film stars (5), about whether she hurts people's feelings. Paragraph 1 starts the essay off with this irreverent, unladylike style. She mocks some of men's less appealing characteristics—their tendency to interrupt or perform "conversational euthanasia," their disregard of household neatness even when it could be achieved without effort, and so on. She then comes on strong and uses some unladylike phrasing to establish her thesis: "there are some real and useful things to learn from men. . . . we're just too *damn* ladylike" (2). Later in the essay, she turns her satiric tone on women; she asks whether macho film heroes would "simper their way through tight spots" or "chatter aimlessly" or "get all clutched up" about possibly hurting another's feelings. In paragraph 7, she uses a smart-alecky tone to recommend to women that "if you're not sure what to do with your face in the meantime, study Clint Eastwood's expressions—both of them." Exaggeration again creates the satiric effect in paragraph 8: "the average man can go 25 minutes saying nothing more than 'You don't say?' 'Izzat so?' and, of course, 'Hmmmm.'" Her tone is again irreverent and blunt in paragraph 9—"If you're taking a vacation from smiles and small talk and some fellow is moved to inquire about what's 'bothering' you, just stare back levelly and say, the international debt crisis, the arms race, or the death of God." In paragraph 11, she again presents a humorous, exaggerated picture of male behavior when angry: "they pound on desks and roar . . . the full basso profundo male tantrum." Finally, her concluding image of how she should have handled the lecherous professor is an exaggerated, humorous "tough-guy" portrayal of a woman "playing it like Bogart" (12).

DIVISION-CLASSIFICATION

OPENING COMMENTS

We confess. We always feel slightly uneasy about teaching division-classification as a distinct pattern of development. After all, the logic at the core of division-classification comes into play a number of times during the writing process. For example, when students generate thoughts during the prewriting stage, when they outline their ideas, when they prepare process analyses, they instinctively draw on the ordering principles characteristic of division-classification. But even though many students automatically use division-classification, we teach it as a discrete method of development. We do so because the pattern helps students understand the demands of logical analysis.

Working with division-classification causes two problems for students. First, they become confused about the difference between division and classification. They think they're classifying when they're dividing and dividing when they're classifying. On page 222, we state as succinctly as we can the difference between these two related but separate processes: Division involves taking a *single unit* or *concept, breaking the unit down* into its parts, and then analyzing the connection among the parts and between the parts and the whole. Classification *brings two or more related items together* and categorizes them according to type or kind.

Second, some students view division-classification as a pointless exercise designed by overly particular composition teachers. When they learn that they've been using division-classification all along (when brainstorming, when outlining, and so on), they begin to understand that division-classification is a valuable tool for logical analysis. In this connection, the student essay "The Truth About College Teachers" (pages 229–30) will provide the class with a good laugh (perhaps even at your expense) and help students see how to use classification to make a point.

This chapter's professional essays show how division-classification can help writers analyze different subjects. Ericsson classifies our everyday falsehoods into categories that lend insight into the complexity of human communication. Zinsser and McClintock classify, respectively, pressures on college students and Madison Avenue propaganda techniques. To illustrate his point about the deceptive nature of "doublespeak," Lutz organizes his proof into four overlapping categories. And Tannen asks us to think before we speak by classifying the main areas of miscommunication between men and women. In-class discussion of any of these essays is bound to raise provocative questions about contemporary values.

ANSWERS FOR PREWRITING ACTIVITIES

Below we provide possible responses for selected prewriting activities at the end of Chapter 6. Of course, other approaches are possible. (p. 235)

1. Division-classification can be used in a variety of ways in these two essays. Below are a few suggestions. It's a good idea to have students share their ideas on the use of division-classification with each other; this will provide a concrete demonstration of the possibilities.

Topic: How to impress college instructors
Divide brown-nosing techniques into types
Classify students according to their favorite technique
Classify instructors according to what impresses them

Topic: Why volunteerism is on the rise
Divide to obtain motivations for volunteerism
Classify people needing help
Classify kinds of people who are apt to volunteer

2. Here are some possible principles of division for each of the topics in Set A. Other principles of division and theses are possible.

   a. **Rock Music**

      Principle of division: According to era
      Thesis: Rock music styles fall into distinct eras: music of fifties, sixties, seventies, and eighties.

      Principle of division: According to audience
      Thesis: Rock music appeals to many audiences: the middle-aged, the yuppie, the college-aged, and the teenaged.

      Principle of division: According to its origin
      Thesis: Rock music has diverse influences: country music, rhythm and blues, and jazz.

   b. **A Shopping Mall**

      Principle of division: According to time of day at mall
      Thesis: At different times of the day, different groups of people inhabit the mall: senior "mall-walkers" in the early morning, business people grabbing lunch at midday, mothers and babies in the early afternoon, and teenagers in the early evening.

      Principle of division: According to what is sold
      Thesis: The types of stores that prosper at Garvey Mall tell much about today's consumer; the majority of shops sell apparel, quite a few sell audio and video tapes, but only one sells books.

      Principle of division: According to places people congregate
      Thesis: The fountain, the fast-food arcade, and the movie theater patio at Garvey Mall are all social spots, but for different types of people.

   c. **A Good Horror Movie**

      Principle of division: According to person being victimized
      Thesis: In "Kennel Horror II," the victim is either an unsuspecting innocent, a helpless poor person, or a law-enforcement officer.

      Principle of division: According to attack location
      Thesis: The victims in "Kennel Horror II" are attacked in their own homes, in pleasant public places, or in isolated rural areas.

      Principle of division: According to film shots
      Thesis: Director Logan Bettari uses extreme close-ups, rapid pans, and jarring cuts to increase the tension in "Kennel Horror II."

Here are some possible principles of classification and thesis statements for the topics in Set B. Your students, of course, may come up with different ones.

Topic: Why people get addicted to computers

Principle of classification: According to types of people
Thesis: Computer addiction is more likely to affect introverts than extroverts, sedentary people than active people, and single people than married people.

Principle of classification: According to types of computer use
Thesis: Computers can be addictive whether they are used for work, play, or simple correspondence.

Principle of classification: According to circumstances of a person's life
Thesis: Computer addiction can be a consequence of boredom, loneliness, or laziness.

Topic: How fast food restaurants affect family life

Principle of classification: According to the effects on the different members of the family
Thesis: Frequenting fast-food restaurants affects each member of the family differently.

Principle of classification: According to effects on various aspects of family life
Thesis: Fast-food restaurants seriously affect the financial, emotional, and physical well-being of a family.

Principle of classification: According to types of consequences
Thesis: Fast-food restaurants have short and long-term consequences for family-life.

Topic: Why long term relationships break up

Principle of classification: According to types of long-term relationships
Thesis: The short distance long term relationship, the long distance long term relationship, and the live-in long term relationship all end for different reasons.

Principle of classification: According to levels of commitment
Thesis: The end of a long term relationship may occur if little commitment is involved, if one person is more committed than the other, or if one person wants a commitment and the other does not.

Principle of classification: According to various aspects of the relationship.
Thesis: Long term relationships often end when the people involved no longer share the same interests, when the people involved lose interest in each other, when the people involved find the relationship no longer suits their needs.

ANSWERS FOR REVISING ACTIVITIES

Below we provide possible responses for selected revising activities at the end of Chapter 6. Of course, other approaches are possible. (p. 235)

3. The essay is based on a principle of division; "experience" is divided according to areas: employment, academic, social.

    The principle of division is applied incorrectly in the second point. Instead of being about an area of experience, this point focuses on "negative" experiences, a broad division that doesn't fit with the other areas. Second of all, the point refers only to "optimists," while all the other points refer to everyone.

    The problem can be remedied by eliminating the second point, since there are already three other solid points to be made in the essay.

4. Make time for your students to share their revisions with each other. Seeing the work of others helps students see all the possibilities in revising.

    This paragraph divides the concept of "play" using as a principle of division how much the child's peers are involved in the play. The paragraph's organization is based on the chronological appearance of the stages in the child's growth. The principle is applied consistently, but there are some problems in organization and in the support offered.

    Here are the specific problems with the paragraph:

    — The discussion of the first stage ("babies and toddlers") needs a specific example or two of "their own actions."
    — The fourth sentence, about elementary children's play, is incorrectly located in the paragraph, which discusses the play of preschool children. Delete this sentence.
    — The discussion of the second stage ("parallel play") could use an example of the "similar activities" the children engage in and how the children might "occasionally" interact. Note the specific examples provided for the third stage.
    — The last sentence is irrelevant and contradictory because no connection is made between the "special delight in physical activities" and the social aspect of children's play. In addition, the second part of the sentence contradicts the topic (first) sentence. This point must be more thought out and more details should be added.

THE WAYS WE LIE

Stephanie Ericsson

Questions for Close Reading (p. 244)

1. Ericsson's thesis is implied. One way of stating it might be, "Lying is common in our society, but an exploration of the types of lies shows that lying is destructive and should be avoided." After the long introduction in which Ericsson establishes a criterion for determining if something is a lie (1–7), the rest of the essay discusses different types of lying.
2. The lies that Ericsson tells are part of a strategy to smooth out small difficulties for everyone concerned. There's a positive result from these four lies. She protects herself by saying traffic delayed her to a business meeting, when it was her own fatigue that caused a late start, and she protects her wallet by telling the bank that the money to cover checks drawn on her account is in the mail, when it's not. To protect her obviously tired partner, she hides her day's little disasters from him. She protects her friend's feelings by saying she's too busy for lunch. Even so, she

debates whether such small lies are harmless: "Sure I lie, but it doesn't hurt anything. Or does it?" (3). She confesses to having a deep voice inside her that says, "When someone lies, someone loses" (5).

During the week of experimental honesty, Ericsson discovered that telling the truth all the time has "serious consequences" (4), and that lying relieves a person of certain painful effects that descend quickly if the truth is revealed. She cites the consequences of the typical lies she named in paragraph 1: that the bank would levy charges, her partner would become overloaded, her client would fire her, and her friend would be offended (4).

3. In appointing these behaviors as lies, Ericsson examines the "meaning of [the] actions" and applies the definitions from *Webster's Dictionary*, two tests she mentions in paragraph 6. Ericsson grants that while sometimes, "ignoring the plain facts" is not "in and of itself a form of lying," such avoiding of reality can fit the dictionary definition of a "false action done with the intent to deceive" (13). She cites the Catholic Church's ignoring information about a priest's abuse of children as a clear example of this type of lie. "Deflecting" attention away from a topic is an effective way to hide the truth, and therefore commits a lie. She provides two serious examples of people who set a false accusation rolling by avoiding a true one about themselves (15–16). "Omission" can create a lie because the partial meaning might "make a difference in how a person lives his or her life" (17). Omissions show the truth of Ericsson's maxim in paragraph 5: "When someone lies, someone loses." She explains how an omission might successfully get you a free pair of replacement glasses (a loss to the optician), or it might affect your whole view of the world, yourself, and religion. She cites the omission of the story of Lilith from the Judeo-Christian Bible as the kind of omission that distorts people's perceptions..

    "Stereotypes and clichés" and "groupthink" are "compound" lies which employ several other techniques of lying. "Stereotypes and clichés" lie by "exaggeration, omission, and denial, to name a few" (23). Her "textbook" example of groupthink involves all these and stereotypical thinking as well—during World War II, Americans denied in the face of plain facts that the Japanese could be smart enough to solve the technical problems of attacking ships in somewhat shallow Pearl Harbor (24).

4. She wonders whether, if she condones lying and practices it herself, she is no better than "slick politicians or . . . corporate robbers" (5). She suspects that "saying it's okay to lie one way and not another is hedging" (5), that is, it's being wishy-washy about a significant moral issue. Her conscience, that "voice deep inside," suggests that "when someone lies, someone loses" (5). Exploring the possible negatives, she wonders if lying protects her at the expense of someone else (6).

5. *travails* (4): burdens and suffering
    hedging (5): avoiding a rigid commitment
    penance (6): punishment received to atone for sins
    pittance (9): a small amount
    facades (10): false fronts
    plethora (11): an overabundant amount
    disenchanted (11): no longer delighted or charmed
    ecclesiastical (12): of the church or clergy
    pedophilia (12): the abnormal sexual desire for children
    irreparable (13): incapable of being repaired or rectified
    blatant (14): obvious
    demonization (18): act of casting someone as a demon
    misogynists (18): people who dislike women
    embodiment (18): physical manifestation

archetype (20): original pattern or model from which something is made

obliterated (22): blot out or erase

dissent (23): difference of opinion

cohesiveness (25): unity

invulnerability (25): immunity to attack

entrenched (25): placed in a position of strength

catatonia (30): mental disease characterized by stupor and rigidity

gamut (31): an entire range

Questions About the Writer's Craft (p. 245)

1. While "white lies" (8–9) and "out-and-out lies" (26–27) are certainly lies, many of the other behaviors Ericsson cites are less obviously examples of lying. In discussing the different types of lying, Ericsson is careful to clarify how each fits the classification of a lie. She establishes how to determine a lie in paragraph six, suggesting that the underlying meaning of a behavior is the determinant. The "meaning" that creates a lie is the "intent to deceive" or "give a false impression," as the *Webster's Dictionary* definition states (6). As Ericsson goes through the various categories of lies, she shows how each one involves deception or intentional falsity. In 11, she provides an example of a man with a sparkling facade who constantly cheated his friends. In 12–13, she shows through an example how "ignoring the plain facts" can be lying; the Catholic Church's conscious covering up of the "plain facts" in the case of Rev. Porter fits the definition, Ericsson says, of "a false action done with the intent to deceive" (13). Deflecting is shown to be a lie through the example of Clarence Thomas, who was able to deceive the country about whether he sexually harassed a colleague by crying racism (15). Omissions are lies, Ericsson indicates, providing an example of suppression of a truth that deceived Christian and Jewish women into "believing they were the lesser sex for thousands of years" (20). Ericsson supports dismissal as a type of lie by citing psychologist R.D. Laing's investigation of the families of schizophrenics, where "deliberate, staunch dismissal of the patient's perceptions" was a universal and likely causal factor. The other types of lying—stereotypes and clichés, groupthink, and delusion—are compound types, incorporating within them several of the other types of lies (22, 23, 34).

2. By using the narrative in her introduction, essentially "fessing up" to being an everyday liar, Ericsson disarms any negative reaction we might have to the idea she proposes in paragraph 3: "We lie. We all do." Since she has admitted to being a liar, we can't feel accused. Instead Ericsson implies we're all members of the same club. In addition, her listing of ordinary, "I'm just coping" types of lies may ring a bell with readers, again encouraging them to concur that lying is common in our lives. Further on in the introduction, in paragraph 4, Ericsson again uses her personal narrative to sketch in scenario that is almost humorous: She says she "tried going a whole week without telling a lie, and it was paralyzing." She then describes what dire and off-beat consequences might have occurred had she not told the four lies mentioned in paragraph 1: The bank levies fees, her partner "keels over" upon hearing of her difficult day, her client "fires her," and she loses her friend. Here, the narrative again seduces the reader to accept the implication that lies might actually be necessary in daily life.

3. Ericsson uses a breezy, jaunty tone, especially at the start of the essay, to steer away from sounding preachy; typically, she says what she wants to say and moves on, resisting any urge to over-analyze or become too reflective. The treatment of her four lies in paragraphs 1–2 is an example; other examples of this speedy discussion of topics occur in paragraphs 4, 5, 6, 8, 17, 22, 26, 29, and 32. Even where she

develops her examples at greater length, she gets right to the point by using direct sentences, as in paragraphs 11, 12–13, 15, 24–25, and 30–31.

Ericsson also employs lots of colloquialisms and contractions, and she writes as if she's chatting with the reader. This down-to-earth word choice begins right in paragraph 1: "It'd been a rough day," she writes. Other examples of colloquial diction include "one more straw might break his back" (2); "Sure I lie . . ." (3); "my partner keels over" (4); "my friend takes it personally . . ." (4); "slick politicians or corporate robbers . . ." (4); "saying it's okay to lie one way and not another is hedging" (5); "pay my penance because I ducked out" (6); "when he looks like hell" (6); "a vote of no confidence" (8); "quite so cut-and-dried" (9); "putting on another face" (9); "suits rather than sweatpants"; "get the kids off to school" (10); "all talk and no walk" (10); "I saw less than a hundred bucks" (10); "a crowded graveyard of disenchanted former friends" (11); "the victim is fully tamed and crawls into a hole . . ." (16); "a rowdy game of basketball" (17); "attempted negotiations"; "said adios" (19); "Eve the Rib" (20); "often shuts down original thinking"; "a candy bar of misinformation" (21); "a textbook example" (24); "'good-ole-boy' cohesiveness"; "The rest is history" (25); "the bald-faced lie" (26); "the common thread" (30); "runs the gamut"; "can be quite handy" (31); "I could write the book on this one" (32).

Finally, Ericsson uses a colloquial exaggeration and strong, emotionally tinged language to imbue her essay with feeling, sometimes humorous, sometimes indignant. Exaggerated descriptions include "sit at my computer in my pajamas until four in the afternoon" (10), "fabulous books to read and fascinating insights"; "a crowded graveyard of disenchanted former friends" (11); "from a highly charged subject to a radioactive subject" (15); "a brilliant maneuver" (155); and "information in nanoseconds" (21). Emotionally tinged language includes "actually providing him with a fresh supply of unsuspecting families and innocent children to abuse" (12); "The church became a co-perpetrator with Porter" (13); "Clarence Thomas exploded with accusations"; "it was a brilliant maneuver"; "unlike sexual harassment, which still regards those who can get away with it" (15); "who understandably screams something obscene out of frustration" (16); "I was stunned"; "[it] felt like spiritual robbery . . ." (18); "renegade Catholic feminists" (19); "a patriarchal strategy to keep women weak" (20); "Unfortunately, it often shuts down original thinking" (21); "they are always dangerous. . . . They close minds and separate people" (22); "the slipperiest of all lies" (28); "a powerful lying tool" (32); and "it shamelessly employs dismissal . . ." (34).

4. Throughout the essay, Ericsson admits that most of the types of lies have a harmless or useful side. For example, her introduction presents an everyday scenario in which little lies are told and no great evil results, implying that telling the truth is sometimes more destructive than fibbing (14). In the case of each type of lie, however, she argues that despite the possible practical advantages, that type of lying is damaging and therefore wrong. In paragraph 8, for example, she concedes that the "white lie assumes that the truth will cause more damage than a simple, harmless untruth." By the end of this paragraph, however, she takes a stand against this type of lie, calling it an "act of subtle arrogance." In paragraph 10, she begins by acknowledging that "we all put up facades to one degree or another," but her examples move from the harmless to the destructive, again suggesting that a facade is not an acceptable deception. Her conclusion points directly to this contrast or tension between the possible "functional" use of a lie and deceitful lying ("living a lie"), thereby clearly establishing the poles of the argument she has been making. Then she firmly takes a side: against lying. She quotes a country music song to the effect that "you've got to stand for something or you'll fall for anything."

COLLEGE PRESSURES

William Zinsser

Questions for Close Reading (p. 254)

1. Zinsser states his thesis explicitly in paragraph 7, at the end of his long introduction to the essay: "I see four kinds of pressure working on college students today: economic pressure, parental pressure, peer pressure, and self-induced pressure."

2. The pressures come from the economy, parents, peers, and the individual students themselves. The notes to Carlos reveal the emotional harm students suffer as a result of these pressures, and in the rest of the essay, Zinsser explains that these pressures cause more than just psychological pain; they also inhibit students' intellectual growth and narrow the range of their college activities. He points out such harms as excessive studying and overexertion (27–29), rigid career choices and half-hearted concurrence with parental wishes (19–22), lack of experimentation (33), failure to get a liberal education (11), retreat from creativity (22), rivalry between friends (24), and deemphasis of extracurricular activities (36). As Carlos Hortas puts it, "Violence is being done to the undergraduate experience" (32).

3. The four pressures that Zinsser cites do not exist independently, but are "intertwined" or related to each other. In discussing the "intertwining" of pressures, Zinsser divides the four pressures into two pairs. In paragraph 14, he says, "Along with economic pressure goes parental pressure. Inevitably, the two are deeply intertwined." He means that economic pressure affects students as parental pressure, because the parents pay the bills, for the most part, and often expect compliance in the form of high grades and a practical major. Zinsser introduces the other pair of pressures in paragraph 23: "Peer pressure and self-induced pressure are also intertwined . . . ." The example of two roommates, each of whom suffered feelings of academic inferiority in relation to the other, points out that such peer pressure is often created or imagined by students who feel a great inner compulsion to excel.

4. Students must "break the circles in which they are trapped," Zinsser writes (31). As individuals, they need to stop following their parents' dreams and reacting to their classmates' fears. They must start to believe in their own uniqueness and their own power to achieve a future right for them (31). Zinsser quotes the dean Carlos Hortas, who agrees that students "ought to take chances" (33). Specific remedies are implied rather than stated directly; they include joining extracurricular activities (36–37), risking experimentation and failure (5), going ahead with creative aspirations (22), sampling a wide variety of courses (11), and taking time to relax and enjoy life (25).

5. *privy* (3): made knowledgeable to secret or special information
   venerated (6): worshipped, highly regarded
   exhorted (13): urged
   tenacity (15): perseverance, persistence
   vacillates (22): wavers
   furtively (22): secretly
   circuitous (4): roundabout, indirect

Questions About the Writer's Craft (p. 254)

1. Zinsser's pairing of the pressures on college students is quite logical and reflects the reality of students' lives. The first pair, economic and parental pressure, is external. These two pressures come from society at large and from parents. The other two

pressures, mass competitiveness among peers and an inner obsession to excel, affect students psychologically. These pairs make the essay's argument easier to grasp, because they reduce the four points to two larger ones; also, the pairing of pressures helps the reader to understand how the pressures interlock and overwhelm today's students.

2. The pressures on students to drive themselves hard and have a practical goal are essentially causes, and the desperate feelings and compulsive behaviors of the students are the results or effects of these causes. The essay can thus be viewed as an example of a *causal analysis* as well as of division-classification. Zinsser uses a pattern of first discussing effects and then showing the causes. For example, paragraphs 8 and 9 focus on some effects of the economic pressures: the beliefs that grades and decisions about majors determine a student's life; the economic causes underlying these beliefs are revealed in paragraphs 12 and 13. The next section follows this same pattern; paragraphs 15 to 19 present a student reluctantly pursuing an M.D., and paragraphs 20 and 21 discuss the causes of such pragmatic decisions. In the section discussing peer pressure and inner pressures, Zinsser again begins with an anecdote demonstrating the effects of the pressures (29) and follows with an analysis of the causes. Paragraph 27 presents a *causal chain* in which the effects become causes of still further effects.

3. The students' notes to Carlos make an engrossing lead-in to the essay. They capture our attention because they are so colloquial and yet so terse, so packed with emotion and occasional black humor. Also, these notes focus our attention on the theme, that many students today experience college as agony because of the pressures they are under. The self-portraits painted by these notes show that students are not, as a reader might imagine, carefree or rebellious, driven to irresponsible frivolity or to serious challenges of society. They are, instead, overwhelmed and frightened victims. On the positive side, they do maintain a sense of humor ("Hey Carlos, good news! I've got mononucleosis."), struggle valiantly with their problems ("I stayed up all night . . . & am typing . . . . P.S. I'm going to the dentist. Pain is pretty bad.") and are not afraid to reach out for help.

4. Such an exaggerated description of what students want shows sarcasm on the part of the author; the description here is almost a put-down of students who succumb to the idea that they must map out their lives completely. Other examples occur in paragraphs 1 ("Who are these wretched supplicants, . . . seeking such miracles of postponement and balm?"), 9 ("The transcript has become a sacred document, the passport to security. How one appears on paper is more important than how one appears in person"), and 15 ("They go off to their labs as if they were going to the dentist"). This ironic tone is found mainly in the beginning of the essay, as Zinsser is still luring his readers into the article. As he examines the intertwining of pressures, he drops the hyperbole and uses a more analytic tone.

DOUBLESPEAK

William Lutz

Questions for Close Reading (p. 261)

1. Paragraph 2, in its entirety, constitutes a statement of Lutz's thesis. And several sentences in paragraph 19 restate the thesis: Doublespeak "is carefully designed and constructed to appear to communicate when in fact it doesn't. It is language designed to distort reality and corrupt thought." The body of Lutz's essay illustrates this

thesis by identifying four categories of doublespeak—euphemism, jargon, gobbledygook, and inflated language.

2. The four questions are stated in paragraph 3: "Who is saying what to whom, under what conditions and circumstances, with what intent, and with what results?" In certain contexts, one must consider the desired outcome of language. In such cases, evasive or esoteric language may be permissible—for example, the euphemism "passed away" to express condolences or the special language used within the medical profession. According to Lutz, language is doublespeak when its intent is to confuse, mislead, or deceive—in other words, when it does exactly the opposite of what language is meant to do: communicate. Thus euphemisms such as "radiation enhancement device" (the neutron bomb) and jargon used outside the special group that understands it are doublespeak; gobbledygook and inflated language, which invariably evade or confuse the issue, are *always* doublespeak.

3. Lutz divides doublespeak into four categories—euphemism, jargon, gobbledygook, and inflated language—and illustrates each with many examples. As a result, individual responses to the question will vary, but here are some possibilities. Euphemism is "an inoffensive or positive word or phrase" designed "to mislead or deceive" a listener about a "harsh, unpleasant, or distasteful reality" (4). The State Department uses euphemism when it substitutes "unlawful or arbitrary deprivation of life" for "killing" to cover up damaging political evidence in a human rights' report (6). Jargon, "the specialized language" of a particular group, can be used outside that group context to confuse a listener. Lutz points to "the involuntary conversion of a 727" as an example of the legal jargon National Airlines used to conceal the source—a plane crash in which three people died—of a profitable insurance settlement (11). With gobbledygook, a speaker tries to "overwhelm an audience with words," and Lutz cites long examples from Alan Greenspan (12), Dan Quayle (14), and Jesse Moore (15). Quoting such impenetrable language, Lutz wonders if any of the men "had any idea what he was saying" (15). Finally, inflated language "make[s] everyday things seem impressive," as when mechanics become "automotive internists" and used cars are reborn as "pre-owned" or "experienced cars" (16).

4. In Lutz's schema, gobbledygook and inflated language are *always* doublespeak. In contrast, Lutz suggests that euphemism and jargon *can* have legitimate uses. As a "tactful word or phrase which avoids directly mentioning a painful reality," euphemism respects social convention and demonstrates concern for a listener's feelings (3–5). Euphemism becomes doublespeak only when it is used to thwart expectations and deliberately deceive a listener (6). Similarly, jargon has a useful purpose in the appropriate context. Jargon is the "specialized language" of a particular group, and Lutz concedes that "Within a group, jargon functions as a kind of verbal shorthand," allowing members "to communicate with each other clearly, efficiently, and quickly" (8). Jargon becomes doublespeak only when it is used outside of the group context, either to "impress" listeners or to confuse them willfully (10–11).

5. *variance* (6): difference or disagreement
   esoteric (9): specialized and restricted to a small group
   profundity (9): deep or profound
   dividend (11): a sum to be divided; money paid to stockholders
   initiative (14): beginning plan of action

Questions About the Writer's Craft (p. 261)

1. Lutz's four categories overlap considerably. For example, the Chrysler corporation's use of the term "career alternative enhancement program" to signal that they are

"laying off five thousand workers" (17) is an illustration of inflated language. But the term could also be considered a euphemism, which Lutz defines as an "inoffensive or positive" wording meant "to avoid a harsh, unpleasant, or distasteful reality" (14). The same is true of "negative patient care outcome," meaning "the patient died" (17). Although Lutz describes this example as inflated language, it also seems euphemistic—as does a "discontinuity," meaning a crack in a beam, which is cited to illustrate jargon (9). In the same vein, "radiation enhancement device," the Pentagon's term for a neutron bomb (7), is classified as euphemism, but it might also be seen as a kind of military jargon. And "rapid oxidation," classified as inflated language (17), could be considered jargon or euphemism as well.

Lutz's classifications overlap because of the nature of his subject: doublespeak. People who resort to doublespeak, as Lutz shows, may do so in different situations (a corporate or military context), and their specific motivations may differ (to hide something embarrassing, to puff themselves up). But their basic intent is always to deceive, and their basic technique is to use confusing, misleading words. Therefore, it is not surprising that the particular words they choose cannot be strictly or rigidly categorized.

2. In addition to classification, Lutz uses *exemplification, comparison-contrast,* and *definition.* He gives numerous and specific *examples* of doublespeak, such as the Pentagon's use of "backloading of augmentation personnel" (18) for "retreat" and "unlawful or arbitrary deprivation of life" (6) for "killing." These are examples of doublespeak in actual situations, and so they support Lutz's thesis that one can learn to spot doublespeak by paying close attention to the context in which such language is used.

Lutz uses *comparison-contrast* when he "translates" doublespeak into plain language. For instance, he explains that "rapid oxidation" means "a fire in a nuclear power plant" (17). With such contrasts, he not only reveals the truths that euphemism, jargon, gobbledygook, and inflated language are meant to conceal but also points up the absurdity and slyness of doublespeak. Lutz also contrasts harmless doublespeak with dangerous doublespeak: for instance, he makes a sharp distinction between euphemism that is simply tactful or sensitive, such as "passed away" for the harsher "died" (5), and euphemism that is designed to mislead, such as "incontinent ordnance" (7). The effect of this contrast is to emphasize the purpose of doublespeak: deception.

Lutz uses *definition* as well. At the outset of his discussion of each category, he carefully defines the type of doublespeak under examination (4, 8, 12, and 16).

3. Greenspan's words quoted in paragraph 12 are gobbledygook. If they mean anything at all, it seems impossible to say what. But the remark that Lutz quotes in paragraph 13 is plain language—in fact, the only plain language quoted in the entire selection. Lutz probably included it to show two things: first, that Greenspan was capable of speaking coherently if he so chose; and second, that Greenspan, able to speak clearly, was guilty of deliberate deception when he used doublespeak.

4. Unlike an activist or radical reformer, Lutz presents an even, distanced, and objective tone. While he believes that some doublespeak "can have serious consequences" (18), he does not call it "dangerous" or "evil" or "oppressive"; instead, doublespeak is described as "mislead[ing]" (6). Avoiding polemic, Lutz breaks his topic into four constituent parts. He supports his divisions with ample citations from official statements and documents, and it is only in the discussion of these citations that Lutz's distanced voice gives way to something sharper. By the third kind of doublespeak, Lutz seems ready to poke fun at gobbledygook speakers like Alan Greenspan and Jesse Moore, noting that "Mr. Greenspan's doublespeak doesn't seem to have held back his career" (13) and wondering "if Mr. Moore had any idea what he

was saying" (15). Generally though, Lutz's tempered tone ensures that his examples stand out; by choosing this tone and restraining his own response to the material, he seems certain that doublespeak will speak for itself. As Lutz notes in paragraph 3, "Most of the time you will recognize doublespeak when you see it or hear it."

PROPAGANDA TECHNIQUES IN TODAY'S ADVERTISING

Ann McClintock

Questions for Close Reading (p. 268)

1. McClintock's thesis is located at the end of the first paragraph: "Advertisers lean heavily on propaganda to sell their products, whether the 'products' are a brand of toothpaste, a candidate for office, or a particular political viewpoint."
2. Propaganda is the "systematic effort to influence people's opinions, to win them over to a certain view or side" (2) in terms of product choices, political candidates, or social concerns. Many people associate propaganda solely with the subversive campaigns of foreign powers or with the spreading of outrageous lies to an unwitting, innocent populace. But actually, propaganda is all around us; it is used by all the special interests that vie for our attention, our dollars, and our votes. American advertising is pervaded with propaganda in its attempt to sell us commercial products, and our political climate suffers from blizzard after blizzard of propaganda before each election.
3. Advertisers use "weasel words" to "stack the cards" and distort facts so that their products appear superior. Weasel words are words that say more than they mean and suggest more value than they actually denote. For example, an ad might say a shampoo "helps control dandruff," but we might understand this to mean that it cures dandruff (19).
4. Consumers should be aware of propaganda techniques so they can resist the appeal of ads that distort the truth or pull at our emotions. Only when we can separate the actual message and evaluate it for ourselves are we doing the hard work of clear thinking: "analyzing a claim, researching the facts, examining both sides of an issue, using logic to see the flaws in an argument" (23).
5. *seduced* (1): enticed, entranced; misled
   warmongers (5): people who attempt to start wars
   elitist (17): belonging to an exclusive or privileged group

Questions About the Writer's Craft (p. 269)

1. The definition of *propaganda* informs us about the term's true meaning and also clears up misunderstandings about the extent to which average Americans are subjected to propaganda. The broader purpose of providing us with this definition is to persuade us that advertising is indeed propaganda. McClintock hopes to motivate us to learn more about the various techniques of propaganda, so we can protect ourselves from its daily onslaughts.
2. "Seduced" and "brainwashed" are both words with strong negative connotations; we are likely to be shocked or disbelieving when we read that "Americans, adults and children alike, are being seduced. They are being brainwashed" (1). By using these terms, McClintock challenges our belief in our independence and free will. Through

the use of these and other terms ("victims"), she provokes us to continue reading the essay. Ironically, this use of loaded words manipulates the readers' reactions in a manner similar to that of propaganda.

3. Questions appear in the discussions of Glittering Generalities and Card Stacking and in the conclusion to the essay. In both the sections on propaganda techniques, the questions are rhetorical, in that they need no answers. They are questions used to make a point. For example, McClintock asks, "After all, how can anyone oppose 'truth, justice, and the American way'?" (6). The implied answer is, "No one can." In her discussion of specific empty phrases, the author asks questions to point out the meaninglessness of such statements as "He cares . . ." and "Vote for Progress" (7). These questions are meant not to be answered, but to show the vagueness of glittering generalities. In the section on card-stacking (18–20), she suggests that readers ask questions to test the validity of a political accusation such as "my opponent has changed his mind five times. . . ." The questions in the essay's conclusion, however, are real questions to which she provides answers.

4. Tied to McClintock's explanation of why propaganda works is a warning: that to remain blind to the power of propaganda is to consent "to handing over our independence, our decision-making ability, and our brains to the advertisers" (24). In order to prevent this fate, McClintock advises us to do the work that clear thinking requires. This ending is an example of a call-for-action conclusion.

BUT WHAT DO YOU MEAN?

Deborah Tannen

Questions for Close Reading (p. 276)

1. Tannen's thesis appears in paragraph 2. She explains there that "conversational rituals common among women are designed to take the other person's feelings into account" while the "rituals common among men are designed to maintain the one-up position, or at least avoid appearing one-down." These conversational differences, Tannen affirms, often place women at a disadvantage, particularly in professional situations. She writes: "Because women are not trying to avoid the one-down position, that is unfortunately where they may end up" (2).

2. Tannen finds that "women are often told they apologize too much" because, in men's speech, "apologizing seems synonymous with putting oneself down" (4). But women, Tannen explains, do not perceive apology as self-negating. They see it as a means "of keeping both speakers on an equal footing" (4). To illustrate this point, Tannen recounts in paragraph 4 a personal anecdote involving an apology ("Oh, I'm sorry") that isn't an admission of wrongdoing, but an attempt to provide reassurance of equality. This drive to foster equality often carries over into apologies that *are* intended to acknowledge wrongdoing. Frequently, Tannen states, a woman claims fault in expectation that the other speaker will also share the blame (5). In this way, both speakers apologize for some component of a mishap, and neither party loses status (6). To men unschooled in sharing blame, a woman's frequent apologies unfairly place her—again and again—in the one-down position (8).

3. As Tannen reports, in "straight" criticism an evaluator delivers commentary directly—"Oh, that's too dry! You have to make it snappier!" (10), while in "softened" criticism the evaluator offers reassuring markers—"That's a really good start" (10). Tannen believes that "women use more softeners" (11) in delivering criticism, but she states that "neither style is intrinsically better" (12). To those

familiar with softened critiques, a straight approach can be too blunt. However, to the straight talker, softened criticism is evasive and overly concerned with providing reassurance and protecting feelings (12). As Tannen sees it, the straight talker imagines that the subject of criticism does not need reassurance and "can take it" (12). Recipients of either approach, Tannen suggests, should recognize straight or softened criticism as first and foremost an *approach*—a style with a specific logic and goal (12). Such a view is consistent with Tannen's aims and conclusions. As she writes in the end of her essay, "There is no 'right' way to talk" (30). Problems in communication are better seen as problems in style, "and *all* styles will at times fail with others who don't share or understand them," just as English won't help one communicate with a speaker of French (30). One must learn to recognize the different speaking styles (just as English speakers traveling in France will find it advantageous to learn some French).

4. Tannen believes that men discuss ideas through a "ritual fight" or "verbal opposition": Men "state their ideas in the strongest possible terms, thinking that if there are weaknesses, someone will point them out, and by trying to argue against those objections, they will see how well their ideas hold up" (16). In short, for men, this battle-like scenario of proposal and interrogation is seen as a means of helping speakers sharpen and clarify their views. Women, however, may view such "verbal sparring" as a personal attack and consequently "find it impossible to do their best work" (18). As Tannen points out, "If you're not used to ritual fighting, you begin to hear criticism of your ideas as soon as they are formed" (18). As a result, a woman may doubt and not sharpen her ideas. She may also equivocate or "hedge in order to fend off potential attacks" (18), thereby making herself and her proposals look weak. This perceived weakness may, in turn, invite actual criticism and attack.

5. *synonymous* (4): having the same meaning
   self-deprecating (4): self-critiquing (often negative)
   reciprocate (14): to give and receive mutually
   contentious (18): prone to argument
   dumbfounded (20): speechless with surprise
   soliciting (23): asked repeatedly
   commiserating (23): sympathizing
   malcontent (26): a discontented person

Questions About the Writer's Craft (p. 277)

1. Although Tannen divides her essay into the seven "biggest areas of miscommunication" (3) between men and women—apologies, criticism, thank-yous, fighting, praise, complaints, and jokes—her categories actually describe *two* gendered tendencies. As Tannen explains, "conversation rituals common among women are designed to take the other person's feelings into account," while those "common among men are designed to maintain the one-up position" (2). As a result, Tannen's seven areas are not mutually exclusive, but demonstrate different instances of the same behaviors. Within each category, women's speech involves reciprocity, placing speakers "on an equal footing" (4)—one speaker apologizes, thanks, or complains, and the second speaker responds in kind—while men's verbal fighting, problem-solving, and teasing, conversely function to determine a speaker's status. For example, when Tannen asks a female columnist for a forgotten telephone number, the columnist responds, "Oh, I'm sorry," even though *she* had not forgotten anything (4). However, when men fail to thank in turn, like the male assistant who did not return the novelist's pleasantry (14), they are following their status-seeking goals. Demonstrating the difference between women's exchanges and men's

positioning across her categories, Tannen reveals repeatedly that women, who "are not trying to avoid the one-down position" (2) in conversation, often end up there.

2. In paragraphs 7–9, Tannen explores several branching effects that she considers damaging to women. Early on, in paragraphs 4–5, she demonstrates how women use apology not to acknowledge mistakes but to preserve parity. Having established that point, she introduces the anecdote about Helen. When Helen frequently apologized at a company meeting, her attempts to foster parity set in motion a series of effects. Her apologies fell on completely male ears, "mask[ed] her competence" (8), placed her in a one-down position, decreased her status in the company (the prime concern of men's conversations), and ultimately compromised her compensation. This causal chain supports Tannen's concern that in male-dominated contexts, women's conversational rituals effectively relegate professional women to subordinate positions.

3. Tannen's essay focuses on conversational rituals—"things that seem obviously the thing to say, without thinking of the literal meaning" (1). In detailing how these obvious but empty words are used differently by men and women, Tannen tries to evoke the everyday world where such language occurs. Her aim is not to explain scientific or sociological data; instead, she uses the first-person point of view to comment directly on those social interactions we all share. Refusing to be a distant observer, the essay's "I" becomes an active participant in the described behaviors. Tannen places herself in rituals like apology (4) and criticism (11), demonstrating what the behaviors signify to each speaker. Through her example and that of the world she knows, Tannen wants readers to recognize their own conversational approaches and understand those of others. Seen in this light, Tannen's use of the first person is not unlike a woman's conversational ritual: her aim is to establish parity between herself and readers and not to assert or secure her status. She does not, as a man might, propose her categories "in the strongest possible terms" (16), bracing the prose for interlocutors to examine holes or flaws in her theory. Instead, the first-person point of view builds rapport and supports Tannen's thesis: that speech is not "a question of being 'right'; it's a question of using language that's shared" (30).

4. Tannen's purpose is to explain how conversational rituals often place women at a professional disadvantage, yet she never adopts a strident tone to make her point. Rather than employing language rich in invective or anger at women's linguistic bind, Tannen remains non-abrasive and impartial throughout. When she writes, she always keeps clarity and common ground in mind. She begins the essay with a simple definition of conversation itself (1), and then moves on to observe that "unfortunately, women and men often have different ideas about what's appropriate, different ways of speaking" (2). While she emphasizes each sex's "different ideas"—that women seek rapport in conversation while men seek status—Tannen is at pains to distinguish these differences from notions of right and wrong. As she emphasizes in her conclusion, "there is no 'right' way to talk" (30), only various styles of talking. Since she suggests that conversation is "not a question of being 'right'; it's a question of using language that's shared—or at least understood" (30), Tannen does the same. Speaking in the first person and drawing on informal anecdotes, Tannen tries to explain how conversational rituals can cause "miscommunication" (3) between men and women. In explaining each of the seven categories, she sometimes addresses women directly; for example, in discussing ritual fighting in paragraph 19, she writes: "Although you may never enjoy verbal sparring, some women find it helpful to learn how to do it." Other times, she addresses men by implication, pointing out why Lester's employees might be dissatisfied with his lack of praise (20). In this way, Tannen works to explain to

each sex, in a deliberately objective and fair fashion, the gendered speech of the other. Tannen's tone—personal, informal, engaging—suits her purpose; because she threatens neither men nor women, readers remain open to her analysis and leave with a clear understanding of gendered miscommunication.

PROCESS ANALYSIS

OPENING COMMENTS

Like many of our colleagues, we cover process analysis early in the semester. This pattern of development teaches students a great deal about selectivity ("Which steps should I cover?" "How many examples should I provide?"), organization, and transitional signals. Process analysis also highlights the importance of audience analysis. To explain the steps in a process clearly, the writer must identify what readers need to know and understand.

Students often expect process analysis to write itself; they expect it to unfold naturally and automatically. But once they get feedback on their first draft, they realize that the sequence of steps was self-evident only to them and that they need to work harder to make the process accessible to their readers.

This chapter includes process analyses that vary widely in subject. Students should enjoy starting with Bryson's "Your New Computer," a spoof on the typical "how to" computer manual. By evoking shock and revulsion, Mitford's "The American Way of Death" underscores the effectiveness of highly specific details. In contrast, the essay by Roberts shows students how humor can be used to make a serious point. And Stoll, meanwhile, provides a tongue-in-cheek how-to for computerizing—and dehumanizing—America's schools. Finally, Rego uses directional process analysis to offer a series of pragmatic suggestions for making sure complaints are heard and acted upon.

ANSWERS FOR PREWRITING ACTIVITIES

Below we provide possible responses to selected prewriting activities at the end of Chapter 7. Of course, your students are bound to come up with their own approaches. (p. 294)

1. Process analysis lends itself to these essay topics in several ways. Below are some possibilities. In class, we suggest you have students share their responses. They will be delighted to discover that their neighbors have devised different uses for process analysis in these essays.

    Topic: Defining comparison shopping
    How a person might use a consumer magazine to compare VCRs' quality
    How a person might compare sneakers at a mall
    How someone might call up car dealers to get the best price

    Topic: Contrasting two teaching styles
    How two teachers respond to student questions
    How two teachers deal with students who don't understand
    How two teachers convey complex information

74

ANSWERS FOR REVISING ACTIVITIES

Below we provide possible responses to selected revising activities at the end of Chapter 7. Of course, your students are bound to come up with their own approaches. (p. 295)

3. Encourage students to work together on this activity or have them share their revisions. Other students' responses will help them discover weaknesses in their choices they otherwise might overlook. Here is a revised version of the list:

    The tone of the opening comments is very important
    Use a friendly tone in opening comments
    Don't introduce the product right away
    Try in a friendly way to keep the person on the phone
    Keep customers on the phone as long as possible to learn what they need
    The more you know about customers' needs the better
    Gently introduce the product
    Describe the product's advantages—price, convenience, installment plan
    If person is not interested, try in a friendly way to find out why
    Don't push people if they're not interested
    Don't tell people that their reasons for not being interested are silly
    Explain payment—check, money order, or credit card payment
    Encourage credit card payment—the product will arrive earlier
    End on a friendly tone

    The points that undermine the paper's unity are:

    Growing rudeness in society. Some people hang up right away. Very upsetting.
    Many people are so lonely they don't mind staying on the phone so they can
      talk to someone—anyone
    How sad that there's so much loneliness in the world

4. We suggest you offer your students the chance to read each other's revisions of this paragraph. Exposure to other versions helps them see many more possibilities in revising. Here are the main problems in the paragraph:

    — To preserve the paragraph's chronology, the sixth sentence (beginning "Before heading to class . . .") and the seventh should come earlier in the paragraph. These two sentences should be placed after "lessen the trauma."
    — Throughout the paragraph, there's a shift in person; for instance, "they" is used in the second sentence, but the third sentence shifts to "you"; it goes back and forth from there. The writer should choose one or the other and stick to it.
    — The tenth and eleventh sentences, running from "A friend of mine . . ." to "volunteers to participate" are irrelevant and should be deleted.
    — The point that you should "never, ever volunteer to answer" should be moved up to occur immediately after the advice about where to sit in sentences 8 and 9.
    — The transition, "however" (sentence 12), doesn't work when the paragraph is reorganized as described above. A transition such as "also" would work well.
    — The last two sentences, though in keeping with the paragraph's light tone, nevertheless seem a bit jarring. Furthermore, since they don't develop the essay's overall point, they should probably be eliminated.

YOUR NEW COMPUTER

Bill Bryson

Questions for Close Reading (p. 300)

1. The thesis is implied and may be stated as: "Computers and their accompanying users manuals are incomprehensible, illogical, and utterly frustrating." The reader can infer the thesis through the highly wry and sarcastic nature of the selection, which parodies the impenetrable and circular language of computer manuals.

2. Both paragraphs emphasize the contradictions and maze-like illogic of computer instructions. Paragraph 6 opens with "Unpack the box and examine its contents. (Warning: Do not open box if contents are missing or faulty . . . . Return all missing contents in their original packaging with a note explaining where they have gone . . .)." Of course, if the box cannot be opened, then the contents cannot be examined, and if the contents are missing, they cannot be explained for or returned. Through this exaggerated example, Bryson accuses computer manufacturers of perhaps deliberately confusing consumers and establishing irrational and unjust policies regarding their products. Similar circular illogic is targeted in paragraph 13. First, "Disc A" is nonsensically labeled "Disc D" or "Disc G." Then, the paragraph goes on to explain a vicious circle where in order to operate the computer, the user must enter a "License Verification Number," which can be found by "entering your Certified User Number, which can be found by entering your License Verification Number." Hence, the user makes no progress. Here, Bryson again emphasizes manufacturers' utterly confusing, impenetrable configurement of computers, as well as the lack of assistance provided by computer manuals.

3. In paragraph 8, Bryson accuses computer manufacturers of dishonesty as they force consumers to buy additional equipment that they hadn't been told about before purchasing the computer. The heading for this paragraph, "Something They Didn't Tell You at the Store," highlights consumer misinformation. The paragraph itself then goes on to list the highly technical-sounding auxiliary software needed "[b]ecause of the additional power needs of the preinstalled bonus software." Bryson intends the irony that the preinstalled software, itself auxiliary, necessitates much additional software—and additional money spent by consumers.

4. The essay opens by congratulating the reader for purchasing the "Edsel/2000 Multimedia 615X Personal Computer with Digital Doo-Dah Enhancer." However, after a lengthy explanation of how to set up and operate the computer, the selection finally acknowledges that the computer "is a piece of useless junk" (31). The manual concludes, "You are now ready to upgrade to an Edsel/3000 Turbo model, or go back to pen and paper" (32). This ending completes a vicious circle in which the user buys the Edsel/2000 only to discover that it is faulty and then is encouraged to buy the Edsel/3000. Bryson condemns the luring of consumers to buy a state-of-the-art computer which immediately has to be replaced by a newer model which will, in all probability, be no more user-friendly than the earlier model. The ultimate irony rests in the conclusion that the owner can either buy the Edsel/3000 or return to pen and paper, the latter of which (Bryson implies) may very well be the better option.

5. *diversion* (1): entertaining distraction
   configured (4): designed or arranged for specific uses
   invalidate (6): nullify, make unacceptable
   miscellaneous (7): various
   auxiliary (8): supplementary, extra

convention (11): accepted or prescribed practice
pylons (24): steel towers supporting high-tension wires

Questions About the Writer's Craft (p. 301)

1. On the most basic, superficial level, this selection appears to guide the reader in setting up the new Edsel/2000 computer, and, as such, is ostensibly directional. But the obviously ironic and parodic underpinnings of the selection reveal that the selection is not meant to provide actual instruction. Through humorous exaggeration of manuals' impenetrable, useless information, Bryson shows how poor and misleading the guides are. By entertaining his readers, Bryson is able to achieve his larger objective: instructing readers in the pitfalls of computer ownership.

2. Bryson knows that playful irony and humor can win the attention and sympathy of readers—and let him make his point clearly. Rather than lecturing readers on his position, he allows the problems he cites to reveal themselves by means of his parodied computer manual. Though bursting with hyperbole, this mock user's manual also contains a strong semblance of reality, enough to deliver Bryson's point effectively. In addition, though Bryson's complaints are legitimate, they are not of dire significance to the human race; hence, it is appropriate that he use humor to poke fun at the problem he targets.

3. The selection's entire format signals Bryson's parodic intention, with the selection posing as a step-by-step guide to setting up a new computer. Bryson's manual voice mimics the detached, instructional tone of computer guides, while also using the kind of technical language (though exaggerated) found in computer guidebooks. Additional features that mimic computer manuals include the selection's title ("Your New Computer"), its question-and-answer troubleshooting section, and, perhaps most effectively, its subheads. Computer manual writers usually employ subheads to organize information, particularly when outlining step-by-step instructions. But Bryson, besides imitating this subhead format, also manipulates the subheads to playful, satirical ends. While some of the headings are legitimate and conventional ("Getting Ready," "Setting Up," "Saving a File," and "Troubleshooting Section"), others are highly ironic and humorous ("Something They Didn't Tell You at the Store" and "Advice on Using the Spreadsheet Facility" followed by the one-word reply, "Don't"). In short, the subheads serve as valuable weapons in Bryson's arsenal of humor.

4. The word "Congratulations" appears six times in the course of the selection. Bryson includes the word as part of his parody of computer manuals, which often begin by congratulating the new computer owner on his or her purchase, hence, the first "Congratulations" (1). Yet, as with most other features of the user's manual, Bryson derisively and hyperbolically twists this convention of congratulations. In paragraph 3, the user is congratulated for having "successfully turned the page." Congratulations may indeed be in order; given the complexity of the manual, turning the page is perhaps the only thing the reader can do. Similarly, in paragraph 9, the user is congratulated for being "ready to set up," even though he or she has done nothing more than unpack the contents of the box and learn that additional equipment must be purchased. By this point, the congratulations have begun to ring with a patronizing, inauthentic note, as users are praised for the most basic and inane of actions. This condescending use of praise is heightened in paragraph 18, where the new owner is congratulated after having submitted personal information to a variety of consumer-hungry businesses, and then in paragraph 19, where the owner is praised for typing a short, simple letter and signing his or her name. The final and most stinging repetition of the word appears in the final paragraph (32). There the

selection acknowledges that the computer "is a piece of useless junk" (31) and smugly concludes, "[C]ongratulations. You are now ready to upgrade to an Edsel/3000 Turbo model, or go back to pen and paper" (32). This instance of congratulations is particularly biting because the reader is congratulated for realizing that he or she has been duped into buying the inherently defective Edsel/2000 and can be duped again into buying the next, probably similarly-flawed model, the Edsel/3000.

THE AMERICAN WAY OF DEATH

Jessica Mitford

Questions for Close Reading (p. 307)

1. Mitford's thesis is implied by her introductory comments that "Embalming is indeed a most extraordinary procedure . . ." (1) and that it is very difficult to obtain information about what goes on behind the "formaldehyde curtain" (3). One way of stating the thesis might be: "Americans should know exactly what they are paying for when they have a relative embalmed." Another version might be: "Knowing the details of embalming is every American consumer's right and responsibility."
2. Ignorance about embalming has a number of causes. On a pragmatic level, bookshops and libraries do not stock texts on the subject, Mitford says (1). Also, while at one time deceased people were prepared for burial at home with a relative standing by, our current custom is to hand over the body to "professionals" who perform their rituals in the mortuary. Mitford suspects that morticians would discourage any family member who wished to witness the procedures because they do not want the information about embalming to become widely known. In addition, the author points out, the law forbids others than the family or mortuary students to watch. Finally, while Mitford says she doubts "the secrecy surrounding embalming can . . . be attributed to the inherent gruesomeness of the subject" (2), since everything from heart surgery to birth is televised these days, students will probably admit to some squeamishness about the subject themselves.
3. Mr. J. Sheridan Mayer reminds us that the goal of mortuary science is to present the deceased in a lifelike manner: "Our customs require the presentation of our dead in the semblance of normality . . . unmarred by the ravages of illness, disease or mutilation" (11). Mitford's treatment of this notion is ironic. After quoting Mayer's guidelines, she makes the wry comment, "This is rather a large order since few people die in the full bloom of health. . . ."
4. The dead person's body can be made to look even better than when he or she was alive by repairing visible damage caused by illness or accident. In paragraph 12, Mitford grimly describes the remedies taken if a body part is missing or if the face is bruised and swollen: replacements are fashioned out of wax, heads are sewn back on with the stitches hidden under a high collar or scarf, and swollen tissue is cut out from the inside. Additionally, emaciation's ravaging can be repaired, Mitford explains in paragraph 13, through the injection of cream, and the effects of diseases on skin color can be rectified through cosmetics, colored lights and careful attention to color-coded casket interiors (15).
5. *docility* (1): the quality of being easily led or managed
   intractable (3): stubborn
   reticence (3): silence, unwillingness to speak

raison d'être (3): reason for being

augers (5): tools for making holes

distend (5): to stretch, expand, or inflate something

stippling (12): applying by repeated small touches

jaundice (15): an illness characterized by a yellowish discoloration of the body

Questions About the Writer's Craft (p. 308)

1. There are two main stages in the process of preparing the body for the funeral. First it is embalmed. This is the procedure by which blood is replaced with "about three to six gallons" of some sort of embalming fluid (9) and body fluids in the torso with "cavity fluid" (10). The deceased's eyes are closed with cement, the mouth sewn shut, and the face "creamed" to protect it from burns by the caustic embalming chemicals (10). The second stage of the process, restoration, occurs eight to ten hours later. During this stage the mortician, using the combined skills of a sculptor and a cosmetician, repairs the appearance of the body and makes it look lifelike. This process involved making casts of missing limbs (12); modeling the face to be neither too emaciated or too swollen (12–13); positioning the jaw, perhaps by dislocation, so the lips stay shut (14); and finally, washing, shaving (if male), shampooing, and dressing the body (16). The final step of this process is "casketing" (17).

    Mitford uses very clear transition words to delineate the steps of the two stages, embalming and restoration. Embalming is described sequentially, so she uses transitions of time and addition: "The body is first . . . (4); "another textbook discusses . . ." (7); "a contrasting thought is offered by another writer" (7); "To return to Mr. Jones . . ." (8); "meanwhile" (9); "the next step is . . ." (10). Mitford also employs repetitions of sentence structure to signal she is adding detail to detail: "There are cosmetics, waxes and paints . . . There are ingenious aids . . ." she writes in paragraph 5. "If Flextone is used . . ." (8) and "If he should be buck-toothed . . ." (9) are other examples of this strategy. Mitford uses this transition technique again in the section on restoration, where details are added in response to a series of similarly worded questions and conditional clauses: "If hand missing? . . ." "If a lip or two, a nose or an ear should be missing . . ." "Head off? . . ." "Swollen mouth? . . ." "If too much is removed . . ." (12); "If Mr. Jones happens to have no teeth . . ." (14); "If Mr. Jones has died of jaundice, does this deter the embalmer?" (15).

    Mitford separates the two stages of the mortician's job by devoting the end of paragraph 10 to making the transition: "He had been embalmed, but not yet restored." And, in paragraph 12, Mitford orients us to the start of the second stage by stating, "The embalmer, having allowed an appropriate interval . . ." (12). The discussion of restoration uses many transitions indicating contrast: "The opposite condition . . ." (14); "however" (14); "on the other hand" (15 and 17); and of addition: "another method" (14). Paragraph 14 begins with a reference to "a problem," so that we know the paragraph will discuss its solution process. Also in this section, there are some transitions referring to process: "sometimes . . . then . . ." (14). Many other details, however, are piled on without transition (16 and 17). Paragraph 16 begins with a summation of the process so far and moves us on to the next stage: "The patching and filling completed, Mr. Jones is now shaved, washed and dressed. . . ." And paragraph 17 introduces the last stage by a transition of process: "Jones is now ready . . ." (17).

2. "Mr. Jones" is an "everyman" name; using it for the corpse conveys that this procedure is universally applied in our country. The name also gives the dead man an identity—it is a constant reminder that this is a human being, being subjected to

grotesque and dehumanizing techniques. We can feel shock and shame as these processes are performed on a "Mr. Jones" instead of on a "body." The use of the particular name helps Mitford draw her readers over to her point of view. However, Mr. Jones is never given any particular physical characteristics, life history, or cause of death, so that while he is a person, not just a dead body, he could still be any person.

3. The quotations from mortuary science textbooks let us know that Mitford has done her homework; she has acquired some of those hard-to-get books on embalming and studied them. The quotations thus increase her authority on the subject. Since the process of embalming is a mystery to most of us, the quotations verify the almost incredible details of the procedures (see paragraphs 12, 15, 16, 17) and convey the theory behind the process as well (6, 7, 11). The particular quotations often combine the subject of barbaric mutilation with a self-congratulatory or sanctimonious tone. The style is usually excessively pompous and marked by terminology designed to underscore the logicality or necessity of the procedures: "It is necessary to   . . ."; "removes the principal cause of . . ." (6); "for every hour that elapses . . . will add to the problems . . ."; "we must conclude that . . ."; "In the average case . . ."; "One of the effects of . . ." (7); "Our customs require   . . ."; "This is the time . . ."; "all doubts of success vanish . . ."; "It is surprising and gratifying . . ." (11).

4. For the most part, Mitford's tone is reportorial; she describes the odd and fantastic processes without much comment or overt interpretation. Occasionally, however, there are touches of irony and sarcasm, enough so that one can tell that Mitford is not objective about the funeral industry. For example, her discussion of how to place the body in a coffin is clearly meant wryly: "Proper placement of the body requires a delicate sense of balance. It should lie as high as possible in the casket, yet not so high that the lid, when lowered, will hit the nose." She points out that placing the body too low will cause the body to look as if it is in a box. Likewise, the questions in paragraph 12 mock the mortician's blasé attitude toward dead bodies: "Head off?" . . . "Swollen mouth?" Also, her word choice can be evaluative, as in paragraph 5: "*appropriately corrupted* . . . as 'demisurgeon'" "equipment . . . *crudely* imitative of the surgeon's . . ." "a *bewildering* array of fluids . . . ." Finally, her choice of quotations from texts in the field contributes to our sense that practitioners of mortuary science are self-aggrandizing and pretentious, if not actually charlatans.

CYBERSCHOOL

Clifford Stoll

Questions for Close Reading (p. 313)

1. Though Stoll's position is evident from the outset of his essay (when he refers to the "pessimal view of the schoolroom of the future"), he does not express his thesis until the ironic close of the essay's final paragraph: "Yep, jut sign up for the future: the parent-pleasin', tax-savin', interactive-educatin', child-centerin' Cyberschool. . . . No learning. Coming soon to a school district near you." Students may wish to refine this statement using their own words. Here is one possibility: "Though the computerization of the classroom seems to be inevitable, this trend will result in disastrous educational consequences for the students subjected to it."

2. The process of fully computerizing schoolrooms—or creating a "cyberschool"—is as follows: First, the school district buys a computer for every student (5), as well as

educational software that matches the curriculum (6). This software will be customized to students' educational levels and personal tastes, but most importantly, to the standardized tests students are required to take (7–8). The computers will track students' progress and convey this information to parents and administrators (9). Classroom desks will be replaced by cubicle workstations, essentially eliminating all student contact (11). Teachers and librarians will be fired or retrained as data entry clerks and replaced by computer specialists and security guards (11–12). "Luxuries" such as art class and field trips will be eliminated to save money, while new profits can be derived from arranging corporate sponsorship of the cyberschool (14). Online extracurricular activities will allow students to "experience" community service and "interact" with people from around the world (18). As a result, test scores will rise dramatically, while costs decrease (13).

As is made apparent throughout by Stoll's sarcastic phrases, such as "Yee-ha!" (1) and "naw" (4), he opposes the over-reliance on computers in the classroom. Overall, Stoll's dismissive yet cuttingly ironic attitude toward his subject is summarized in the sentence "Yep, just sign up for the future: the parent-pleasin', tax-savin', teacher-firin', interactive-educatin', child-centerin' Cyberschool" (18).

3. In paragraph 3, Stoll points the finger at "harried" school board members and other administrators, especially elected ones. These individuals are pressured to reduce educational costs while improving students' performance and placating taxpayers. In the minds of these individuals, Stoll asserts, the cyberschool model of education presents numerous benefits. First, the computerized classroom allows long term reduction in education spending achieved through the firing of full-time teachers (3, 11–12, 15), as well as the possibility of future profit through teaming with corporate supporters (14). Proponents also believe computers will allow students more customized learning, especially with regard to standardized test preparation (6–8). They could facilitate instant feedback and surveillance of students' progress to parents and administrators (9, 18) while reducing contact—troublesome and otherwise—among students (10). In the eyes of proponents, computers could even be seen as fostering healthy extracurricular activities such as distance mentoring or international student buddying (17)—all vicariously through the computer and never through firsthand contact.

4. According to Stoll's characterization of the cyberschool, teachers will play little to no role. As he says, tongue-in-cheek, in paragraph 11, "Teachers are an unnecessary appendix at this cyberschool." Rendered "irrelevant" by the new multimedia computer capabilities (11), by a "cadre of instructional specialists, consultants, and hall monitors" (12), and by "real-time instructors" available through "distance learning displays" (15), teachers and librarians will be "laid-off" and some can be "retrained as data entry clerks" (10).

Stoll's attitude, though tongue-in-cheek, also carries ominous overtones regarding the dehumanization of children's education. This becomes especially apparent in his vision of a Big Brother-esque online instructor available only via "distance learning displays" and "two-way video" (15). Similarly alarming is the idea of the school board's monitoring of everything that students learn "without idiosyncratic teachers to raise unpopular topics or challenge accepted beliefs" (16)—when in fact teachers' fostering of independent thinking among students is what many people value as essential to a good education. Stoll also seems to mock the idea of teachers being replaced by "instructional specialists, consultants, and security guards" (12), as if those functions are the only ones that teachers fill in children's lives.

5. *infrastructures* (1): underlying foundations, especially for an organization or system
optimal (1): most favorable or desirable

harried (3): distressed by repeated attacks or harassment

placate (4): appease; allay the anger of, especially by making concessions

adept (8): very skilled

standardized (8): conforming to a standard

cubicles (10): small compartments for work or study

compartmentalized (10): separated into distinct parts

cadre (12): small, tight-knit group of trained personnel

recoup (14): return as an equivalent for; reimburse

idiosyncratic (16): having a behavioral characteristic peculiar to an individual or group

Questions About the Writer's Craft (p. 313)

1. This is a "trick question" of sorts, given the irony at the heart of Stoll's essay. On its surface, the process being described could seem directional in nature, laying out the procedure for implementing the cyberschool model of education. Stoll goes into relative detail regarding the set-up and administration of the cyber-classroom as well as the implications of doing so. The speaker of the essay, in all his ostensible enthusiasm for the cyberschool, almost provides a handbook to interested parties. But on closer look, it becomes apparent that this process analysis is, in fact, informational, primarily because Stoll presents the mechanics of a cyberschool in order to actually advocate *against* its implementation. He does so by offhandedly presenting the cyberschool's serious flaws and defects as though they are benefits; these include the reduction of precious interaction among teachers and students, elimination of independent or creative thinking, concentration solely on learning content of standardized tests, and so on.

2. Stoll's tone is dismissive and definitely ironic. In presenting the cyberschool, Stoll adopts a persona much like the voice in an infomercial—synthetic, hyper, and ultimately trying to sell junk. However, Stoll's actual cynical agenda comes through in much of the wording that disrupts the pro-cyberschool façade. The phrase "whatever that means" blows the cover on the self-important tech-speak of paragraph 1, as do the artificially enthusiastic "Yee-ha!" (1) and "Naw—it's easy to solve all these problems" (4). The words "edutainment" (6) and "edu-games" (8) that Stoll coins reveal a cynical view of the education trends he challenges, implying their watered-down nature. This is reinforced by the image of a "chatty pony" or "Fred the Firefighter" assuming the instructional role that trained professional teachers currently occupy—an absurd and demeaning image. In fact, regarding teachers in the cyberschool, he says, "No need for 'em" (11), a phrase that's obviously suspect in its flippancy. And the phrase "Virtual Compassion Corps" (17) is bursting with bitter contradiction, as is the statement "All without ever having to shake hands with a real person . . . or (gasp!) face the real problems of another culture" (17). Overall, Stoll's dismissive yet cuttingly ironic attitude toward his subject is summarized in the sentence "Yep, just sign up for the future: the parent-pleasin', tax-savin', teacher-firin', interactive-educatin', child-centerin' Cyberschool" (18). By referring to educational computers and their supporters in such dismissive terms, Stoll diminishes the stature of computers as a viable vehicle for teaching children, and he reinforces the central idea that computers are flashy distractions from the serious work of learning. The gravity of his message is resoundingly conveyed in the simple phrase "No learning."

    Regarding the effect of Stoll's tone on his overall message, students' answers may vary, though it is likely that many will argue his apparent flippancy and humor in handling the topic helps capture readers' attention and send home his point more effectively than a straightforward, dry argument would.

3. Based on the information conveyed about Stoll, he appears to have airtight credibility in writing on the topic of computers and their effect on children's education. As an astronomer and programmer of computers "since the mid-sixties," Stoll has both an intimate working knowledge of computers and a highly informed long-term perspective on their effects on society; this expertise indicates that he is a well-reasoned and well-intentioned computer user, not a fanatical technophobe. As a teacher of children and young adults, he has accumulated firsthand observations of the increasing emphasis on computers in the classroom and the effects of this emphasis on young people. Finally, as a father, he has likely seen the impact of computers on the various facets of children's lives as they grow. His passionate desire to stave off the crippling effects on children of computer overuse is therefore legitimized by his roles as scientist, teacher, parent—and avid computer user.

4. In paragraph 15, Stoll addresses the central argument against the computerization of education when he says, "Concerned that such a system might be dehumanizing? Not to worry." His speaker then goes to present a series of quasi-human interactions—all involving computers—to "allay" the fear of mechanized learning. These include "interactive chat sessions" among kids (instead of conversation, play, or in-person group work), help from a "trained support mentor" via Internet (rather than a trained, in-person teacher), and, if necessary, assistance from a real-time instructor via "distance learning display" and "two-way video" (and certainly not in person). Clearly, these examples—all of which demonstrate complete reliance on computer rather than human contact—offer little to no comfort regarding the concern that computerized classrooms will result in dehumanized education for children. For as long as computers are the sole conduit of communication between individuals, the charge of dehumanization will remain valid. Stoll has deliberately selected these examples to sabotage the counterargument because; in fact, his essay seeks to undermine the idea of the cyberschool.

HOW TO SAY NOTHING IN 500 WORDS

Paul Roberts

Questions for Close Reading (p. 327)

1. Roberts states the thesis at the end of paragraph 6: "But there are some things you can do which will make your papers, if not throbbingly alive, at least less insufferably tedious than they might otherwise be."
2. The hypothetical student author of the essay on football seems to assume several things about the assignment: 1) that a student writer should try to hold an opinion that the professor will approve of or agree with, 2) that ending up with the exact number of words is one of the writer's top priorities, and 3) that the intelligence or vitality of the ideas in the essay is not very important.
3. Colorful words are those that create emotions in a reader or that draw a picture. Roberts calls them "dressy," specific, and "loud." Colored words are those that convey strong favorable or unfavorable associations in addition to their basic meaning; another term for them is "connotative language." Colorless words are those so general and vague that they hardly have a meaning at all—words like "nice" or "aspect." Roberts would like students to be more attuned to the qualities of words, and he does wish students to beware of colorless words. He does not, however,

indicate a blanket preference for any particular type of word. Instead, he suggests that a writer should decide whether highly colored language is appropriate for the subject matter, the readers, and the purpose of the writing. Writers should use judgment in incorporating colorful words, because, he writes, "it should not be supposed that the fancy word is always better" (36). In paragraph 43, he points out, "The question of whether to use loaded words or not depends on what is being written."

4. The author's main commandments are to avoid stating the obvious, try to hold an unusual position, speak in specifics, pare down your writing, be frank, and avoid clichés. You can look at the headings for sections 2 through 7 for brief statements of his main recommendations.

5. *bromides* (6): hackneyed remarks or ideas
   insufferably (6): intolerably, unbearably
   inexorably (7): relentlessly
   dissent (13): differ, disagree
   abolition (16): the act of doing away with something
   adept (20): competent
   euphemism (27): use of inoffensive term instead of a more accurate, unpleasant term
   insensible (41): unconscious

Questions About the Writer's Craft (p. 327)

1. Roberts first presents the process by which he believes many students write papers—a description "exaggerated a little," he admits, but "not much" (5). Then he describes how students should write a paper; in paragraph 7 he tells how a student should begin, and he follows with advice on how to choose words and edit one's writing. The reader can compare the two processes and see how much more valid is the one Roberts recommends. The description of "how to say nothing" is presented for our information and amusement and to lay the groundwork for the discussion of how to say something interesting in a composition. This process is intended to be directional and instructive.

2. Writing to the reader directly as "you" helps Roberts establish a personal, friendly rapport with the students he intends as his audience. Most students will say that they come away from the essay with an image of Roberts as an understanding and warm teacher; he seems to speak directly to their concerns and to anticipate their reactions: "Well, you may ask, what can you do about it?" (6). He comes across as someone who knows them and knows how they think, and, most important, respects them while still urging them to improve their work. Note that the headings are in the imperative, as if preceded by "You should. . . ."

3. The tone is warm, human, almost playful at times, but it is also a tone of frankness and directness. The informality and humanness result from a number of different techniques. Addressing the reader directly as "you" is one; in addition, Roberts uses colloquial language: "This was still funny during the War of 1812, but it has sort of lost its edge since then" (13). He has a surprising, sometimes sardonic, way of putting things: "All subjects, except sex, are dull until somebody makes them interesting" (6). He enjoys overstatement, just for effect, as when he provides possible specifics for a paper on college football (15). The sense of directness results from the author's frequent use of short sentences: "Then you go to the heart of the matter" (9) and from his willingness to expand on his points, provide examples, and give specific directions: "Don't say . . . . Say . . ." (18). The tone is quite effective; in fact, it may be the only tone possible for conveying this complex information about the high-level ability of writing to an audience of potentially hostile college students.

4. Yes, Roberts does follow his own advice. His starting recommendations that students seek out unpopular, uncommon, or hard-to-defend topics and points of view for their compositions is itself an example of "avoiding the obvious content" and "taking the less usual side." Roberts also "avoids the obvious content" by choosing to speak in a personal, informal tone, instead of the typical teacherly authoritarian tone most students (and teachers) would expect. He certainly "slips out of abstraction," using numerous examples of weak or potentially successful topics, sentences, phrases, and images. Paragraph 21, for example, illustrates his use of specifics. The essay is quite lengthy, and so it may not be obvious that Roberts has "gotten rid of obvious padding." Yet he does not repeat himself and is certainly not guilty of "circling warily around" his ideas (22). Rather, as he recommends in this section, he conscientiously illustrates and proves his points; see paragraphs 17 and 18 for examples of how he states his idea and then develops it rather than "pads" it. Roberts "calls a fool a fool" by directly confronting the inanities of the typical student composition: "All bloodless, five hundred words dripping out of nothing . . ." (5); "insufferably tedious . . ." (6). In fact, his portrait of the hypothetical student writer clearly reveals the folly of the student's writing process (3–4). Finally, students will have a hard time finding any clichés or euphemisms in Roberts' writing; some may cite his use of familiar expressions, such as "you're off" (3), "good ripe stuff" (3), "the brink of lunacy" (7), and "a general wringing of the hands." These are not really "pat expressions" in the sense that Roberts means, but familiar phrases used in a new context or in an interesting way. They do not "stand like a wall between the writer and thought"; they are colloquialisms that help Roberts make his ideas meaningful to his audience.

THE FINE ART OF COMPLAINING

Caroline Rego

Questions for Close Reading (p. 332)

1. Rego states her thesis in paragraph 4. Noting that many people go to extremes when dealing with annoyances, she writes that both milquetoasts and table-pounders need "a course in the gentle art of *effective* complaining." She proceeds to define this term (paragraphs 5–6) and then to give guidelines on how to achieve this art (7–24).
2. Acting self-important, raising one's voice, and making threats are counterproductive because they are likely to create hostility in the other person. Likewise, Rego suggests that demeaning oneself by begging and explaining is not productive either. Finally, she cautions against apologizing because the problem is not your fault (6).
3. The letter should explain the problem and include facts to convey the seriousness of the problem (12). It should also directly convey what remedy for the problem is desired (16) and what recourse will be sought if the remedy is not provided (19). It should not include details that are not to the point, such as how repairs were attempted (9), and it should not threaten extravagant action or aggression (21).
4. She advises us to keep complaining and to make sure the complaints are always heard by the same person. A single complaint may not be enough to achieve the desired results, and persistent complaining may wear down the person's resistance (23). Finally, she suggests threatening action, as long as it is a reasonable action. Notifying the Better Business Bureau or a consumer affairs agency (21) and taking the case to small claims court are valid recourses that may inspire the company to solve the problem (22).

5.	*hapless* (3): unfortunate
	venture (3): to go despite risk or uncertainty
	patsy (3): (slang) a person easily victimized or cheated
	milquetoasts (4): people with meek, timid, or retiring natures
	apoplectic (4): seizure-like
	Neanderthal (4): (slang) crude, boorish person
	indiscriminately (5): randomly; without making any distinctions
	disembodied (7): without or outside the body
	credible (21): believable

Questions About the Writer's Craft (p. 332)

1.	Rego provides both information and directions about performing an effective complaint, but most of the essay is devoted to a directional approach. She gives numerous examples of what to do and not to do (5–6), allowing the reader to visualize what it's like to make a complaint effectively. These examples also help persuade the reader that holding the line on emotion and projecting a businesslike image serve a complaining patron well. In paragraphs 7–8, the author provides more in-depth directions for conducting the in-person complaint, and in paragraphs 9 through 22, she details how to write a letter of complaint. Providing such step-by-step information about complaining and giving a well-developed example of a complaint letter help Rego be all the more persuasive that complaining can be done effectively.

2.	Throughout the essay, Rego uses short narrative scenarios to add vividness, variety and humor to what might otherwise have been a dry set of instructions. The narratives also serve to show exactly what she means at each step of the process. The narratives begin in the first paragraph, where Rego sketches three brief stories about unappetizing food, a shrunken T-shirt, and a car repair. She then recalls these at the end of the second paragraph. Paragraph 3 provides more mini-narratives, about people who flare up and shout in offices, restaurants, and stores as a way of complaining. In paragraph 6, Rego includes a scenario of effective complaining about delayed car repairs. The details in paragraph 9 about a broken vacuum cleaner and its resistance to repair by "Uncle Joe" also convey a narrative. The sample letter of complaint also invokes a more detailed narrative about a balky appliance, poor service, and faulty repairs (13–20).

3.	Rego relies upon oppositions to create drama and a touch of humor, as well as to provide clear and persuasive images of what does and does not work in the "fine art of complaining." These oppositions begin in paragraphs 2 and 3, where Rego first describes a wimpy reaction to consumer problems and then an overly combative style. She repeats this contrast between "milquetoasts" and "Neanderthals" in paragraph 4, and invokes it again in paragraph 5, where she discriminates between apologetic and aggressive complaining. In paragraph 5, Rego opposes effective to ineffective complaining by defining what effective complaining is not: it is not "apologetic and half-hearted," nor is it the opposite, "roaring away indiscriminately."

	Next, Rego provides details about what an effective complainer is, and opposes each quality to a negative. She defines "businesslike and important" as not "puffing up your chest," but treating your own request as reasonable and fair (6). At the end of this paragraph, she uses examples to contrast a polite, firm request for action with a hesitant, self-effacing style.

	In the following paragraph (7), Rego compares the effectiveness of speaking in person and complaining by phone, and in paragraph 8, of complaining to a convenient person instead of to someone who can take or order action. Paragraph 9 introduces the letter of complaint by comparing its use to a personal complaint. Additional contrasts follow the example of the letter. In 21 and 22, Rego contrasts effective and useless threats. By constantly contrasting winning and self-defeating styles, Rego enlivens the essay and makes her strategies for successful complaining irresistible.

4. Rego begins the essay in the second person, giving hypothetical examples which dramatically put the reader right on the scene. In the second paragraph, she moves to the first person plural to describe the typical reactions people—"we"—have in dealing with annoyances and faulty products. Through this switch, she includes herself among those who find complaining an awkward and to-be-avoided eventuality. In paragraph 4, she makes another switch, to the third person, as she labels the two extremes in complaining with pejoratives: "milquetoasts" and "Neanderthals." Her description of how to complain effectively is couched, for the most part, in the third person (4–6). She then returns to the second person in paragraphs 7–9, in order to give advice about whom to complain to. In paragraph 8, she uses the imperative form to instruct the reader in how to complain: "complain to the right person. . . . Getting mad doesn't help. . . make sure from the start that you're talking to someone who can help. . ." (8). The italicized explanations between the paragraphs of the sample letter continue in the imperative, giving instructions about what each section of the letter should contain. After the letter, Rego continues with the use of "you," first, in advising upon the strategy to be used in the postscript (21–22), and then in coaching her readers to persist with complaints, since action may not result immediately. In concluding, she offers an upbeat image of a future devoid of complaint-inducing annoyances and then reminds us that, in the present, complaints are necessary. This final paragraph ends with two sentences that punch home the importance of complaining well. Using the second person, she asserts, "You can depend upon it—there will be grounds for complaint. You might as well learn to be good at it." The use of multiple points of view allows Rego to inject personality and warmth into the essay and to place the reader and the writer at the center of the complaint process.

COMPARISON-CONTRAST

OPENING COMMENTS

Students learn early that comparison-contrast questions are one of the mainstays of essay exams: "Compare and/or contrast the organizations of the Senate and the House of Representatives"; "Discuss the similarities and/or differences between psychotic and neurotic behavior."

But we've found that students' familiarity with comparison-contrast doesn't necessarily mean they know how to structure their answers. On the contrary, students tend to prepare helter-skelter papers that ramble every which way and back. Yet, once they are introduced to some basic strategies for organizing a comparison-contrast discussion, their overall ability to write clearly and logically often takes a quantum leap.

When first using comparison-contrast, students may have trouble organizing their thoughts. Overly concerned about making their ideas fit into a neat symmetrical pattern, they may squeeze their points into an artificial and awkward format. We find it helpful to remind students that comparison-contrast is not an end in itself but a strategy for meeting a broader rhetorical purpose. Our reminder loosens them up a bit and encourages them to be more flexible when organizing their papers. The student essay, "The Virtues of Growing Older" (pages 345–46), helps students appreciate that a well-organized comparison-contrast paper does not have to follow a rigid formula.

We selected the readings in this chapter because, in addition to being just plain interesting, all of them illustrate key points about the comparison-contrast format. Carson uses the one-side-at-a-time approach to dramatize the difference between two extremes. Suina employs both comparison-contrast strategies to evoke a confusing and painful time of adaptation in his childhood. And Rodriguez organizes his essay around an entire network of comparisons and contrasts. To illustrate his point that men and women view their looks differently, Barry gives both sides equal time, balancing the humorous with the serious in this point-by-point method of analysis. By comparing and contrasting punishments in Islamic and American society, Chapman exposes and questions the values underlying our system of jurisprudence.

ANSWERS FOR PREWRITING ACTIVITIES

On the next page, we provide possible responses to selected prewriting activities at the end of Chapter 8. Of course, other approaches are possible.   (p. 349)

1.   There are numerous ways to use comparison-contrast in these two essays. Below are some possibilities. In going over this activity in class, we suggest you have students trade responses so that they can see how diverse the responses are.

Topic: The effects of holding a job in college
Comparing/contrasting job-holders' and non-job-holders' grades
Comparing/contrasting on-campus and off-campus jobs
Comparing/contrasting part-time and full-time jobs

Comparing/contrasting job-holders' and non-job-holders' involvement in campus activities

Topic: How to budget money wisely
Comparing/contrasting formal and informal budgets
Comparing/contrasting following a budget to buying on impulse
Comparing/contrasting those who budget and those who don't
Comparing/contrasting reasonable and unreasonable budgets

ANSWERS FOR REVISING ACTIVITIES

Below we provide possible responses to selected prewriting activities at the end of Chapter 8. Of course, other approaches are possible. (p. 349)

3. a. This statement works well as a thesis.
    b. This statement is unworkable as a thesis; it is too vague and broad since "assistance" could refer to academic, financial, or other kind of aid. A possible revision: "This college provides much more comprehensive job placement services to students than other colleges in the area."
    c. This statement would be effective as a thesis if revised to state an attitude toward the candidates' use of television, for example, if one made legitimate use of the medium and the other none. A possible revision: "Joe Cooper's overwrought campaign tactics gained extensive media coverage, while Cooper's opponent, Nancy Ashbury, conducted a more subdued campaign that emphasized issues and failed to attract much attention."
    d. This statement would not work as a thesis. First of all, it points out the obvious and sets up the writer for a pedantic recital of known information. Secondly, the statement is far too inclusive; in attempting to cover the topic, the writer would have to use a ream of paper. A possible revision: "Applying their technological know-how, Japanese car manufacturers learned how to make small engines more powerful, while American companies, showing very little foresight, simply added power to their cars by reintroducing larger engines."

4. Have students read each others' versions of this paragraph so that they get a stronger sense of what changes needed to be made and the revision strategies possible.
    Here are the main problems with the paragraph:

    —   Since the paragraph discusses a boss and then a manager, the topic sentence should be reversed to read, "A boss discourages staff resourcefulness and views it as a threat, while a manager encourages creativity and treats employees courteously."
    —   The second sentence ("At the hardware store . . .") begins abruptly; a transition, such as "for example," would be helpful here.
    —   The boss's helter-skelter system is introduced awkwardly: "What he did was . . . ." Something like this might be more effective: "He organized overstocked items. . . ."
    —   The phrase "created chaos" is vague, possibly a bit extreme, and also somewhat slangy. Briefly describing the actual problems his system created would be helpful, as long as the paragraph doesn't veer off-track and focus entirely on the chaos.

89

- Some language is possibly too judgmental: "helter-skelter" (4), "slapdash" (7), and "eccentric" (9). Students may want to describe the system with enough telling details so the readers can see for themselves the system's inefficiency.
- No reason is given for the boss's anger at the new system—or perhaps there was no reason other than that his ego was deflated. In either case, the source of his objections should be clarified.
- Some ideas are repeated at the end; sentences 8 and 9 ("I had assumed he would welcome my ideas. . .") repeat material conveyed at the beginning of the paragraph.
- The phrase "to scrap" is perhaps a bit slangy in tone.

A FABLE FOR TOMORROW

Rachel Carson

Questions for Close Reading (p. 352)

1. Carson's thesis comes at the end: "A grim specter has crept upon us almost unnoticed, and this imagined tragedy may easily become a stark reality we all shall know." Carson is referring to the potential devastation of plant and animal life by herbicides, insecticides, and other environmental hazards.
2. The lovely sights include orchard blossoms (1), autumn foliage (1), wildflowers (2), and birds (2).
3. She is adopting the point of view of the townspeople, who find the spreading illness "mysterious" and "unexplained" (3). The people are "puzzled and disturbed" (4).
4. Plants, animals, and humans die; an eerie silence replaces bird-song and other customary animal sounds; the landscape turns increasingly ugly ("browned and withered vegetation"); and animals fail to reproduce normally.
5. *viburnum* (2): a tree or shrub of the honeysuckle family
   alder (2): a tree or shrub of the birch family
   moribund (4): dying
   specter (9): something fearful that appears unexpectedly

Questions About the Writer's Craft (p. 353)

1. The one-side-at-a-time method enables Carson to highlight the drastic difference in conditions before and after the blight. The selection is so short that a point-by-point comparison would only reduce the impact.
2. The first paragraph is developed primarily through lush visual description, such as "white clouds of bloom drifted above the green fields" and "a blaze of color that flamed and flickered across a backdrop of pines." It refers, as well, to foxes' barking and deer's silence. Paragraph two is dominated by visual description. Paragraphs 4, 5, and 6 all mention sounds no longer present: "chorus of robins" (4), "no bees droned" (5), and "silent roadsides" (6). Paragraphs 4, 6, and 7 each contain at least one visual detail that creates a harsh, disturbing image unlike the luxurious, peaceful description that opens the essay. All of the sensory images reinforce Carson's thesis by making the reader experience the fullness of life before the blight.
3. The biblical tone adds an air of authoritative prophecy.
4. In the last paragraph, Carson steps outside her fable and writes direct argumentation-persuasion. She no longer shows, using description and narration, but instead warns the reader directly that the situation is a dangerous one. The effect of the last

paragraph is to base the fable in reality by stating that "every one of these disasters has actually happened somewhere."

AND THEN I WENT TO SCHOOL

Joseph H. Suina

Questions for Close Reading (p. 359)

1. Suina's thesis is implied by the comparison of his preschool lifestyle with his life after school begins. It could be stated as, "Attending school began the destruction of Suina's strong Indian self-image and of his attachment to Indian customs and values." Paragraph 16 also provides a thesis-like statement: "life would never be the same again. . . . the ways of the white man. . . . would creep more and more into my life."

2. Values were instilled through story-telling, praise, and direct instruction. Suina mentions several typical story-telling sessions; for example, his grandmother would tell him about "how it was when she was a little girl" (3). When the relatives gathered, a nightly occurrence, they too would tell stories to "both children and adults" (4). Praise was showered upon him by his grandmother so that he would be proud of his accomplishments; "her shower of praises," he writes, "made me feel like the Indian Superman of all times" (6). Finally, his grandmother teaches him about his culture by taking him along with her to various ceremonies and teaching him "appropriate behavior" for these occasions. She also models how to pray, so that he learns both the words and the proper attitude (7). When Suina goes to school, he is shocked by the very different methods of teaching. Instead of praise, he receives "a dirty look or a whack with a ruler" when he speaks his native language (13). Personal hygiene is impressed upon him through a cruelly administered shampoo and caustic, embarrassing comments about his background (12). The language barrier meant that he couldn't comprehend all the lessons, but "yet [he] could understand very well when [he] messed up . . . The negative aspect was communicated too effectively. . ." (11).

3. The village begins to take in some non-Indian influences. There are automobiles, albeit very few of them. Suina's grandmother possesses a dresser in which she keeps some of her possessions; the dresser, a European type of furniture, was acquired by trading some of her famous hand-made pottery. And, in the dresser, she keeps goodies, which include "store bought cookies and Fig Newtons." (3). Even the tradition of going nightly to visit relatives to chat and tell stories is on the decline as radios and televisions cause people to stay home instead of going out (4). And, the children have access to some 10-cent comic books, which they read and use as the basis for fantasy games when their families get together at night. They imitate the cowboys-and-Indians plots in the comics, with, ironically, all the children wanting to be cowboys because they always won the conflicts. Suina sums up the encroachment of white culture in paragraph 16: "The schools, television, automobiles and other white man's ways and values had chipped away at the simple cooperative life I grew up in. The people of Cochiti were changing."

4. In paragraph 13, Suina indicates that the adults around him wanted him to attend school so that he "might have a better life in the future" (13). This idea is in itself confusing to him, because he felt he "had a good village life already" (13). Near the end of the essay, he recognizes that "there was no choice but to compete with the white man on his terms for survival" (16).

91

Many elements of the school lifestyle are confusing to him. The teaching style, with whacks of a ruler, dirty looks, scoldings and embarrassing comments, is very alien to him. "The strange surroundings, new concepts about time and expectations, and a foreign tongue" were other elements that bewildered him (8). The teacher is so different in appearance from his grandmother that he thinks she is ill; she is also unfriendly and, he thinks, not very smart, because she couldn't speak his language. The classroom is so large it seems cold and ominous; the artificial building style and the fluorescent lighting also seem forbidding and alien. Instead of running freely, he must sit all day long. The most confusing thing to him, however, is that he must give up his language and speak English.

Going to the boarding school clinches his separation from his native village culture. He lives in a white-style building and learns the comforts of indoor plumbing, spacious rooms, and ventilation. By the time he returns for a four-day break at Thanksgiving, the village lifestyle does "not feel right anymore" (15). Now living with whites 24-hours a day, he finds himself unaccustomed to the culture he was raised in. He soon "gets back with it" (15), he says, and then finds returning to school extremely difficult. His life has been transformed; he "could not turn back the time just as [he] could not do away with school and the ways of the white man" (16).

5. *adobe* (5): sun-dried clay, usually in bricks

ego (12): sense of self-importance

belittled (15): to criticize something as unimportant or trivial

Questions About the Writer's Craft (p. 359)

1. The essay is predominantly organized according to the *one-side-at-a-time* pattern. First, Suina discusses his life as a preschooler residing in his grandmother's house (1–7). Then, he discusses what life was like for him after he was required to attend school (8–16). This pattern works well because the essay compares "before" and "after" stages of Suina's childhood, stages that occurred one after the other. The *one-side-at-a-time* strategy allows Suina to maintain the chronological order of events.

There are some places within the description of his school life where he returns to talk about Indian ways; in these places he uses the *point-by-point* strategy. For example, at the start of paragraph 9, he describes his teacher, comparing her with his grandmother. In paragraph 10, he compares the fluorescent lighting to "the fire and sunlight that my eyes were accustomed to" and sitting at a desk all day with his previous life of "running carefree in the village and fields, . . ." In paragraph 13, he compares the attitude of the school towards his native language and his own childhood view of it: "This punishment was for speaking the language of my people that meant so much to me. It was the language of my grandmother and I spoke it well. With it, I sang beautiful songs and prayed from my heart" (13). Later, Suina compares the beloved home cooking that his family brings to him once a month with the school food: "I enjoyed the outdoor oven bread, dried meat, and tamales they usually brought. It took a while to get accustomed to the diet of the school." Finally, the last paragraphs of the essay use *point-by-point* organization to express the conflicts he felt when he returned home from boarding school for four days. In 16, he describes how disappointed he felt with his old home: "Home did not feel right anymore. It was much too small and stuffy. The lack of running water and bathroom facilities were too inconvenient. Everything got dusty so quickly and hardly anyone spoke English. I did not realize I was beginning to take on the white man's ways, the ways that belittled my own."

2. The numerous places where Suina evokes the Pueblo lifestyle and values include paragraph 3, where he describes the inside of his grandmother's one-room house in great detail. Most of the details here are visual, although Suina does mention the "sharp odor of mothballs" in the dresser and the flour sack containing the " goodies," which made a "fine snack" at night. We also learn that he frequently hears stories or a softly sung song from a ceremony in the house. There are further references to the foods they shared with relatives in paragraph 4, and in the next paragraph he notes the sound and glow of the fire and the smell of stew cooking. He contrasts these sensory descriptions with details about the school he attends. There, he notices the teacher's appearance is very different from his grandmother's; he smells her odor, which makes him sick (9). He provides details of the classroom: its "huge" size and medicine-like smell, its artificial walls and ceiling, its "eerie" and blinking fluorescent lights. He feels the hardness of the desk to which he is confined. Towards the end of the essay, he returns to some beloved details about his Indian culture, things that he savors when his parents visit him at boarding school: "outdoor oven bread, dried meat, and tamales" (14). Yet, once home for a four-day break, he discovers he longs for some of the conveniences of the school, for his home "was much too small and stuffy. The lack of running water and bathroom facilities were too inconvenient. Everything got dusty so quickly . . ." (15).
3. Into the simple factual information of the first two sentences, Suina inserts a word with strong negative connotations: "invade." This word is used metaphorically to suggest that the coming of electricity to the pueblo began a conquest of the Indian culture by that of the whites. Portraying the Indians as "unsuspecting" suggests their innocence in not being aware that they were being transformed. These images establish an ominous tone and convey Suina's ambivalence about the material goods and other elements of white lifestyle that altered his native culture. However, while suggesting negative forces are at work in the pueblo, Suina's tone remains calm, almost matter-of-fact. There is no sense of blaming or rage; because of this tone, the changes seem inevitable changes.
4. The last four sentences of paragraph 14 all begin with the phrase, "I longed for. . . ." This repetition drums into the reader the grief and yearning Suina felt at being parted from his home culture. The sentences seem to cry out with pain. In addition, the shortness and simplicity of the sentences effectively convey the depth and sense of unallayed need. The final sentence moves away from specific needs for his grandmother and siblings, his home, and the familiar ceremonies to asserting that he needs to be free to be himself, instead of being confined in the alien world of the boarding school.

WORKERS

Richard Rodriguez

Questions for Close Reading (p. 366)

1. The thesis of "Workers" is implied. One way of expressing it might be: "A summer of hard physical labor is not enough to teach a young middle-class college graduate what it is like to be poor or Mexican, or what it means to make construction work one's livelihood."
2. Rodriguez writes that desire for the job "uncoiled" in him as soon as he heard about it. This surprised him, although he was in need of money at the time (1). In the weeks leading up to the job, he realized that he felt challenged to learn, after four

years in college, what it was like to work hard physically (3). In doing so, he would overcome his father's scorn that the young Rodriguez did not know what "real work" was. He was also intrigued by the thought of the sensations that would come from working in the open, under the sun, and by the chance to become "like a *bracero*" (4).

3. Very quickly the contrast between the "real laborers" and Rodriguez becomes apparent to him. He is only flirting with being a construction worker before going on to graduate school, while the other men do construction work for a living. Unlike them, he appreciates the sheer physicality of the work. When the older men try to show him how to shovel efficiently, so as not to waste energy or strain his back, he feels resistant to their instructions. "I liked the way my body felt sore at the end of the day," he writes (7).

4. Rodriguez comes to recognize he has little in common with *los pobres*, the Mexican aliens who occasionally cut trees and haul debris, although at first he seems to think there might be some natural kinship between himself and them. After all, they are Mexicans, like Rodriguez's parents; he is "physically indistinguishable" from them (17). He even speaks a rudimentary Spanish and can communicate with them in their native tongue. They treat him as an outsider, however, and he realizes he is of a different world. He earns a wage, while they are paid "for the job," as if they had no individual identities. They stay apart from the regular workers, work with little rest, converse rarely, and are powerless to change their situation. "They lack a public identity. . . . They depend upon the relative good will or fairness of their employers each day" (19). In addition, they must be submissive to retain the good will of employers; they are vulnerable in a way Rodriguez will never be. Rodriguez has a self-determined future ahead of him, the result of his college education. He says he can "act as a public person—able to defend my interests, to unionize, to petition, to speak up—to challenge and demand" (18). He states the difference philosophically at the end of paragraph 17: "What made me different from them was an attitude of *mind*, my imagination of myself."

5. *menial* (1): servile, subservient
   skepticism (4): doubt
   luxuriating (5): wallowing in pleasure
   diversity 9): variety, quality of difference
   ludicrous (16): laughable, absurd
   nouveau riche 18): the newly rich
   pathos (20): quality of arousing pity or sorrow

Questions About the Writer's Craft (p. 366)

1. The author is more like the American construction workers than the Mexican laborers; the details provided in paragraph 9 make his similarity to the Americans clear. He is able to find other workers that he can relate to, because some, like himself, have college degrees; one is an abstract painter in the off-hours. Also, these workers accept him, while the Mexicans do not. "I felt easy, pleased by the knowledge that I was casually accepted, my presence taken for granted by men (exotics) who worked with their hands," he writes (9). Other details reveal that these workers are "middle-class Americans," like himself, who follow football, vacation in Las Vegas, and consider the merits of different campers, presumably in view of purchasing one (9). The details about the Mexicans, on the other hand, show them to be alienated, silent, and submissive (11, 15).

2. There are four narrative segments in the piece: the stories of how Rodriguez heard about the job and how he came to take it (1–3, 4); the story of the older workers

teaching him how to shovel (6–8); the narrative of his Spanish conversation with the Mexican workers (12–15); and the description of how the boss pays the Mexicans (16). The anecdotes about the Mexicans come last because the experience of working with them generates Rodriguez's most important point—that he will never be like them, that his attempt to recover a more elemental, ancestral self was a failure. The anecdotes occur in chronological order at first: hearing about a job, getting it, and learning to do the work. In putting the Mexican anecdotes last, Rodriguez switches to emphatic organization.

3. The subjective descriptions of how it feels to do hard physical work occur mostly in paragraph 5. Students will probably find two phrases especially striking: "my chest silky with sweat in the breeze" and "a nervous spark of pain would . . . burn like an ember in the thick of my shoulder."

4. Rodriguez mixes in a few Spanish words to suggest his origins. In terms of the theme, these foreign words express the author's uncertain identity: as a highly educated American of Mexican descent, he feels neither like an "all-American worker" nor like a Mexican laborer; the Spanish terms convey his middle position between the two groups. Also, Spanish in general and the words he chooses in particular (such as *bracero*) represent his desire to vindicate himself in terms of his father's value system, which celebrates "real work."

THE UGLY TRUTH ABOUT BEAUTY

Dave Barry

Questions for Close Reading (p. 370)

1. The selection's main idea is expressed in the fourth paragraph: "The problem is that women generally do not think of their looks in the same way that men do." Throughout the essay, Barry addresses a serious topic—the way men and women develop their self-images—with tongue-in-cheek humor. Most men, he argues, "think of themselves as average-looking," and "being average does not bother them" (paragraph 5). He illustrates this claim with the humorous observation that men's "primary form of beauty-care is to shave themselves, which is essentially the same form of beauty-care that they give to their lawns" (5). Most women, on the other hand, believe that their appearance is simply "not good enough" (6) and obsessively seek to narrow the gap between themselves and the images of ideal beauty that pervade society. Women "grow up thinking they need to look like Barbie, which for most women is impossible" or "like Cindy Crawford, who is some kind of genetic mutation" (8).

Though he pokes fun at the behaviors of both men and women regarding how they view themselves, Barry implies that women's obsession with how they look can be highly detrimental to the psyche as well as a colossal waste of time.

2. The reason for men's unwavering unconcern with their appearances, Barry states, is that men are not inundated with images dictating how they should look. For instance, while girls grow up subjected to an impossibly-proportioned, utterly-unrealistic model of female beauty—the Barbie doll—boys, through their "hideous-looking" but "self-confident" action figures, are socialized to value physical perfection to a much lesser degree (7). So, as women grow up "thinking they need to look like Barbie, which for most women is impossible" (8), men aren't encouraged to spend much time at all considering their looks. In fact, to look presentable—which, Barry implies, is good enough for most men—men only need

engage in a "four-minute . . . beauty regimen" of shaving, "which is essentially the same form of beauty care that they give their lawns" (5). Ultimately, Barry argues, men can content themselves with an average appearance because, unlike women, they are not subject to a "multibillion-dollar beauty industry devoted to convincing [them] they must try to look perfect" (8).

3. From a woman's point of view, Barry argues, personal beauty is a matter of measuring up to the "difficult appearance standard" that pervades society (7). He says that "women grow up thinking they need to look like Barbie, which for most women is impossible, although there is a multibillion-dollar beauty industry devoted to convincing women that they must try" (8). TV shows, such as *Oprah,* perpetuate these negative values in featuring "supermodel Cindy Crawford" and her ludicrously-detailed lessons on make-up application (8). Eventually, women become convinced they must strive for what is actually an unattainable image, and they "spen[d] countless hours . . . obsessing about the differences between [themselves] and Cindy Crawford" (13), whose apparent flawlessness Barry identifies as "some kind of genetic mutation" (8). Because the image that women pursue is virtually impossible to achieve, most women feel they fall far short of the mark when it comes to attractiveness. Thus, women believe that their appearance is simply "not good enough" (6), and they often wind up developing negative self-images and low self-esteem (7).

In addition to Barbie dolls, the all-powerful beauty industry, and the media (represented by TV shows like *Oprah*), Barry addresses another potential source of women's obsession with their appearance: men. He says that "many women will argue that the reason they become obsessed . . . is that men WANT them to look that way" (10). But he then undermines this claim in two ways. First, he says that women should know better than to be misled by men, that "just because WE'RE idiots, that does not mean YOU have to be" (11). Next, he claims that "men don't even notice 97 percent of the beauty effort you make anyway" (12). Ultimately, despite his humorous take on his subject, Barry seeks to point out the negative consequences of women's obsession with beauty and to persuade women away from this misguided mentality.

4. Barry implies that, ideally, women should not align their sense of self-worth with their appearance and should reject the unrealistic beauty standards with which they are bombarded in society. Though this is not an easy feat, Barry implies that women have the intelligence and strength of character to resist society's damaging messages about beauty: "just because WE'RE [men are] idiots [in appreciating supermodels], that does not mean YOU have to be" (11). In fact, though Barry cautions that he's "not saying that men are superior" (9), he does imply that men's indifference to matters of their own appearance is a worthwhile model for women to emulate.

5. *regimen* (5): routine or process
municipal (6): community or public
societal (7): shared by society or by the group
dispensed (8): handed out
genetic (8): inborn, hereditary
mutation (8): alteration or deviation from the norm
demeaning (9): humiliating
bolster (9): reinforce, strengthen

Questions About the Writer's Craft (p. 370)

1. Barry uses the point-by-point method of organization to contrast how men and women perceive their personal appearances. Paragraphs 4 and 5 explore how men

evaluate their appearance, and then paragraph 6 looks at how women do. Paragraph 7 begins by exploring how girls' toys affect their self-perception and ends by showing how boys' toys affect theirs. Paragraph 8 illustrates women's embracing of beauty role models, while paragraph 9 outlines men's rejection of the same. This animated alternation between women's and men's attitudes toward personal attractiveness both heightens and lends immediacy to the contrast between the two. Barry's point-by-point contrast, maintained with a great deal of humor, encourages both women and men to laugh at themselves and their efforts (or lack thereof) to be good-looking. Yet the sharply-delineated disparity between men's and women's self-evaluations emphasizes the fundamental absurdity of what women put themselves through.

2. Throughout the selection, Barry tends to overstate ideas in order to maximize their impact on readers. For example, to demonstrate men's quandary when women ask how they look, Barry suggests that men should "form an honest yet sensitive opinion, then collapse on the floor with some kind of fatal seizure" (3). In this and other instances, Barry's humor draws upon highly-exaggerated visual images. For example, when illustrating men's unchanging, generally positive opinion of their looks, he says that men who decide early on that they are "stud muffins" remain steadfast in this opinion "even when their faces sag and their noses bloat to the size of eggplants and their eyebrows grow together to form what appears to be a giant forehead-dwelling tropical caterpillar" (4). Barry likewise employs exaggeration in demonstrating that women are perpetually dissatisfied with their appearances. He says that "no matter how attractive" a woman may be, "when she looks at herself in the mirror, she thinks: woof" and that "at any moment a municipal animal-control officer is going to throw a net over her and haul her off to the shelter" (6). To demonstrate the negative impact on women of Barbie's unrealistic figure, he provides another humorous overstatement: If the doll were a human, "it would be seven feet tall and weigh 81 pounds, of which 53 pounds would be bosoms" (7). Similarly, in conveying the unattainable beauty standards set by supermodels, Barry calls Cindy Crawford "some kind of genetic mutation" (8). And in dismissing the claim that men encourage women's painstaking efforts to be beautiful, he claims that "[t]he average woman spends 5,000 hours per year worrying about her fingernails, while [m]any men would not notice if a woman had upward of four hands" (12).

The most obvious purpose of this repeated exaggeration is to engage readers by making them laugh. At the very least, Barry shows, people should laugh at themselves for taking their looks and society's standard of beauty too seriously. Yet Barry's overstatement has a serious purpose: to demonstrate how women's obsession with society's inflated beauty standards undermines women's and, by extension, men's psychological well-being. Sadly, Barry's exaggerations may have much in common with many people's distorted mindset about the subject of personal beauty.

3. Barry points out a number of cause-effect relationships in order to make us aware of how our self-perceptions are formed and to persuade us to stop subjecting ourselves to society's impossible standards. The central causal analysis of the selection explores the reasons for and effects of women's appearance-consciousness. Barry begins by illustrating some of the effects of this fixation, the first of which is women's need to know "How do I look?" (2). This question, which strikes fear in the hearts of men who don't know how best to respond, reflects women's need for external affirmation of their appearance. Barry goes on to state that, unlike men, women generally appraise their appearance as "not good enough" (6) and that most women suffer from "low self-esteem" (7). He then proceeds to explore the complex psychological and societal reasons for women's poor self-image, which, he half-jokingly proposes, are summed up in the Barbie doll (7). The doll, complete with its outrageous, unnatural physical proportions, brainwashes young girls about the

way a real woman should look. It is no wonder, then, that women would "grow up thinking they need to look like Barbie, which for most women is impossible" (8). Other sources of women's beauty ideals include the "multibillion-dollar beauty industry" (8) as well as the media (represented by the *Oprah* show), which fuel women's insecurity and beauty-obsession by constantly imposing new standards of beauty. As a result, women squander "countless hours"—and, presumably, dollars—as well as precious self-esteem in "obsessing about the differences" between themselves and the newest unattainable beauty ideal (13).

Since Barry's thesis is that "women generally do not think of their looks in the same way that men do" (4), he offers a second series of cause-effect chains; these focus on men's relative comfort with their appearance and provide a crucial counterpoint to his analysis of women. Unlike women, men "never ask anybody how they look" (5). This is because most men, Barry argues, see themselves as "average-looking" (5); they "form an opinion of how they look in seventh grade, and they stick to it for the rest of their lives" (4). The reason for this mentality, Barry reveals later, is that young boys, unlike young girls, are *not* taught to emphasize their physical appearance. He illustrates this claim with the example of his son's "hideous-looking" but "extremely self-confident" action figure, which contrasts sharply with the inhumanly-beautiful Barbie dolls with which girls are socialized to play (7). As a result, men are not conditioned to obsess about their appearance. Unlike women, men spend very little time and energy on grooming, their greatest exertion being a "four-minute beauty regimen" of shaving, "which is essentially the same form of beauty care that they give their lawns" (5). In fact, men's freedom from beauty-brainwashing causes them aggressively to reject any models of male beauty. Barry argues that men would recognize as "pointless and demeaning" (9) women's eager desire for Cindy Crawford's beauty tips on the *Oprah* show. If men were presented with the challenge to look like Crawford's male equivalent, Brad Pitt, they would respond by making reference to their capabilities—"Oh YEAH? Well, what do you know about LAWN CARE, pretty boy?"—*not* by trying to mirror the beauty standard placed before them (9).

Barry does acknowledge an intersection point between the female and male causal chains when he addresses women's claim that men "WANT women to look like supermodels" (10). Barry, however, debunks this claim by humorously arguing that women should know better than to listen to men, and that "[m]en don't even notice the beauty efforts women make anyway" (12). Yet despite Barry's light-hearted dismissal of women's claim, the fact still remains that men are indeed a cause of women's beauty-mania. Ultimately, a larger effect of both women's and men's attitudes is their different expectations regarding beauty—hence, Barry's advice that when a woman asks "How do I look?" a man would do best to "collapse on the floor with some kind of fatal seizure because he will never come up with the right answer" (3).

4. The title, "The Ugly Truth About Beauty," suggests that our concept of beauty itself is not beautiful. Throughout the essay, Barry outlines the highly detrimental psychological effects to women of the appearance-consciousness they are taught. Women's obsessive pursuit of beauty, in effect, has disastrous—and ugly—consequences on their mental and emotional well-being. Thus, in spite of the humor with which Barry addresses his subject, his title indicates that he takes the matter seriously and wants his readers to do the same.

THE PRISONER'S DILEMMA

Stephen Chapman

Questions for Close Reading (p. 376)

1. Chapman's thesis statement is implied in his discussion of how the American justice system compares to that of Islamic countries. The thesis might be stated this way: "Although we consider the Islamic punishment system cruel, our own is just as frequently cruel, even barbaric, and often unfair." In paragraph 3, Chapman presents the "single device" of our punishment system, incarceration, and through examples of its use, strongly implies its unfair, cruel, and even ludicrous nature. These examples include 1) that some states do not impose a sentence of a specific length on certain convicts, but instead permit parole boards to decide the sentence length during the course of the imprisonment and 2) the imposition of extremely long sentences for small crimes because of multiple offenses or of the use of a weapon.

2. Chapman gives several examples of Islamic punishments: flogging for such crimes as prostitution (1), stoning or scourging for sexual crimes or drinking alcohol, amputation of the hands for thievery, and death for murder or leaving the Islamic religion (2). These punishments are barbaric to us not only in themselves but also in the manner in which they are inflicted. Many punishments are carried out in public, with hordes of viewers, as many as 10,000 at a time, entertained by the spectacle of other people's agony (1). The accused are often punished after summary, immediate trials, and, in the case of flogging, are stripped, marked with red, and virtually attacked by burly, strutting, stave-wielding convicted murderers (1). As Chapman says, these punishments seem barbaric in two ways, by being cruel and by seeming "pre-civilized" (1). Much later in the essay (11), Chapman returns to the issue of why Americans might find the Islamic system barbaric. He cites the lack of due process, that is, of an elaborate and protective legal system such as ours, and the numerous offenses pertaining to what Americans consider personal morality, such as drinking, adultery, and religious offenses. He also points out that the Islamic legal system is full of "ritualistic mumbo-jumbo pronouncements," which Americans find irrelevant and peculiar.

3. There are five goals of imprisonment, according to criminologists cited by Chapman in paragraph 6. These are, first, retribution, the idea that the criminal should pay for the crime. A second goal is "specific deterrence," the idea that the criminal should be discouraged by the punishment from repeating the crime at a later date. There is also the goal of "general deterrence," by which the criminally inclined will take note of the punishment meted out to others and turn away from crime. The fourth goal is prevention, the idea that while in prison, the criminal cannot commit other similar crimes. The fifth and most important goal is supposed to be rehabilitation, by which the criminal is reformed so that he will return to society an upright citizen (6). In terms of success, only on the score of punishment does Chapman believe American prisons achieve their goals. He cites statistics on the increase of crime over the last 20 years to indicate that few criminals are reformed and few are deterred, in specific or in general. In addition, he pronounces that "almost no one contends any more that prisons rehabilitate their inmates" (17).

4. Chapman concludes that both systems are cruel and barbaric, and that ours may be the worse one. The main difference is that our system is hidden from our eyes, and so we find it easy to ignore how cruel it is, whereas the Islamic one is inflicted in full view of the public (12). Chapman finds us admirable in our reluctance to

sanction cruelty and violence in the style of Islamic societies. He sees that this revulsion for deliberate cruelty both forces us to hide our punishment of criminals and might prompt us to someday discover a better way to deal with criminals (13). However, this hidden nature of our cruelty also perpetuates it and causes us to be self-congratulatory about our civilized methods. In other words, we have become unknowing hypocrites.

5. *barbaric* (1): crude and unrestrained
   stipulated (2): specified
   penological (2): having to do with the punishment of crime
   malefactors (2): people who do evil or violate the laws
   effusive (2): unrestrained in expression of feeling
   brazen (3): shockingly bold
   genteel (3): refined; free from vulgarity or rudeness
   indeterminate (3): not specified; not known in advance
   superfluous (3): more than sufficient or necessary
   extortion (4): using force to compel someone to hand over valuables
   criteria (7): standards of measurement
   ostensible (8): apparent, professed, or stated
   recidivism (9): relapsing into or returning to criminal behavior
   corporal (9): affecting the physical body
   blasphemy (11): impious statements about God
   sanctioned (13): authorized or approved

Questions About the Writer's Craft (p. 377)

1. Chapman helps the reader keep track of the goals by using transitional questions as he moves from one function of imprisonment to another. Only with the first goal does he use the numbering system that he relied upon in paragraph 6: "First, do they punish?" The other transitional questions that cue the reader's memory of his earlier list include, "Do they deter crime?" (8); "Do flogging and amputation deter recidivism?" (9); "Do these medieval forms of punishment rehabilitate the criminal?" (10). Note that in paragraph 8, he disregards the difference between specific and general deterrence, and discusses deterrence in response to the question, "Do they deter crime?" (8). By thus collapsing two functions in to one, he needs only to contrast four aspects of punishment in the two cultures.

2. In the first paragraph, Chapman defines "barbaric" for us, although it is a word most readers would already, in some sense, be familiar with. But Chapman spells out two dimensions of this word because he believes both are relevant and need to be acknowledged. To Americans, he says, Islamic punishment seems "barbaric" in two ways: "cruel" and "pre-civilized." He then provides a definition of what "flogging" is in Pakistan, even though the reader most likely has a basic understanding of the term. But by providing an extended definition, involving a horrifying vivid picture of flogging in action, Chapman dramatizes what Americans would find so barbaric. These definitions establish the reader's agreement with Chapman's opening point, that Islamic justice is cruel beyond our conception. In the next paragraph (2), Chapman solidifies the reader's revulsion to Islamic ways by defining scourging.

    In paragraph 6, Chapman uses definition to clarify what is meant by the five separate goals of punishment in the American system. He spells out the five goals carefully, defining them and differentiating them from each other. Later in the essay, he will argue that the American system is a failure by its own standards, meeting only one of five goals (retribution), and that by American standards, the Islamic system may, shockingly enough, be more successful.

100

3. Chapman uses emphatic organization in arranging both these paragraphs. In paragraph 3, he begins with a fairly standard or "typical" example of our punishment system at work, the sentencing of people to three to five years' imprisonment for grand theft and to six to 30 years for armed robbery. He points to longer sentences for repeat offenders and begins to give additional examples, but these examples begin to display the illogicality and cruelty that can crop up in our system. These examples of prison sentences, thus, are arranged from those that seem acceptable to those that seem unfair and even absurd (receiving life for thefts of less than $300 of property or the sentence of "life plus a day," once a sentencing option in Maryland).

In paragraph 4, Chapman offers examples of what it's like to be an American prisoner. Again he moves from the moderate, almost expected negatives to those which are horrific. The first examples consist of routine cruelties, such as overpopulation and overcrowding, unhealthy conditions conducive to infectious diseases, and poor medical treatment. He moves from these fairly mundane examples to those that dramatize the extent of violence and other crimes rampant in our prisons. These last examples, enumerating the numbers of stabbings and fatalities and specifying a list of horrific crimes, are shocking.

4. In paragraph 3, Chapman begins with a judgment on Islamic justice that hints of sarcasm: "Such traditions, we all must agree, are no sign of an advanced civilization." This seems a put-down of the Islamic systems, but as we read the paragraph that follows, describing the application of the "single device" of American justice, imprisonment, we may feel that the entire paragraph is tinged with irony. The examples offered demonstrate that our justice system produces cruel and unfair results equal to those in Islamic countries.

Paragraph 4 begins with a sarcastic question: "What are the advantages of being a convicted criminal in an advanced culture?" The details provided in the paragraph show plainly that "advantages" is hardly the word for the conditions in our prisons and that the term "advanced culture" is misapplied to such a cruel system.

Chapman summarizes these ideas more neutrally at the start of paragraph 5, but then inquires of the reader, "Skeptical? Ask yourself: Would you rather be subjected to a few minutes of intense pain and considerable public humiliation, or be locked away for two or three years in a prison cell crowded with ill-tempered sociopaths?" The tone of this question and that following is teasing. The academic-sounding term, "ill-tempered sociopaths," ironically mocks our complacent distance from the violence within our prisons.

In 8–9, Chapman speaks mockingly of the debate about punishment continuing "in all the same old ruts." Throughout these two paragraphs, his word choice and phrasing are occasionally ironic. He asserts that Islamic punishment succeeds "in a uniquely painful and memorable way" and dryly suggests that "presumably no Western penologist would criticize Islamic punishments on the grounds that they are not barbaric enough" (8). He wryly notes that "it is hard to imagine that corporal measures could stimulate a higher rate of recidivism than already exists [in our culture]" (9). Chapman's use of irony adds passion to his argument and could be effective in creating indignation in a reader newly aware of the flaws in the American justice system.

CAUSE-EFFECT

OPENING COMMENTS

Along with comparison-contrast, cause-effect writing (often called "causal analysis") is frequently required of college students—especially in exams ("Analyze the causes of the country's spiraling divorce rate"; "Discuss the impact of the revised tax laws on middle-income families.") Since students can't deny that an ability to write sound causal analyses will serve them well, they are generally eager to tackle this rhetorical pattern.

Not surprisingly, though, many students run into problems with their analyses. Although they enjoy the intellectual challenge of tracing causes and effects, they sometimes stop at the obvious—overly concerned as they are about getting closure on an issue.

We've found a classroom activity that helps counteract this urge to oversimplify. Here's what we do. We put on the board a broad, noncontroversial statement (for example, "In the United States, many people work hard to keep physically fit"). Then we ask students to take five minutes (we time them and announce when the time is up) to brainstorm the reasons *why* (causes) people are so involved in physical fitness. Then we ask students to spend another five minutes brainstorming the *consequences* (effects) of this concern with physical fitness. Next, we put students in pairs and then in groups of four; each time they exchange, first, their causes and then their effects. As you'd expect, this activity generates a good deal of energy. We hear a number of comments such as, "That's interesting. I never thought of that." Such a reaction is precisely what we hope for. The activity sensitizes students to the complexity of cause-effect relationships and encourages them to dig deeply and not settle for the obvious.

For this chapter, we chose professional selections that dramatize the power of causal analysis to make the reader think. In his essay "Why We Crave Horror Movies," King, a master of horror himself, considers both the obvious and the underlying reasons for the horror film's popularity. With reflective eloquence, D'Amboise identifies dance as a major component in character development. Walker explores a complex causal chain to conduct an in-depth inquiry of human nature. Darley and Latané's "Why People Don't Help in a Crisis" provides a well-researched analysis of the causal factors behind bystanders' typical inaction. Walljasper's causal analysis, by illustrating our tendency to overschedule our lives, asks students to consider the way our fast-paced, hi-tech society distances us from the joys of spontaneous human experience.

ANSWERS FOR PREWRITING ACTIVITIES

Below we provide possible responses to selected prewriting activities at the end of Chapter 9. Of course, other approaches are possible. (p. 395)

1. There are many ways to use cause-effect in these two essays; the lists below suggest only a few of the possibilities. We suggest that you have students share their ideas on ways to use cause-effect in these essays. Seeing others' ideas makes the point dramatically that writing involves invention and individuality.

102

Topic: The need for a high school course in personal finance
  Causes of many young people's casual attitude to money
  Causes of parents' reluctance to teach about finance
  Effects of a young person bouncing checks
  Effects of overspending

Topic: How to show appreciation
  Causes of people's callous disregard for each other
  Causes of an appreciative approach to good manners
  Effects of appreciation in everyday life
  Effects of not showing appreciation

2. Here are some possible causes and/or effects for the various topics. Others are possible. Students' thesis statements, purposes, and outlines will vary widely.

   a. *Pressure on a student to do well*
       Causes:
               High career ambitions
               Parental demands
               Inner pressure; self-esteem
       Effects:
               Restricted social, campus, and physical activities
               Emotional instability, anger
               Less effective academic performance

   b. *Children's access to soft-core pornography on cable TV*
       Causes:
               Lenient parents
               Failure to purchase a TV lock
               Children visiting friends' homes
       Effects:
               Children grow up too soon
               Children get unrealistic view of adult relationships
               Children dating at too early an age

   c. *Being physically fit*
       Causes:
               Media attention to health concerns
               Trend to engage in sports
               Desire to look attractive
       Effects:
               Better health
               Growing enrollments in health clubs
               Preoccupation with fitness

   d. *Spiraling costs of college education*
       Causes:
               Growing costs of faculty and staff
               Modernization going on: computers, for example
               Inflation
               Cutbacks in state and federal funds

Effects:
>
>Students burdened with more loans
>Concern about paying back loans influences career choices
>More students work during college
>Some students drop out

ANSWERS FOR REVISING ACTIVITIES

Below we provide possible responses to selected prewriting activities at the end of Chapter 9. Of course, other approaches are possible. (p. 395)

3.   a. The growing Latin American immigrant population and the crime rate may be correlated, that is, there may be some connection between the two. That both figures are increasing, however, does not mean that the rise in immigration has *caused* the rise in crime. To say so is *post hoc* thinking.

 b. This statement shows *post hoc* thinking because it assumes that one of two parallel events is causing the other; that is, that more women working is causing the divorce rate to rise. However, there are other possible reasons for the increase in the divorce rate: a change in American values regarding the family, for instance, or the "sexual revolution." Moreover, one could cite the same two facts—more women working and the divorce rate rising—and argue the opposite, that the divorce rate is causing more women to work outside the home. In any case, disregarding these other possible points of view and arguing that a clear-cut relationship necessarily exists is an example of *post hoc* thinking.

 c. These two parallel situations do not have a proven causal relationship. To say that one has caused the other is *post hoc* reasoning, unless other proof exists. Such proof might consist of information about what chemicals exist in the landfill, whether they are cancer-causing, whether the chemicals have leached into the soil, water, or air of the town, and whether other causes for the cancer might exist.

4.   It's a good idea to provide time in class for students to read over each other's revisions of this paragraph. Seeing how others handled the activity can give students a stronger sense of their revision options.
    Here are the main problems with the paragraph:

—   Overall, the paragraph asserts that the bank machines have *caused* certain behaviors and attempts to support such a claim with broad generalizations stated in absolute terms. For example, the fourth sentence asserts that automatic tellers have negatively influenced the "average individual." Similarly, the next three sentences state—almost categorically—that people, once they have cash readily in hand, invariably spend their lunch hours shopping. Equivalent absolutes can be found throughout. The paragraph could be rescued if the writer toned down the absolute tone and provided qualifications that suggest that "for *some* people" or "for *many* people" these machines present problems.

—   The writer assumes causation explains the circumstances (use of ATM cards and people shopping during lunch hour) when these may simply be correlated, that is, they may happen at the same time because they are two results of some other earlier event. Or, the simultaneous appearance of increased spending and ATM card use may be a coincidence, meaning that the writer has committed the *post hoc* fallacy.

— Another problem with the paragraph is its lack of supporting examples. Although it isn't necessary for the writer to provide hard evidence in the form of research, he or she should have supported the paragraph with specific references to friends, family, etc., for whom automatic tellers have created problems.

— The point that children don't appreciate the value of money is an unfounded generalization; it also digresses from the paragraph's point and so should be eliminated.

— The last sentence categorically asserts ("There's no doubt. . .") that banking machine fraud is a *cause* of the "immoral climate in the country." This is an unsupported causal statement and would need evidence to be considered valid. It should be deleted.

WHY WE CRAVE HORROR MOVIES

Stephen King

Questions for Close Reading (p. 399)

1. King states the *topic* of his essay clearly in the title, which proposes to explore not only why we watch or enjoy horror movies, but why we *crave* them. He does not, however, state his *thesis* explicitly, but, rather, develops over the course of the essay his main idea: that the horror movie satisfies a type of "insanity in us." He begins with the provocative opinion, "I think we're all mentally ill; those of us outside the asylum only hide it a little better" (paragraph 1). For King, sanity is only "a matter of degree," and we are all on the same continuum as "Jack the Ripper or the Cleveland Torso Murderer" (8). While King is sure that "the potential lyncher is in all of us" (9), he also knows that society works very hard to hide or repress this fact. As a result, "every now and then, [the lyncher] has to be let loose" (9). It is what King calls the "dirty job" of horror movies to satisfy "all that is worst in us" (12). Watching these movies is like "throwing a basket of raw meat to the hungry alligators swimming around in that subterranean river beneath" (12). King concludes that horror movies keep the dangerous psychological gators "down there" and a more ostensibly sane "me up here" (13).

2. In paragraph 8, King wants to collapse the separation between the sane and the insane. Watching a horror movie, we are all invited to "lapse into simplicity, irrationality, and even outright madness" (7) as we enjoy the spectacle of "seeing others menaced—sometimes killed" (6). Our eager participation in this "modern version of the public lynching" (6) proves that "we are all insane" and that, by extension, "sanity becomes a matter of degree" (8). The infamous killers are now invoked to demonstrate this point. Using the second person, King directly addresses the reader, placing him or her on a continuum with famous killers. King writes, "if your insanity leads you to carve up women like Jack the Ripper or the Cleveland Torso Murderer, we clap you away in the funny farm . . . if, on the other hand your insanity leads you only to talk to yourself"—or to crave horror films—"then you are left alone" (8). The extreme examples of the serial murderers are necessary to illustrate King's main thesis: the presence of a shared "insanity of man" which the horror movie satisfies (11). Linking the psychopath and supposedly normal, everyday people (like us) is King's project, and the references to the murderers in paragraph 8 establish this uncomfortable bond.

3. What King calls the "conservative" nature of horror movies should not be understood in terms of politics. Instead, King uses the term more strictly to mean "cautious,"

"traditional," and "staid." While horror films may challenge us to face the darkness, they provide no new understanding of it. King argues that horror movies "re-establish our feelings of essential normality" (4). By watching monsters on the screen, we reassure ourselves that we are not monsters ourselves. As King writes, horror movies remind us that "no matter how far we may be removed from the beauty of a Robert Redford or a Diana Ross, we are still light-years from true ugliness," such as that of the grotesque creatures featured in many films (4). Furthermore, King argues that horror movies encourage us to "put away our more civilized and adult penchant for analysis" and to see the world in "pure blacks and whites" (7). In reinforcing basic definitions like "us" and "them," horror movies touch on the "reactionary," restoring us to primal, absolute attitudes and emotions.

Yet some of these same impulses inspired by horror movies render the films "anarchistic, and revolutionary" (11)—quite the opposite of conservative. Reveling in the dark fun of horror movies, we "exercise" our inherent, universal "anticivilization emotions" (11)—the ones that society attempts to quash out of us, as in the example of the child being punished for deliberately hurting "the little rotten puke of a sister" (10). The "dirty job" of horror movies is highly subversive in nature: "It is morbidity unchained, our most basic instincts let free, our nastiest fantasies realized (12). As we watch these films, we may allow our emotions a free rein . . . or no rein at all" (7). So, while horror films may restore our conservative sense of humanity (as opposed to the extreme monstrousness on the screen), they also incite an anarchy of the psyche, where our delight in the grotesque is free from regulation. In spite of the "civilized forebrain," horror movies feed "the hungry alligators swimming around in that subterranean river beneath" (12).

4. Alligators symbolize the latent, uncivilized tendencies that King argues we all possess but are compelled, by society, to repress. Throughout his essay, King develops his theory that sanity is only "a matter of degree" and that we are all on the same continuum as "Jack the Ripper or the Cleveland Torso Murderer" (8). Society, however, militates against "the potential lyncher . . . in all of us" (9). It encourages actions based on feelings like "love, friendship, loyalty, kindness" while actively discouraging their opposites (10). To King's mind, however, sanctioned emotions are only half of the equation; the rest of our emotions—the aberrant ones—won't disappear, and they too "demand periodic exercise" (11). So, while love may be the sort of emotion endorsed by society, this and other benevolent sentiments cannot be sustained unless we periodically satisfy the other, darker elements in our psyche—the "gators." King argues that one safe way to "feed" these gators is to indulge in horror movies, which function as a safety valve for our potentially destructive emotions.

5. *hysterical* (1): characterized by nervous, emotional outbursts
   reactionary (4): extremely conservative; opposed to progress
   voyeur (6): one who is highly stimulated by watching others
   lynching (6): illegal mob action against a person; a murder carried out by a mob
   penchant (7): a strong preference, inclination, or liking
   immortalized (9): made eternal
   anarchistic (11): lawless, wild
   morbidity (12): an interest in gloom, disease, and death

Questions About the Writer's Craft (p. 400)

1. King may be seen, at different points in the essay, as encompassing each of the three purposes. In explaining why we crave horror movies, King proposes a theory of the human psyche. Unlike a scientific researcher, he offers no statistical, biological, or

106

clinical data. He does not aim to inform us about new psychological discoveries. Instead, he acts like a philosopher and *speculates* about the nature of human emotions and, more specifically, about why we crave horror movies. He develops a theory about the existence of a shared "insanity of man" which the horror movie satisfies (11). But he then attempts throughout the rest of the essay to *persuade* us of this claims validity, providing an abundance of vivid examples and analogies. His purpose may also be interpreted as *informative*; King wants to show us the dark, repressed part of ourselves as well as a benign means of keeping it at bay: watching horror movies.

King's theory also functions as a defense of his own craft—of not only why we crave horror movies, but why King writes them. In persuading us of our psychological need for horror movies, he simultaneously (and implicitly) seeks to persuade us of our practical need for horror writers—like King himself.

2.   The task of King's essay is to spell out the dark psychological tendencies satisfied by horror movies. In order to explain the "simple and obvious" (3) reasons for the horror films attraction, King begins by comparing it to a roller coaster. Like roller coasters, horror movies pose a challenge. As King argues, in both cases "we are daring the nightmare" (2), and we do so "to show that we can, that we are not afraid" (3). In both, we enjoy the sheer thrill of the ride—the possibility that a movie, like a coaster ride, might "surprise a scream out of us" (3) or might just be "fun" (5). But, according to King, horror films fundamentally differ from roller coasters in the source of all that fun. Our enjoyment of horror movies, he demonstrates, originates in a far darker and more complex part of the psyche. In the horror movie, the fun comes not from twists and turns but from "seeing others menaced—sometimes killed" (6). The horror movie returns us to child-like thinking, shutting down adult analysis and recasting the world in "pure blacks and whites" (7). In this way, horror movies invite us "to lapse into simplicity, irrationality, and outright madness" (7). Roller coasters, by implication, do not serve nearly as complicated a function.

King then turns to a second comparison-contrast to explain our response to horror movies. He says that "the horror film has become the modern form of the public lynching" (6). In both cases, spectators derive "a very peculiar sort of fun . . . from seeing others menaced—sometimes killed" (6). This malignant pleasure in morbidity always lurks beneath our socially-adjusted surfaces, King argues, but society systematically represses these "anticivilization emotions" (11). The implied difference between the two is that public lynchings are no longer sanctioned by society, while horror movies still are, even though they exercise the same emotions. As King concludes, horror movies keep the dark side "from getting out, man" (13).

King develops a final comparison-contrast to explain the phenomenon of horror movies: the same "anticivilization emotions" that fuel our enjoyment of the films also incite us to delight in "sick jokes" (11). Sick jokes "may surprise a laugh or a grin out of us even as we recoil" (11)—a response much like the one King attributes to horror-movie watching. He goes a step further in stating that "[t]he mythic horror movie, like the sick joke, has a dirty job to do. It deliberately appeals to all that is worst in us" (12). Our morbid enjoyment of the two serves as evidence of King's larger observation that "we're all mentally ill" (1) and "share in an insanity of man" (11). Another similarity between them is that they both are particularly attractive to young people. Early in the essay, he identifies horror movies as "the special province of the young" (3). Later in the essay, King cites the example of the dead baby joke that he heard "originally from a ten-year-old" (11). Ultimately, both horror movies and sick jokes attest to the "potential lyncher" (9) that we all harbor within.

3.   In explaining our attraction to horror movies, King builds a theory about the shape of our emotional life, a theory that fundamentally includes children. He begins by

observing that "horror movies, like roller coasters, have always been the special province of the young" (3). Ostensibly, this youthful appeal owes to the raw thrills provided by both, but King goes on to suggest several less innocuous reasons for young people's attraction to horror films. In discussing society's repression of malignant human emotions, he cites the example of our youthful reactions to a little sister (10). King demonstrates how "society showers us with positive reinforcement" (often in the form of sweets) when we exercise valued emotions like love or kindness—"emotions," King explains, "that tend to maintain the status quo" (9). However, when we deliberately hurt "the rotten little puke of a sister," "sanctions follow" (10). King explains the problem of such sanctions in paragraph 11, reminding us that, even after a series of punishments, "anticivilization emotions don't go away." We still harbor destructive desires, a fact evidenced in King's example of the "sick joke" told by a ten-year-old. The child's implied enjoyment of the gory "dead baby" joke points to the shared "insanity of man"—King's main point. "We're all mentally ill" (1), he believes, and the perverse impulses that society tries to repress in its young nevertheless remain with us forever. In King's view, children are not innocents; instead, they are an amoral nature run amuck. The use of children as examples simply underscores King's belief that "the potential lyncher is in almost all of us" (9).

4. Each of these paragraphs consists solely of one brief sentence or, in the case of paragraph 14, one sentence fragment. In each case, King's compressed writing style adds emphasis and directs our attention to a single idea. In paragraph 2, King places us in the darkened theater, "daring the nightmare," in order to establish the horror movies conscious and unconscious challenge to viewers. Not only does the film dare us to sit through it, as King will explain in paragraph 3, but the horror movie also dares our darker side to come out and express itself (9). The second brief paragraph—"And we go to have fun" (5)—forces us to think about the unconscious challenge to seek the kind of fun that excites "the potential lyncher . . . in almost all of us" (9). This short paragraph introduces King's thesis about the inherent pleasure involved in "seeing others menaced—sometimes killed" (6). King hopes to deliver the same kind of punch in his sentence-fragment conclusion. In the preceding paragraph, he acknowledges that you, the reader, are taught to believe that civilized emotions are "all you need" (13). But, as his striking conclusion asserts, this is true only "[a]s long as you keep the gators fed" (14). This pithy conclusion, with its vivid imagery, memorably captures King's thesis and promises to resonate in the minds of readers.

SHOWING WHAT IS POSSIBLE

Jacques D'Amboise

Questions for Close Reading (p. 406)

1. D'Amboise states his thesis explicitly in paragraph 8: "When you learn to move your body on a note of music, it's exciting. You have taken control of your body and, by learning to do that, you discover that you can take control of your life." D'Amboise restates and broadens his thesis—that learning dance teaches discipline, control, confidence, and respect—elsewhere in the essay, specifically in paragraphs 16, 22, and 27.
2. Madame Seda is wise in the ways of human nature and in knowing how to find the best in and for her students. For instance, instead of disciplining him and thereby

possibly encouraging his misbehavior, Madame Seda involves young Jacques in the class. Then, knowing that a very active seven-year-old boy would bristle at the suggestion that girls can perform actions that he cannot, Madame Seda challenges Jacques to attempt the *changements*. Finally, knowing also that Jacques needs encouragement to continue and to improve, Madame Seda praises him and then lets him join other dancers during part of the lesson—teaching him patience and self-control as he awaits his turn. She continues to praise and to set further challenges, all the while pulling him into the group of dancers. Finally, in an act of unselfish wisdom, she recommends that Jacques and his sister go to a better dance teacher.

3. D'Amboise relates qualities of the special environment that teaching dance requires in paragraphs 7, 15–16, 19–22, and 27–29. Those special qualities include the following: challenging and praising students; participating actively in students' learning and their struggles; demanding "precision, order and respect"; and, most importantly, continuing to encourage students and never "polluting" them with negativity, bad manners, and disrespect. In short, the ideal environment seems to be one that demands students' best while at the same time nurturing and respecting them.

4. D'Amboise is quick to point out that "polluting" does not refer only or even necessarily to unhealthy air or drugs. The kind of personal pollution he has in mind concerns a metaphorical poisoning of the soul and spirit and sense of self—in short, those qualities that humanity has developed over thousands of centuries that make it civilized. For D'Amboise, these kinds of personal pollution would include violence, disrespect for oneself and for others, "foul language, dirty books and ignorance."

5. *diabolically* (paragraph 1): wickedly, devilishly
   flaying (5): in a lashing motion or manner
   accessible (8): easily entered or understood
   choreography (11): the art of creating and arranging dance movements
   inevitably (12): unavoidably, certainly
   triathletes (23): athletes who compete in a race involving bicycling, swimming, and running

Questions About the Writer's Craft (p. 406)

1. D'Amboise uses both sequences. He begins chronologically, recounting his own childhood experiences, explaining what he learned in Madame Seda's classes, continuing through his later training and professional career, and concluding by examining his later years as a dance instructor. Throughout this chronology, he illustrates the influences that dance had on students, including himself. Complementing the chronological sequence is an emphatic sequence, which moves from immediate effects (self-knowledge and self-confidence) to longer-term effects (control, life-long discipline, and an appreciation for "the best that is available to you from the wealth of human culture").

2. The introductory narrative serves at least two functions. First, as an autobiographical story, it engages readers' interest in the potential conflict developing between the fidgeting seven-year-old and the "wise" Madame Seda. Second, the short narrative introduces one of the themes of the essay—how an "exceptional teacher got a bored little kid, me, interested in ballet" (7). In conjunction with this theme, the narrative illustrates the instructional process Madame Seda—and later the author—employed: setting an initial challenge, complimenting students on completing that challenge, and then further encouraging students by setting a new challenge.

3. The two sentences of paragraph 21 could have gracefully concluded paragraph 20. However, by placing the climax and the point of his brief anecdote in a short,

separate paragraph, D'Amboise succeeds in emphasizing more fully his dual point: that dance teaches self-discipline and that children want (and need) to learn such control over their minds and bodies.

4. In paragraphs 30–31, D'Amboise establishes an analogy between a trunk and a person. He says that whatever people put into a trunk in an attic will be what those people leave behind. Similarly, whatever people fill a child with—violence, foul language, ignorance—will determine what that child will be left with, what he or she will become. But if a child, like a trunk, is filled with good, valuable interests or qualities—"music, dance, poetry, literature, good manners and loving friends"—then the result is a happy, well-adjusted person. These good things, D'Amboise argues, can be taught and learned through the study of dance.

BEAUTY: WHEN THE OTHER DANCER IS THE SELF

Alice Walker

Questions for Close Reading (p. 414)

1. Walker's thesis is not stated explicitly. The following, however, approaches a thesis statement: "for all it [the defect] had taught me of shame and anger and inner vision, I *did* love it" (49). The main idea of the piece is that a physical loss can lead to a spiritual gain. Having suffered from people's negative, superficial judgments of her, Walker eventually overcomes her own tendency to judge by appearances.

2. Before her disfigurement, Walker is garrulous, chattering at her siblings until they demand silence. Three years later, she delivers a long Easter speech "without stammer or pause" (6)—further evidence of self-assurance. After the "accident," however, Walker alternately answers with a monosyllable or "rants" with self-hatred. After her surgery, Walker is once again articulate, with her classroom lessons flowing "faultlessly" from her lips (32). Finally, with her realization that being able to *see* beauty is more important than being thought beautiful, Walker experiences a poetic outpouring.

3. After Walker has developed a strong bond with her cat, she is prevented from being with the cat. Eventually, she is even told the cat cannot be found. Similarly, she becomes attached to a teacher who soon afterward marries and departs for Africa. Both the cat and the teacher, then, represent Walker's feelings of loss, perhaps even betrayal.

4. The title's meaning is not obvious. At the end of the piece, Walker's dream, in which she is dancing with herself, follows her revelation that her daughter's love for her transcends physical appearances. Because of this context, the title seems intended to convey a sense of joy and fulfillment. Walker writes that both dancers are "beautiful, whole and free." It would seem, then, that she intends to communicate a newfound sense of personal autonomy, self-sufficiency, and self-acceptance. At last, she loves herself. At last, she needs no outside approval, no admiring partner.

5. *subversive* (1): rebellious
   chronic (2): habitual
   flocked (4): tufted
   crinoline 4): a stiff petticoat
   cataract (13): an opaque area of the eye's lens
   abscess (25): a localized swelling containing pus

1. The "accident," of course, is the physical cause of Walker's disfigurement, but her brother was first motivated to aim his gun at her. As a result of the physical event, Walker's self-esteem diminishes. Her father, classmates, and others treat her differently after her disfigurement, but her own changed attitude may be a contributing factor. The same is true after her cosmetic surgery—this time, with positive consequences. Those who accept Walker without censure—her lover, her favorite teacher, her daughter—help her to be less affected by externals.

2. The present tense adds immediacy. It also emphasizes how an event or statement can have lasting effect.

3. Walker signals the ages at which some significant change in her life occurred by repeatedly using the phrase "I am" followed by her age: "I am eight years old . . ." (8), "I am fourteen . . ." (32), and "I am twenty-seven . . ." (47).

4. The repetition creates irony and ambiguity. Despite her relatives' claim that she did not change, Walker relates a process of both social and spiritual change. In addition, people *do* appear to treat her differently after her disfigurement. On the other hand, her relatives seem to be speaking sincerely, because Walker tells us they respond with puzzlement to her question. Perhaps, then, Walker wants us to understand that her relatives are right insofar as she remains "fundamentally Alice" whatever her social and physical vagaries. Some support for this view occurs in paragraph 32, where Walker writes that after the corrective surgery she was transformed, or so she *thought*.

WHY PEOPLE DON'T HELP IN A CRISIS

John M. Darley & Bibb Latané

Questions for Close Reading (p. 421)

1. Darley and Latané state their thesis at the end of their introduction, as an answer to the question, "Why, then, didn't they [witnesses to an emergency] act?" (8). They write, "There are three things the bystander must do if he is to intervene in an emergency: *notice* that something is happening; *interpret* that event as an emergency; and decide that he has *personal responsibility* for intervention" (9). They then indicate that the rest of the essay will explains the research that has led the authors to this conclusion: "As we shall show, the presence of other bystanders may at each stage inhibit his action" (9).

2. People need to notice that a problem is occurring before they can help, which means they must be disturbed out of their mental distractions. In addition, Americans are taught to keep their eyes to themselves, to "close our ears and avoid staring," the authors write (10). This principle of polite behavior can cause people to ignore or not really see a critical situation happening near them (10).

Then, after an event has attracted their attention, people must realize that someone needs help. But the presence of others can delay the realization that a problem is going on. Darley and Latané explain that people take their cues from those around them—"if everyone else is calm and indifferent, [a person] will tend to remain so" (14). People simply get the message that there's no problem because, in our culture, people usually try to remain cool and calm in public; "it is considered embarrassing to 'lose your cool'" (15). The collective nonchalance of a crowd can suppress anyone's urge to help, that is, to go against the prevailing passivity and rush to aid.

Finally, even when a person has determined that aid is required, he or she will not feel the personal requirement to perform the assistance if there are many others nearby. Darley and Latané call this the "diffusion of responsibility theory" (21). Such people are not hard-hearted but just confused about what to do when others around them are doing nothing (27). People's "reactions are shaped by the actions of others," be it response or passivity.

3. The researchers wanted to eliminate the possibility that the presence of others would prevent awareness of the emergency, so they designed an experiment in which an obvious crisis occurred and in which the subjects' awareness would not be blunted by others being in the room with them. The subjects were told to discuss with each other over headsets, used with the rationale of protecting everyone's privacy. In this way, the researchers could determine whether, even when one of the students reported a medical crisis, the knowledge that several people knew it was happening and could take responsibility would blunt the individuals' willingness to act. The experiment showed that, indeed, the response of subjects to the emergency deteriorated rapidly when the number of people linked by microphones increased. "The responsibility diluting effect of other people was so strong that single individuals were more than twice as likely to report the emergency as those who thought other people also knew about it" (25).

4. The authors indicate that any one of us could be that unresponsive bystander, because being unresponsive is not a defect of character or a sign of the decay of civility in urban life (5). Rather, the failure to respond occurs in particular situations which could befall any of us. When people are surrounded by others, they notice less (10), they conform to norms of public behavior (14), and they take less responsibility for events around them (20). As Darley and Latané write, "If we look closely at the behavior of witnesses to [emergencies], the people involved begin to seem a little less inhuman and a lot more like the rest of us" (7). Any person could be influenced by the "apparent indifference of others" to "pass by an emergency" (28). "We are that bystander," they conclude (28) and suggest that being aware that groups or crowds might encourage our passivity could help us to "see distress and step forward to relieve it" (28).

5. *megalopolis* (5): an urban region consisting of several adjoining cities
    apathy (5): lacking involvement or interest
    indifference (5): without interest or concern
    alienated (6): to cause to become indifferent or hostile
    depersonalized (6): to make impersonal
    inhibit (9): to block or hold back
    corroborates (11): supports with additional proof
    coronary (13): of the human heart
    slavish (14): deliberately dependent or slave-like
    nonchalance (15): coolly unconcerned or indifferent
    diffused (20): spread widely or thinly
    blandly (27): unemotionally or indifferently

Questions About the Writer's Craft (p. 422)

1. From the way the thesis is introduced to the way the essay is organized, the authors make it easy for the reader to determine the causes of inaction. Darley and Latané introduce their thesis in a dramatic way, as the answer to a one-paragraph question (paragraph 8). Setting off the question in one paragraph creates surprise in the reader.

They then follow this with a clear and direct answer. In this sentence, the three causal factors are italicized to call attention to them (9). They follow up this listing with a direct announcement of their intentions in the essay: "As we shall show, the presence of other bystanders may at each stage inhibit his action" (9). The rest of the essay is divided into sections, the next three of which reflect the three causes: "The Unseeing Eye," "Seeing Is Not Necessarily Believing," and "The Lonely Crowd." Each one of these sections begins with an anecdote about a hypothetical situation in which help is needed. Then after presenting the ambiguities in this situation, the authors present a hypothesis suggesting why people avoid or delay acting and then cite psychological research that has shown the hypothesis to be valid. In addition, the authors use bridging sentences, the beginnings of which link back to previous material. For example, paragraph 13 begins, "Once an event is noticed . . ." which repeats the idea of the previous section. And paragraph 20 uses the beginning clause, "Even if a person defines an event as an emergency . . ." to remind the reader of the previous point.

2. Using the present tense creates a dramatic introduction to draw readers in—or at least, not scare readers away—from a serious and analytic essay. Narratives of crime and danger are intrinsically interesting, but the style used here heightens the shock-effect of the situations. Each narrative begins bluntly, with no lead-in, using a direct statement of the victim's situation: "Kitty Genovese is set upon by a maniac"; "Andrew Mormille is stabbed in the head"; "Eleanor Bradley trips and breaks her leg." The present tense adds a sense of urgency, while the direct style seems almost like a narrative voice-over, telling us events as they happen. In addition, the present tense circumvents the need to provide background data, such as the year of occurrence and so on, data that would slow the reader down and introduce the analytic style too early in the essay. Finally, the present tense conveys the timelessness of the events, in the sense that given human nature, these past responses would hold true at any point in time.

3. The experiments are described in paragraphs 11–12, 16–19, and 22–25. Each experiment is introduced by a clear announcement, and throughout the description of the experiment and the results, numerous transitions make each stage of action crystal clear. In paragraph 11, Darley and Latané write, "Experimental evidence corroborates this. We asked college students to an interview. . . ." Paragraph 16 begins, "To determine how the presence of other people affects a person's interpretation of an emergency, Latané and Judith Rodin set up another experiment." And the third experiment is introduced in paragraph 21: "To test this diffusion-of-responsibility theory, we simulated an emergency . . ." and picked up again in paragraph 22: "For the simulation. . . ."

Within each description of an experiment, the authors use numerous clear signals to indicate the stages of the process. In paragraphs 11–12, they use signals of time, as well as the colon, effectively: "as the students waited. . . . As part of the study, we staged an emergency: smoke was released. . . . Although eventually all . . . —when the atmosphere grew so smoky. . . ."

In the injured-researcher experiment (16–19), narrative and spatial signals help the reader along: "An attractive young market researcher met them . . . and took them to . . . where they . . . Before leaving, she told them she would be working next door in her office, which was separated from . . . She then entered . . . where she . . . After four minutes. . . ."

In the group-discussion experiment (21–25), narrative transitions predominate, along with spatial indicators and enumeration: "Each student was put in an individual room . . . Each person was to talk in turn. The first to talk . . . Then . . .

Other students then talked . . .in turn. When it was the first person's turn . . ." (22–23). The authors interrupt the process to explain the hidden reality of the experiment, using transitions of contrast: "But whatever the apparent size . . . only the subject; the others, as well as the instructions . . . were present only on . . . tape" (23). Returning to the process of the experiment again in paragraph 24, the authors use a narrative transition plus an enumeration and a signal of repetition: "When it was the first person's turn to talk again. . . ."

The authors also often use balanced sentence structure to compare the reactions of subjects who were alone with those who were in groups of various sizes. In the leaking-vent emergency (11–12), they write, "Solitary students often glanced idly about while filling out their questionnaires; those in groups kept their eyes on their own papers" (11); "two thirds of the subjects who were alone noticed the smoke immediately, but only 25 percent of those waiting in groups saw it as quickly" (12). In the injured researcher experiment, the results are presented in two separate paragraphs, one for those who were alone (18), and one for those who were in groups of various sizes (19). Short direct sentences which put in the foreground the percentages of how many subjects responded in what way make the data easy to follow, and signals of contrast help the reader sort out the details: "Seventy percent . . . offered to help. . . . Many pushed back the divider . . . ; others called out to offer their help" (18). "Among those waiting in pairs, only 20 percent . . ." (19).

In reporting the results of the group-discussion simulation, Darley and Latané again rely upon direct statements that list the percentages explaining who responded how: "Eighty-five percent of the people who believed themselves to be alone. . . . Sixty-two percent of the people who believed there was one other bystander. . . . Of those who believed there were four other bystanders, only 31 percent reported. . . ."

4. At the start of the essay, the reader is likely to think of witnesses who do not help a victim as monsters, as aberrant and mean-spirited human beings. Darley and Latané wish to show that inaction is in fact a natural result of ordinary human psychology; as they write in paragraph 7, "If we look closely at the behavior of witnesses to these incidents, the people involved begin to seem a little less inhuman and a lot more like the rest of us." One of their goals is to show that the failure to take action is typical in certain situations, situations, in fact, in which there are multiple bystanders. "As we shall show, the presence of other bystanders may at each stage inhibit his action" (9).

At the end of the essay, they indicate that their ultimate purpose is to create the awareness that inaction is the norm when people are in a group. With this awareness, people might be able to counteract the paralyzing effect of other people and get involved in helping in a critical situation. "Caught up by the apparent indifference of others, we may pass by an emergency without helping or even realizing that help is needed. Once we are aware of the influence of those around us, however, we can resist it. We can choose to see distress and step forward to relieve it" (28).

OUR SCHEDULES, OUR SELVES

Jay Walljasper

Questions for Close Reading (p. 427)

1. Although Walljasper reiterates variations of his thesis throughout the essay, he states it most succinctly in paragraph 3: "On the job, in school, at home, increasing

numbers of North Americans are virtual slaves to their schedules." Students might alternatively identify as the thesis the first sentence of paragraph 2: "Welcome to the daily grind circa 2003—a grueling 24–7 competition against the clock that leaves even the winners wondering what happened to their lives."

2. In paragraph 3, he mentions Palm Pilots and day planners, which though they are "precise" and presumably convenient means of tracking time, also prevent spontaneity and result in overscheduling. As opposed to enjoying "luxurious leisure"—the anticipated result of technological progress—we have instead become saddled with "a dizzying timetable of duties, commitments, demands, and options." Walljasper then focuses more explicitly on the "onslaught of new technology" in paragraph 5, where he discusses cell phones, e-mail, and laptop computers. While these technologies "promised to set us free"—presumably by freeing us from our offices and desks—they have instead "ratcheted up the rhythms of everyday life," making us more reachable and busier with work than we've ever been. And while these technologies have, in fact, allowed us to live more of our lives outside the physical confines of the workplace, the downside is that now "[i]t's almost impossible to put duties behind" us since we can be reached anywhere, at any time. He makes this point with the example of the boss or committee chair being able to reach us at a restaurant, concert, or even "on vacation in Banff or Thailand." Ultimately, Walljasper points out, the fact that we are now "never out of the loop" is simultaneously a benefit and a serious drawback of these technological devices.

3. Walljasper explicitly outlines the causes of the overscheduling problem in paragraphs 4 through 6. The first and "chief culprit" he addresses is the "acceleration of the global economy" and the decline in people's control over their "wages and working conditions" (4). Presumably, because the working world has become increasingly competitive, workers can't afford to restrict their commitment to work and instead find themselves working even during off-time. Poorer people have a harder time making ends meet and have to work more hours; wealthier workers are overwhelmed by pressures to accomplish more and more in their workday. The second cause of the schedule crunch is "the onslaught of new technology" which keeps people connected to work at all times, in all places (5). Instead of increasing leisure time (3), these technologies—including Palm Pilots, cell phones, e-mail, and laptops—have resulted in people feeling they need to work even more because they can. The final factor Walljasper explores is "[o]ur own human desire for more choices and new experiences" (6). The burgeoning number of "cultural offerings" for adults and children that have become available over recent years, as well as "the number of different social roles" that one can now play, have resulted in a glut of extracurricular activities crowding our schedules.

    After exploring the causes of overscheduling, Walljasper then immediately turns to its effects. In paragraphs 7 and 8, he describes the most profound consequence: the loss of spontaneity and the concurrent piling on of obligations, which drain pleasure out of life. "Our 'free' hours," he says, "become just as programmed as the work day" (7). As he states in paragraph 2, "the idle moment, the reflective pause, serendipity of any sort have no place in our plans"—these are the moments that "make us feel most alive" (8) and that "nurture . . . [the] soul" (13).

4. Although Walljasper addresses the issue of class, his analysis is relatively brief and underdeveloped. In discussing the accelerated globalized economy as a culprit of the overscheduling phenomenon, he first discusses "[f]olks at the bottom of the socio-economic ladder," who he perceives "feel the pain most sharply." Because of difficulties making ends meet, these individuals are forced to work multiple jobs, usually with few or no benefits or vacations of any sort. Walljasper then very briefly addresses another class, that of "successful professionals." He uses the example of

115

doctors, who are subject to extreme time and money pressures. While this example is underdeveloped, presumably the rest the essay pertains to this class of people. In fact, Walljasper's essay, overall, seems most pertinent to the lives of the middle and upper classes. People belonging to lower strata generally don't have the time or money to indulge in the activities and technology that cause their middle and upper class counterparts to overbook themselves. One might conclude, then, that Walljasper's essay displays class bias and is not universal. As a result, some students might disagree with his observations. But for other students, his analysis might resonate perfectly. Therefore, answers to the second question may vary.

5. *circa* (2): approximately; about
    grueling (2): physically or mentally demanding to the point of exhaustion
    serendipity (2): instance of making fortunate discoveries by accident
    virtual (3): existing in essence though not in actual fact
    onerous (3): troublesome or oppressive; burdensome
    allotments (3): things assigned as a portion
    onslaught (5): overwhelming outpouring
    ratcheted (5): caused to increase or decrease by increments
    instill (5): implant by persistent efforts
    smorgasbord (6): buffet meal featuring a varied number of dishes
    roster (10): list
    preordained (11): appointed or determined in advance
    sabbatical (11): leave of absence, often with pay
    clout (11): influence
    shucking (12): casting off

Questions About the Writer's Craft (p. 428)

1. Walljasper employs reverse emphatic order, beginning with the *most* significant cause and then proceeding to the least. This becomes evident in paragraph 4 when Walljasper uses the phrase "the chief culprit" in discussing the economy's role in the problem. He doesn't use any signal devices in discussing the next factor, new technology, but he does use the less impactful phrase "also plays a role" when addressing the final factor, our desire for more choices and experiences.

    While saving the most significant point for last is usually considered the most effective way to organize items emphatically, reverse order makes sense in this case for a few reasons. First, the essay does not end by discussing the causes of the problem, but rather continues to discuss effects and then remedies. As a result, there's less of a reason for Walljasper to want to end on the strongest cause since so much more follows. In addition, the ideas of the paper flow well in the current configuration. The final (and weakest) *cause* he discusses, in paragraph 6, leads directly into the first *effect*, in paragraph 7; both of them address the common issue of enriching experiences in life. It wouldn't have made sense for Walljasper to have begun his discussion of causes with the weakest point about experiences and activities, then discuss technology and economy, only to have to return to the life-experience topic again in the later section on effects. The current arrangement, therefore, provides for a smoother and more coherent progression of ideas.

2. Walljasper's purpose in discussing the overscheduling of our lives is to *persuade* us to curtail this phenomenon. While there is an instructive component to his essay when he discusses the causes and effects of the problem, he uses clearly charged language in order to persuade readers that this is a dire problem requiring rectification. His emotional pitch is evident when he calls people "virtual slaves to their schedules" (3) and refers to what people's lives have become as "the daily

grind" (2), "a grueling 24–7 competition against the clock" (2), "dizzying" (3), and "an obligation obstacle course" (7). In addition, Walljasper's persuasive purpose is reinforced when he offers suggestions for how to correct the problem of overscheduling; he seeks to persuade his readers to act against this phenomenon.

3. Overall, the clusters of abundant, undeveloped examples in the essay reinforce the harried pace of life that Walljasper examines. By presenting numerous examples in a rapid-fire manner, he mimics in language the fast-paced, overbooked reality he observes in the world around him.

4. Walljasper constantly shifts among points of view in the course of the essay. He begins the essay by using 2nd person in introductory anecdote (1) as a means of drawing the reader into his subject matter and making the subject very immediate. In paragraphs 2–3, Walljasper shifts to 1st person plural, showing he is just as vulnerable to and guilty of the overscheduling phenomenon as everyone else. He moves into 3rd person in paragraph 4 when examining socioeconomic issues; most likely he adopts this more neutral point of view to avoid identifying with any one class. Then, in paragraph 5, he adopts 2nd person seemingly for rhetorical force, to mimic the invasion of personal space and time that technology is facilitating. He then returns to 1st person again in paragraphs 6–8, speaking for a collective group that includes himself. In doing so, he reduces the distance between author, subject, and audience. And finally, he relies on 1st and 2nd person in paragraphs 11–14, where he provides a process analysis that everyone should follow in order to mitigate the problem of overscheduling.

In general, one can make the following observations about Walljasper's shift in use of point of view. When he wants to establish common ground and identify with his audience, he uses 1st person. He uses 2nd person for a similar reason, as well as to draw his readers into his subject matter. And he uses 3rd person for more analytical sections when he seeks to create greater distance between himself and the subject matter.

Answers will vary regarding the final question. While some might argue that the constant shifts in points of view reflect a level of sloppiness and inconsistency in the essay, others might observe reasons why these shifts are appropriate in various instances.

DEFINITION

OPENING COMMENTS

In high school and certainly in college, students frequently answer questions that ask for definitions: ("Define 'mitosis'"; "Explain what 'divestiture' means.") Even so, we hold off discussing definition as a method of development until the last quarter of the course. Here's why.

Since extended definitions can be developed through a variety of patterns, students need to be familiar with those patterns before they can prepare a well-supported definition essay. At the very least, they need to know how to marshal well-chosen *examples* so that their definitions can be grounded in specifics. Similarly, the *comparison-contrast* format can show students how to go about organizing a definition by negation. And *process analysis*, explaining how something works, is often critical when developing a definition. Once students feel comfortable with these and other rhetorical strategies, they can approach definition essays with confidence, knowing that they have a repertoire of techniques to draw on.

For this chapter, we selected readings that illustrate a variety of approaches for writing definition essays. Touching on a wide range of topics, the pieces show how definition can explain difficult-to-understand scientific concepts, as well as demonstrating that the pattern can challenge the meaning we attach to common everyday words. We often start with Cole since she mixes a number of strategies (examples, facts, personal anecdotes) to develop her definition of entropy. Gleick, in a careful analysis of behavioral research, asserts that the traits typically associated with Type A behavior are actually characteristics we all exhibit, directly related to the world we live in today. Naylor's essay treats the reader to glimpses of middle-class African American life while disclosing unexpected meanings. With the help of abundant examples, Robbins and Wilner coin a new term—"the quarterlife crisis"—and make a case for its pervasiveness in contemporary culture. Finally, Raspberry's essay relies on a series of definitions to compare the positive and negative effects labels can have on people's self-images.

ANSWERS FOR PREWRITING ACTIVITIES

Below we provide possible responses to selected prewriting activities at the end of Chapter 10. In many cases, other responses are possible. (p. 443)

1. There are many ways to use definition in these two essays. Below we've listed some of the possibilities. In classroom use of this activity, we suggest you have students share their responses. They will be surprised and often delighted to discover that their neighbors have quite different answers.

    Topic: How to register a complaint
    Define "effective" complaining
    Define a "no-win situation"
    Define "conflict resolution"
    Define "diplomacy"

Topic: Contrasting two stand-up comics
Define "black humor"
Define "improvisational humor"
Define "political humor"
Define "put-down" humor

ANSWERS FOR REVISING ACTIVITIES

Below we provide possible responses to selected revising activities at the end of Chapter 10. In many cases, other responses are possible. (p. 443)

3. Here's our appraisal of the effectiveness of the definitions:

    a. This definition is circular because it repeats the words of the term itself. In addition, the "is when" format is awkward if not ungrammatical. Here's one way to revise the definition: "Passive aggression is a personality disorder in which a person chronically performs poorly as a way of unconsciously showing resentment of the demands of an employer, teacher, or other person."
    b. This definition is also ineffective because of its circularity. One way to rewrite it might be: "A terrorist uses violence against innocent people to intimidate those in power."
    c. This definition is effective and clear.
    d. This is a circular definition that tells us nothing about the term being defined. A better version would be: "Pop music typically contains simple lyrics, a strong beat, and appealing harmonies."
    e. This definition needs rephrasing to eliminate the awkward "is when"; otherwise, it is a workable definition. "Standing by another person during difficult times is the essence of loyalty."

4. It's a good idea to have your students read each other's revisions of this material. Doing so gives them helpful exposure to alternative ways of rewriting a problem paragraph.

    Here are our recommendations for rewriting the paragraph:

    — The opening sentence is weak; relying on the dictionary only tells us (boringly) what we already know. The sentence should be rewritten to catch the reader's interest.
    — Since the second sentence states the obvious, it should be deleted.
    — The listing of times people feel tense (sentences 3, 4, and 5) consists of obvious, general situations. Dramatic examples would be appropriate here.
    — Similarly, "Wear and tear on our bodies and on our emotional well-being" is overly general. "Wear and tear" is a cliché as well. Specifying some actual damage that can result from tension would be an effective revision strategy.
    — The thesis (how to relieve tension with walking) seems tacked on. A transitional phrase or lead-in is needed to build more naturally to the thesis.

ENTROPY

K. C. Cole

Questions for Close Reading (p. 448)

1. Cole's thesis is located at the start of paragraph 3, after her two-paragraph introduction: "Disorder, alas, is the natural order of things in the universe."
2. Entropy is unique in being irreversible; most physical properties "work both ways" (3). In nature, things fall apart and decay, and they do not naturally reverse and come together. The "arrow of time" image helps us understand that entropy occurs in relation to time; as time passes, disorder naturally accompanies it. Entropy is the "arrow" also in the sense that it is the weapon time uses to destroy things.
3. The creation of life is the ordering of the particles of matter into a living thing, be it a plant or a person, and so represents the major contradiction to entropy. Such creation, however, requires energy in the form of nutrients such as, for a plant, soil, sun, carbon and water, and for a person, "oxygen and pizza and milk" (9). Cole's other examples show that countering entropy does generally require energy in the form of physical work, the work of cleaning up children's rooms, painting old buildings (4), or maintaining skill at flute-playing (12). Creating order and countering entropy require energy whose expenditure causes an increase in entropy in another part of the system; Cole uses as an example our society's creation of electricity by burning oil and coal, only to produce smog.
4. Entropy is "no laughing matter" because it is inevitable, and it operates not only in nature, but in society as well. There are "always so many more paths toward disorder than toward order," Cole writes (14), and unless we are diligent, entropy will get the better of us individually and societally. This ever-present threat of disorder is especially distressing in the area of social institutions and international events. Cole believes that the ultimate randomness of entropy endangers us—the "lack of common purpose in the world" (15) threatens to create more and more disorder.
5. *futility* (1): sense of uselessness
    dissipated (6): scattered, spread out
    buffeted (7): hit, slapped, pushed
    tepid (7): lukewarm
    atrophied (12): deteriorated

Questions About the Writer's Craft (p. 448)

1. Entropy is a phenomenon we surely have noted—rooms getting messy, wood rotting, metal rusting—but it is not likely we have understood it to have a name or be a "principle" of the universe. So Cole's definition is informative about this scientific law. In explaining the need for energy to counteract entropy (10–12) and in relating entropy to societal and world events, however, Cole adopts a persuasive tone. In paragraph 16, she cautions, "Friendships and families and economies all fall apart unless we constantly make an effort to keep them working and well oiled." Clearly, she is making a pitch for us all to work harder at keeping order in our world.
2. Speaking like a common person with average concerns, such as her refrigerator breaking and her tooth needing root canal work, Cole encourages a reader to follow her into a discussion of entropy as an explanation for these ordinary problems. She achieves a friendly, almost breezy tone by using the first person, contractions, short

sentences, and colloquialisms such as "lukewarm mess" (5), "to get ourselves together" (10), and "the catch is" (10). The question in the second paragraph is another example of her personable, casual tone.

3. These terms are blunt and jarring and carry an intense impact. Throughout the essay, Cole uses these emotional words to keep us aware of the personal dimensions of entropy. While entropy is a scientific concept, she wants us to understand that it also pertains to our personal lives and has effects we can respond to emotionally. Some other similar terms are "unnerving" (4), "lost and buffeted" (7), "distressed," "afraid," "terrified," and "upset" (15).

4. This sentence pattern emphasizes contrasts—it contains an inherent opposition between the elements of the first and second half. Cole may find this pattern useful because she is trying to dramatize the effects of entropy and convince us to counteract its power as best we can. The first example compares the two "roads" to disorder and creation, finding one downhill, the other uphill. The second example compares ways to do "a sloppy job" and a "good one." Other examples occur throughout the essay: "Once it's created, it can never be destroyed" (3); "When my refrigerator was working, it kept all the cold air ordered in one part of the kitchen. . . . Once it broke down the warm and cold mixed into a lukewarm mess that allowed my butter to melt. . ." (5); "Though combating entropy is possible, it also has its price"; "That's why it seems so hard to get ourselves together, so easy to let ourselves fall apart" (10); "creating order in one corner of the universe always creates more disorder somewhere else"; "We create ordered energy from oil and coal at the price of the entropy of smog" (11); "The chances that it will wander in the direction of my refrigerator at any point are exactly 50–50. The chances that it will wander away from my refrigerator are also 50–50" (13); "there are always so many more paths toward disorder than toward order. There are so many more different ways to do a sloppy job than a good one, so many more ways to make a mess than to clean it up" (14); "The more pieces in the puzzle, the harder it is to put back together once order is disturbed" (17).

LIFE AS TYPE A

James Gleick

Questions for Close Reading (p. 454)

1. The thesis is clearly stated in the first sentence of paragraph 4: "We believe in Type A—a triumph for a notion with no particular scientific validity." Prior to paragraph 4, Gleick illustrates the cultural pervasiveness of the Type A category and traces its identification to Friedman and Rosenman's studies; these studies attempted to link heart disease to a set of personality traits clustered around the "theme of impatience" (paragraph 2). Following the statement of his thesis, Gleick challenges the scientific validity of Type A, while observing its compelling cultural relevance. He concludes the essay in paragraph 12 by reiterating the thesis; he says that linking the Type A phenomenon to cardiac problems "made for poor medical research," but "it stands nonetheless as a triumph of social criticism."

2. Friedman and Rosenman's study, "Association of Specific Overt Behavior Pattern with Blood and Cardiovascular Findings," looked at connections between heart disease (including high blood pressure) and Type A behaviors. Gleick gives several reasons why the study was "obvious and false" and "a wildly flawed piece of research" (5). First, only a small number of people were studied. Group A consisted

of only 83 people. Second, the subjects were all men. Third, the research subjects were not chosen at random. Instead, Friedman and Rosenman selected subjects who shared similar professional and personal characteristics. They were generally "white-collar male employees of large businesses" (5) who exhibited stressed behavior, who smoked, and who were overweight. Fourth, rather than acknowledging these shared characteristics and the possibility that they might be associated with heart disease, Friedman and Rosenman instead claimed that the Type A personality—rather than the subjects' unhealthy behaviors—was responsible for Group A's medical problems. Gleick also cites the researchers' amorphous definition of Type B as evidence of their flawed understanding of Type A.

3. "The notion of Type A has expanded, shifted, and flexed to suit the varying needs of different researchers," writes Gleick in paragraph 7. He calls Type A a "grab-bag" of traits; researchers pick and choose those characteristics that reinforce their predetermined conclusions. Such researchers, each with a definite agenda, jump on the Type A bandwagon, producing sometimes alarming, sometimes ludicrous, but usually problematic results. For instance, researcher V.A. Price associated hypervigilance with the Type A personality. And researcher Cynthia Perry applied her interest in the study of daydreams to the Type A phenomenon and was able to conclude that Type A's daydream less often than other people. Similarly, National Institutes of Health researchers looking at the effects of petlessness on particular groups connected the incidence of heart disease in Type A people with the condition of petlessness. Further, researchers interested in the behavior of children—even babies—have extended the reach of the phenomenon to include this group: babies who cry more are Type A (7).

    Gleick concludes that even before they begin their studies, these researchers already have in mind how Type A will be tied into their findings, and they manipulate the studies "until they find some correlation, somewhere . . ." (8). He concludes: "The categorizations are too variable and the prophecies too self-fulfilling" (9).

4. Gleick demonstrates that the Type B personality has been "defined not by the personality traits its members possess but by the traits they lack" (10). He remarks somewhat disparagingly that Friedman and Rosenman were able to find only eighty men—municipal clerks and embalmers—"in all San Francisco" who, unlike Type A sufferers, did *not* feel that they were under any time constraints (10). The researchers labeled these men as having the Type B personality. Gleick implies that this identification by default of a small, nonrepresentative sample is further evidence of the researchers' unscientific practices. As the "shadowy opposites" of Type A's, Type B's, according to Gleick, "do *not* wear out their fingers punching the elevator button. They do *not* allow a slow car in the fast lane to drive their hearts to fatal distraction; in fact, they are at the wheel of the slow car" (10). In essence, Gleick implies that scientists' vague, amorphous definition of Type B reinforces the dubious scientific validity of Type A.

5. *coinage* (1): an invented word or phrase
    harrying (2): harassing, annoying
    canonical (2): authoritative, officially approved
    circuitously (2): indirectly
    sanctimoniously (4): hypocritically righteous
    overt (5): open, observable, not hidden
    incipient (5): beginning to exist or appear
    sedentary (6): inactive
    hypervigilance (7): excessive watchfulness
    correlation (8): mutual relation of two or more things

strident (9): loud, harsh, grating, or shrill
staccato (9): disjointed, abrupt
foil (10): opposite
totem (12): venerated emblem or symbol

Questions About the Writer's Craft (p. 454)

1. Although Gleick questions the scientific basis of Friedman and Rosenman's link between heart disease and Type A behavior, he seeks to show the universality of many of the Type A personality traits ascribed to Paul. Gleick counts on the fact that we've all met a Paul and could well have some of Paul in us. As Gleick goes on to argue, Paul's Type A personality is shaped not by personal psychology, but by the society in which he lives—the same society that, to some extent, has engendered Type A traits in us all.

2. The three fragments—"Excessive competitiveness. Aggressiveness. 'A harrying sense of time urgency'"—are, according to Gleick, how Friedman and Rosenman describe the Type A personality. Gleick likely intended these choppy, clipped fragments to mimic the hurried, fast-paced lifestyle of the Type A person.

3. Gleick uses the personal pronouns "we," "us," and "our" throughout his essay. In the first paragraph of the essay, for instance, he asserts that Type A "is a token of our confusion" and asks, "[A]re we victims or perpetrators of the crime of haste? Are we living at high speed with athleticism and vigor, or are we stricken by hurry sickness?" These queries involve and hook us; they are *about* us; they cause us to want to read on. Because he knows that most readers will identify with these Type A characteristics, he seeks to show that Type A is less a medical condition than a cultural one. We are members of the society that has embraced the Type A phenomenon. We are Type A people because of the high-intensity society in which we live. It is also important to note that the pronouns "us," "we," and "our" also include Gleick himself; he, too, is a member of the society that has embraced and perpetuated the Type A lifestyle.

4. Gleick's sarcasm reflects his frustration and annoyance with the medical establishment's attempts to find scientific correlations where no valid ones exist. Other examples of sentences, phrases, and words which strike a similar tone include: "standard medical knowledge untainted by research" (4), "cardiovascular comeuppance" (4), "the original Type A grab-bag" (7), "This is sweet, but it is not science" (7), "even more bizarrely" (11) and the last sentence of paragraph 11, which asserts: "No wonder they omitted Type C from the subsequent publicity." Considered together, these sentences and phrases establish the author's stance: one of bemused dismay, even disappointment, at the unscientific treatment the scientific community has given the Type A phenomenon.

"MOMMY, WHAT DOES 'NIGGER' MEAN?"

Gloria Naylor

Questions for Close Reading (p. 459)

1. Naylor's thesis is implied. One way of stating it would be, "The word 'nigger,' like other words, takes its meaning from its context and from the consensus of those who use it. Hence, it can have a positive as well as a negative meaning." This complex

idea is sketched briefly in the introductory paragraphs (1–2), but is given body by the examples and extended narrative that comprise the rest of the piece.

2. The boy's use of the term was clearly meant as a negative. Naylor says he "spit" the word at her (3) in retaliation for her pointing out his inferior grade. She knew that the word was "something he shouldn't have called me" (3). She receives confirmation of this fact when she reports him to the teacher and "watched the teacher scold him for a 'bad' word" (3). Her bafflement over the meaning of the term occurs, not because she has never heard the word 'nigger' before ("I realize that this could not have been the first time the word was used in my presence") (4), but because she has heard it used to mean only something positive. In paragraphs 5–9, she describes the several ways people in her family used 'nigger' in a positive way. Sometimes, the word was used as a compliment or an indicator of "strength, intelligence or drive" (6). It could also be a "term of endearment" when used by a woman about her boyfriend or husband (9). Finally, it could refer to the "essence of manhood," that is, to the inner force that helped men survive despite the tough odds of racism (9).

3. Besides its usual reference to a young female, the word 'girl' could take on other meanings when spoken in a certain way in certain situations. It could, for example, convey approval and "confirming worth" (11) when spoken in a kind or upbeat tone. It was used as the feminine equivalent of 'nigger,' as a "token of respect" (11). This kind of exchange, however, could only occur between women of the same generation or from an older woman to a younger. Like the word 'nigger,' 'girl' could also have a negative meaning of "communal disapproval" when spoken with a negative tone, "snapped out of the mouth" (13).

4. Naylor rejects the idea that the use of 'nigger' within the African American community was a symptom of low self-esteem or "internalization" of racism (14). Rather, she believes that her family, and many other African Americans, adopted and altered the fearsome negative term used by whites so that it played up the positive strengths they knew they possessed. Through such a transformation, "they rendered it impotent" as a pejorative, Naylor writes (14), and converted it "to signify the varied and complex human beings they knew themselves to be" (14). She says that African Americans used the word to demonstrate that, in its negative sense, it was not accurate about them or the lives "they were determined to live" (14).

5. *transcendent* (1): going beyond ordinary experience or thought
   dynamics (1): movements or interactions
   intermittent (2): alternately beginning and ceasing
   reprieve (2): temporary relief
   consensus (2): general agreement
   innocuous (2): harmless
   nymphomaniac (3): woman with uncontrollable sexual desires
   necrophiliac (3): person attracted to corpses
   gravitated (4): propelled or revolved
   mecca (4): center of activity
   anecdotes (5): brief tales
   inflections (5): vocal tones
   disembodied (9): without a body
   unkempt (10): disheveled or messy
   trifling (10): frivolous or shallow
   connotation (11): suggestion or echo of meaning
   communal (13): group or community
   internalization (14): process of making something external part of oneself

degradation (14): lowered dignity or rank
impotent (14): ineffective

Questions About the Writer's Craft (p. 459)

1. The first contrast occurs in paragraph 3, where Naylor describes the little boy spitting out the word to show his hatred and her own confusion at the precise meaning of the term. A second contrast occurs as she listens to the teacher scold the child for using a bad term, a term that ironically everyone else but her seems to know, even though it pertains to her. This negative sense of the word is contrasted with her descriptions of how 'nigger' was used in her extended family, portrayed in paragraphs 5–10. The uses of 'nigger' within her childhood community were multiple and diverse, with the context establishing the exact meaning. Naylor then develops variations of the *positive* uses of the word: the approving meaning (6), its use as a sign of affection (9), and the sense in which it played up, almost as an archetype, the survival power of the oppressed African American male (9). Naylor contrasts these with the ways in which 'nigger' could be used as a *negative* in her community: to refer not to people who had fallen on hard times but to those who had stopped trying and who hurt those around them, those who "had overstepped the bounds of decency as my family defined it" (10). She further contrasts the use of 'nigger' as a term for men with how the term 'girl' was used both approvingly and pejoratively for women. This complex array of meanings shows the subtle and richly textured use of one single term in her community's vocabulary. As a result, we learn in a concrete way how context determines the definition and—if we are outsiders—we see a hidden dimension of African American culture. In her conclusion, Naylor underscores the contrast between the little boy's use of 'nigger' as a racial epithet and her family's positive use of it. The contrast in the ways the word is used by whites and by African Americans is so great that as a child she failed to recognize the word when it was used to put her down.

2. The dialogue that Naylor provides shows the rhythms of informal expressive speech. She seems to catch snatches of conversations on the fly, offering up examples that burst with energy and personality. In addition, the quotations provide snapshots of successful members of her family's community. The first quotation, "I'm telling you, that nigger pulled in $6000 of overtime last year" (8), demonstrates the use of the term to express admiration and at the same time sketches a picture for us of a hardworking, successful person. The next quotation, "Yeah, that old foreman found out quick enough—you don't mess with a nigger" (9), shows us a snapshot of a person standing up for his rights. The final quotation, "G-i-r-l, stop. You mean you said that to his face?" (12), again provides to the reader who is outside the author's community an image of spunk and fortitude.

   Overall, the dialogue can be said to serve several purposes. Through it, Naylor can provide strong examples of how the word 'nigger' was used and how the situation determined whether it meant something positive or negative. Naylor's belief that words take meaning from their use in speech could be a difficult concept to get across, but the specific situations she describes and the lively quotations put her concept across accessibly and concretely. Finally, the quotations, so colloquial and expressive, sing out the cadences of her community's aural traditions. Through this dialogue, we can sample and appreciate the variety, subtlety and richness of African American culture, even though, as Naylor maintains at the start of the essay, the written word is never as dynamic as the spoken.

3. The discussion of what her childhood environment was like is crucial to our understanding of what the term 'nigger' meant when it was used in her family's

125

home. Since Naylor believes the meaning of words derives from the contexts of their use, she has to make the context of how 'nigger' was used very clear to her readers. The details she provides let us know some very important facts about this family that used 'nigger' so freely. They were a broad group of people—relatives, friends, tenants—and therefore, likely a representative group, not just a small family of a few people with an idiosyncratic habit of language. In addition, they formed a close and stable network of families and friends, owners of property and full-time wage earners (4), in other words, staunch and upright members of American society. That there was "a rigid set of rules about what was said and how" informs us that there was a decorum and sense of decency regarding the innocence of children, again a very mainstream American value.

The use of 'nigger' by these people, in other words, was typical of working middle-class African Americans and is not a sign of economic failure, poverty, or any other kind of "worthlessness or degradation" (14). Since the term 'nigger' conveys, to white society, such explosive negatives, Naylor takes precautions against any chance that some white readers might picture her family as the degraded stereotypes typically conveyed by the word.

4. Paragraph 14 provides an abstract reflection on the reasons why African Americans have adopted and transformed the devastating slur 'nigger' into a term conveying strength, endearment, and even heroism in the face of oppression. Naylor refutes a common understanding of this phenomenon, that 'nigger' used by African Americans constitutes self-hatred, an "internalization of racism." Rather, she attributes its use to a valiant defiance of racism, to an attempt to '[meet] the word head-on" and disqualify it as a label of inferiority. This analysis balances the drama and personal force of her examples and counters any reservations forming in her readers' minds about how to interpret African Americans' use of 'nigger.'

In the final paragraph, Naylor moves away from this analysis back to the narrative of her childhood confusion. This narrative returns us to the scene where 'nigger' is by and large a positive word, a world where people support and love each other instead of tear each other down. The touching scene of her climbing into her mother's lap to be taught how 'nigger' can be used to destroy provides a final and powerful critique of white culture which has been so vicious toward other groups.

WHAT IS THE QUARTERLIFE CRISIS?

Alexandra Robbins & Abby Wilner

Questions for Close Reading (p. 466)

1. In paragraph 4, the authors provide a series of statements that could be identified collectively as the thesis: "[This crisis] may be the single most concentrated period during which individuals relentlessly question their future and how it will follow the events of their past. It covers . . . an age group that can range from late adolescence to the mid-thirties but is usually most intense in twentysomethings. It is what we call the quarterlife crisis, and it is a real phenomenon." However, students might want to refine and slightly expand this thesis using their own words; one possibility is: "The quarterlife crisis, a period of intense confusion and anxiety about the future typically experienced by twentysomethings, is a real phenomenon that should be acknowledged in our society."

2. The authors say that individuals anywhere from "late adolescence to the mid-thirties" are prone to this crisis. However, they specify that twentysomethings—the twenties

being the age when people typically complete their education and are confronted with the "real world"—are most vulnerable.

3. Robbins and Wilner commence their comparison-contrast in paragraph 4, before they've officially named the "quarterlife crisis," calling it the "other crisis" and saying it "can be just as, if not more devastating than the midlife crisis." What the two crises have in common is that they "stem from the same basic problem," which is major life change (5). And both result in tremendous anxiety and upheaval in the lives of their sufferers. But in every other way, the quarterlife and midlife crises are opposites.

The contrast begins on the most fundamental level: the age of the sufferers, indicated by the name of each respective crisis. On one hand, uncertainty about the future causes quarterlife crisis sufferers to fear change and instability (6), while the feeling of stagnancy experienced by middle-agers causes them to seek out change (5). As the authors observe, "the midlife crisis revolves around a doomed sense of stagnancy" while "the quarterlife crisis is a response to overwhelming instability, constant change, too many choices, and a panicked sense of helplessness" (8). In addition, the responsibility levels that characterize each of the two groups contribute to their differences. Midlifers have more responsibilities, which they may seek to flee, while quarterlifers have fewer commitments, resulting in a dizzying array of possibilities (17). Another key difference between the two crises is the level to which they are acknowledged in society. Midlife crisis, the authors assert, is the "widely acknowledged" subject (8) of "hundreds of books, movies, and magazine articles" (3). As a result, midlifers know about and even expect this crisis; they can choose from a variety of helpful resources, including "support groups, books, movies, or Internet sites" (8). In contrast, despite its pervasiveness, the quarterlife crisis remains unacknowledged in society and unexpected by young people, causing them to be blindsided when it strikes (8). In fact, no crisis-related statistics exist for this younger age-group; quarterlifers and their specific issues have not been studied by the mental health or the medical communities.

4. The authors state in paragraph 18 that the feeling of doubt is the "most widespread, frightening, and quite possibly the most difficult manifestation of the quarterlife crisis." Doubt is especially threatening because it can strike anyone in any situation, from the most to the least socially and professionally successful, regardless of "levels of self-esteem, confidence, and overall well-being." While doubting oneself is a normal, healthy part of life, the excessive self-doubt that characterizes a quarterlife crisis can immobilize a person. And because this doubting as it relates to the quarterlife crisis remains unaddressed in society, people's anxiety is increased by the feeling they are alone in self-doubt, sending them "spiraling downward."

5. *pertinent* (3): relevant
chaotic (4): disorderly; confused
disarray (4): disorder
interval (4): time between two periods
phenomenon (4): an occurrence, circumstance, or condition that can be perceived
stagnancy (5): motionlessness; state of lacking vitality
nexus (7): place of connection
monotony (8): tedious sameness
ramifications (8): consequences
trepidation (9): apprehension
virtually (17): practically
ramen (15): Japanese dish of noodles in broth, usually very affordable
excruciatingly (17): very painfully; agonizingly

manifestation (18): obvious demonstration
barrage (18): overwhelming outpouring

Questions About the Writer's Craft (p. 466)

1. The authors do not seek to define their term in a vacuum; rather, there is a distinctly persuasive aspect to their essay, one which seeks social change. Robbins and Wilner posit that the quarterlife crisis is an unacknowledged social phenomenon whose effects are rendered more acute because it is undiscussed. This lends immediacy and importance in their attempts to define the term and "get the word out" about its existence. To deliver home to readers the importance of their mission, the authors use high-impact words and phrases in explaining the dire effects of the quarterlife crisis: "Twentysomethings . . . face a crisis that hits them with a far more powerful force than they ever expected" (8); "The slam is particularly painful because today's twentysomethings believe that they are alone . . ." (8); "[T]he ramifications can be extremely dangerous" (8). In addition, in paragraph 13, the authors provide a compelling quote from an expert, Robert DuPont, to validate their claim that the quarterlife crisis is a pervasive and potentially serious condition.

2. This narrative anecdote, presented and discussed in paragraphs 1 through 3, serves multiple purposes. First, its familiar, stereotypical subject matter—of a man having a midlife crisis—is an inviting way to draw readers into the essay. But the mere familiarity of the anecdote's subject also serves a more pointed purpose: It proves the authors' point about midlife crisis being common knowledge in society. This, in turn, sets up the contrast with the quarterlife crisis which, the authors argue, is as pervasive but remains unacknowledged. Additionally, the humor implicit in the opening anecdote sets the comfortable, conversational tone of the piece. This, too, draws readers into the essay and helps make them more sympathetic to what the authors have to say.

3. It would not be inaccurate to say that an exploration of causes and effects of quarterlife crisis is at the heart of the authors' definition of the term. While other patterns of development allow the authors to set up the term and explain the importance of defining it, causal analysis provides the structure and content of the definition itself.

   Robbins and Wilner logically begin their causal analysis with an exploration of the causes of quarterlife crisis. In a nutshell, they say that it is "a response to the overwhelming instability, constant change, too many choices, and a panicked sense of helpless" (8) and then proceed to explain each of these causes in subsequent paragraphs. They discuss causes including the feelings of uncertainty and instability following completion of school (6–7), as well as the sense of being overwhelmed by the massive amounts of options suddenly available to them (7–8) and the "whirlwind of new responsibilities, new liberties, and new choices" (9).

   The effects of the crisis, briefly stated, are "overwhelming senses of helplessness and cluelessness, of indecision and apprehension" (8). Whole paragraphs are devoted to explaining how the following conditions can result from the quarterlife crisis: hopelessness (12); depression, anxiety, and even addiction (12–14); disappointment (15); and self-doubt (18).

4. In discussing the similarities between the two crises, the authors use signals including "same" and "both" (5), and then later, "Just as . . . so, too" (8). But overwhelmingly, the authors focus on contrasting the two crises, a shift clearly marked by the phrase "In contrast" at the beginning of paragraph 6 and marked by the following signal devices: "while" (8), "by contrast" (8), and "But" (17).

THE HANDICAP OF DEFINITION

William Raspberry

Questions for Close Reading (p. 471)

1. Raspberry implies the thesis when he introduces the concept of "handicap of definition" in paragraph 1. The thesis might be stated as, "Black youth are handicapped by the associations of the word 'Black' in our society." The rest of the essay explains through examples what "black" has come to mean—something limited rather than something open-ended. He asserts this position clearly in paragraph 7: "My point is the harm that comes from too narrow a definition of what is black." Near the end of the essay he includes a statement that crystallizes the situation: "But the real problem is not so much that the things defined as 'black' are negative. The problem is that the definition is much too narrow"(14). This sentence is the clearest statement of the thesis in the essay.

2. Black culture, according to Raspberry, includes assumptions that certain talents are "black"—that is, that Blacks possess them in abundance—while other talents are not Black, or are "white." The Black talents are athletic, musical, and performative, while whites own all the talent in business, language, reasoning, academics, and so on (6). As a result, Blacks do not strive to achieve in "white" fields, even if they have ability, and so failure is all but guaranteed. Another effect of this limited view of blackness concerns the way being a "man" is defined in Black culture. Blacks are led to assume that maleness is related to "physical aggressiveness, sexual prowess, the refusal to submit to authority" (13). The prisons, Raspberry comments, "are full of people who, by this perverted definition, are unmistakably men."

3. "Positive ethnic traditions" are "myths" (9) or assumptions (11) that portray ethnic groups as having innate talents or traits. Raspberry cites the beliefs that Jews are strong in communication and that the Chinese have a facility for mathematics. He believes that such talents result as much from the assumption they exist as from actual genetic inheritance. The assumption that Blacks excel in sports and entertainment is another example of a "positive ethnic tradition." He would like Blacks to expand their sense of what is naturally Black. He writes, "Wouldn't it be wonderful if we could infect black children with the notion that excellence in math is 'black' rather than white, or possibly Chinese? Wouldn't it be of enormous value if we could create the myth that morality, strong families, determination, courage and love of learning are traits brought by slaves from Mother Africa and therefore quintessentially black?" (9)

4. Raspberry perceives that the assumptions about what it means to be Black are inhibiting African American youngsters from success. Too many of the qualities necessary for success are attributed to white heritage and not to Black. Raspberry believes that the African American community needs to convey to its youth that Blacks are naturally competent, smart, and capable. Once it is accepted that academic achievement, success, hard work, and so on are not limited to whites, African American children will be freed from the inhibiting narrowness of the definition of "black" (15). Then they would be able to succeed in mainstream culture instead of becoming "failures—by definition" (16).

5. *diction* (3): clarity of enunciation
    scrimping (5): economizing in the extreme
    array (6): impressive display of numerous items
    quintessentially (9): most typically or most purely

elocution (10): the art of public speaking; vocal ability
sustained (10): prolonged or repeated
inculcated (11): instilled or taught by frequent repetition
concede (12): yield or grant

Questions About the Writer's Craft (p. 471)

1.   Raspberry defines three additional terms besides "black": "white" (5–6), "positive ethnic traditions" (11), and "man" (13). Raspberry defines "white" as a term which Blacks use to describe qualities which they feel they do not have but which whites do. The effect of this definition is that "white" has become a negative label among Black youth, who criticize each other for speaking well (talking "white") and striving academically (acting "white") (5–6). Describing this use of "white" helps Raspberry explain through contrast what he means by the "narrowness" of the word "black." The second term which Raspberry defines is "positive ethnic traditions" (11). By giving examples, he explains that such traditions are assumptions about talents supposedly innate to various ethnic groups: communication ability for Jews, math ability for the Chinese. The qualities associated with ethnic groups are merely assumptions; they are in the realm of psychology, not genetics (11). He believes these myths have the effect of encouraging hard work and dedication in the ethnic youth who believe themselves talented in these areas. Thus, by discussing the term "positive ethnic traditions," Raspberry shows by contrast the negative effects of the narrowness of the meaning of "black." Finally, in paragraph 13, Raspberry explains the definition of "man" in the Black community. This definition is a parallel to the definition of "black," for it consists of assumptions about innate qualities, assumptions that aren't necessarily true and that are very limiting and even damaging in their effects. For Black youth, a "man" is physically and sexually aggressive and combative towards authority. The tragic effect of this "perverted definition," according to Raspberry, is that such "men" often wind up in prison.

2.   In his introduction, Raspberry discounts the effects of a series of commonly recognized negative factors—"bad schools, mean politicians, economic deprivation, and racism"—on Black youth, suggesting they are not the "heaviest burdens." Rather, he says, there is a different burden that is especially influential, and this is the "handicap of definition," the burden imposed by the associations commonly held with the term "black." This refutation of the sociological factors affecting Black achievement creates a credible tone; here is a writer, the reader might think, who knows the facts, the reality, the explanations, and can cut to the essence. Raspberry shows himself to be forthright and direct, someone who doesn't "soft-pedal" the truth. Also, beginning with this refutation permits Raspberry to present his thesis right away, without a lot of beating around the bush; this would be very important for him stylistically, since the essay first appeared as a newspaper column.

3.   Although the readership of the *Washington Post* is predominantly white, Raspberry appears to be addressing Blacks rather than whites. He uses the first person to emphasize he is a participant-critic of Black culture and uses "we" and "our" to join with Black readers in thinking about their own culture. Raspberry uses "I" in paragraphs 1, 2, 7, and 11; since the essay is critical of the Black community for its narrow, handicapping use of the words "black" and "white," Raspberry uses the personal pronoun "I" to keep the readers aware that he is a Black writer. Especially for Black readers, knowledge of Raspberry's race might defuse resistance they feel toward his criticism of an aspect of Black culture. Raspberry shows his awareness that people might be upset by his thesis when he begins the second paragraph by

saying, "Let me explain quickly what I mean." He doesn't want readers to get the wrong impression, that he is "anti-black."

The pronouns "we" and "our" occur in paragraphs 9, 12, 15, and 16. In paragraph 9, the "we" could refer to Americans as a whole: "Wouldn't it be wonderful if we could infect Black children with the notion that excellence in math is 'black' . . . Wouldn't it be of enormous value if we could create the myth that morality, strong families, determination, courage and love of learning are traits brought by slaves . . .?" But the references to "we" at the end of the essay clearly refer to the Black community: "many of the things we concede to whites . . ." (12); "we have to make our children understand that they are intelligent, competent people. . . . What we seem to be doing, instead, is raising up another generation of young Blacks who will be failures . . ." (15–16). By creating this link with the Black community, Raspberry includes himself among those who are responsible for the attitudes of the future generation.

4. Raspberry makes use of several techniques to keep us interested in his subject. He includes numerous recognizable examples, establishes a personal tone, employs balanced sentences for dramatic effect, and chooses informal transitions. His specific examples begin in paragraph 2, where he refers to basketball star Larry Bird and well-known singer Tom Jones. He also names Teena Marie, a singer some readers might recognize, and refers to a rock group called "The Average White Band"—a humorous reference even if we have no familiarity with the group. In addition to these and other specifics later in the essay, Raspberry establishes a lively, personal, forthright tone that keeps us involved. "Let me explain quickly what I mean," he writes in starting off paragraph 2, showing his directness. He then uses parallel structure and the imperative form to draw the reader in: "Tell pop singer Tom Jones he moves black. . . . Say to Teena Marie or The Average White Band that they sound 'black' . . ." In the next paragraph he continues this tone: "But name one pursuit. . . . Tell a white broadcaster he talks 'black' . . . Tell a white reporter he writes 'black' . . . Tell a white lawyer he reasons 'black' . . ." He returns to this memorable style in paragraph 5: "Think of all the ways black children put one another down . . ." Finally, Raspberry uses informal transitions that keep the essay moving, such as "But" (3 and 14), "And" (7), and "So" (13).

ARGUMENTATION-PERSUASION

OPENING COMMENTS

First-year composition courses often end with argumentation-persuasion. There are good reasons for this. Since an argumentation-persuasion essay can be developed using a number of patterns of development, it makes sense to introduce this mode after students have had experience using a variety of patterns. Also, argumentation-persuasion demands logical reasoning and sensitivity to the nuances of language. We've found that earlier papers—causal analysis and comparison-contrast, for example—help students develop the reasoning and linguistic skills needed to tackle this final assignment.

When teaching argumentation-persuasion, we stress that the pattern makes special demands. Not only do writers have to generate convincing support for their positions, but they also must acknowledge and deal with opposing points of view. Having to contend with a contrary viewpoint challenges students to dig into their subjects so that they can defend their position with conviction. Students should find the material on pages 484–88 helpful; it illustrates different ways to acknowledge and refute the opposition.

Despite their initial moans and groans of protest, students enjoy the challenge of argumentation-persuasion. To help them become more aware of the characteristics of this rhetorical pattern, we often ask them to look through current newspapers and magazines and clip editorials and advertisements they find effective. In class, these items provide the basis for a lively discussion about the strategies unique to argumentation-persuasion. For example, the endorsement of a health club by a curvaceous television celebrity raises the issue of credibility, or *ethos*. An editorial filled with highly charged language ("We must unite to prevent this boa constrictor of a highway from strangling our neighborhood") focuses attention on the connotative power of words.

We often conclude our composition courses with an assignment based on a controversial issue. Depending on the time available and the skill of our students, the assignment may or may not require outside research. If it does call for research, we begin by having the class as a whole brainstorm as many controversial social issues as they can. Then, for each issue, the class generates a pair of propositions representing opposing viewpoints. Here are a few examples of what our classes typically come up with:

Controversial Subject	*Propositions*
School prayer	Prayer in public schools *should / should not* be allowed.

Controversial Subject	*Propositions*
Drug abuse in professional sports	Professional sports *should / should not* implement a program of mandatory drug-testing.

Adoption	Adopted children *should / should not* be given the means to contact their biological parents.

If the assignment does not include research, we focus attention on more immediate local problems. Using the sequence described above, we start the activity by asking the class as a whole to brainstorm as many controversial campus problems as they can. Here are some argumentative-persuasion topics that have resulted from this activity:

Controversial Subject   Propositions

Cheating	A student found guilty of cheating on an exam *should / should not* be suspended.
Fraternities and sororities	Fraternities and sororities *should / should not* be banned from campus.
Drinking	The college pub *should / should not* be licensed to serve liquor.

Once the propositions have been generated, the activity can go in one of two directions. We might ask students to pair up by issue, with the students in each pair taking opposing positions. Or, unconcerned that both sides of an issue be covered, we might have students select a position on any issue identified by the class. In either case, students base their argumentation-persuasion essays on the proposition they have selected. Though they may eventually qualify their propositions, starting with a definitive thesis helps focus students' work in the early stages of the activity.

We try to schedule the assignment so that there is enough time at the end of the course for students to deliver their arguments orally. The presentations take about one class; we call this class either "Forum on Contemporary Social Issues" or "Forum on Critical Campus Issues." Students tell us that they enjoy and learn a good deal from these brief oral presentations. (We do not, by the way, grade the talks—just the papers.)

We have been pleased by the way this final activity energizes students, pulling them out of the end-of-the-semester slump. The forum creates a kind of learning fellowship—not a bad way to end the course.

This chapter's professional readings illustrate the mix of logical support and emotional appeal characteristic of argumentation-persuasion. To develop her assertion that the threat of failure should be regularly utilized to motivate students to work up to their potential, Sherry relates her experiences as a teacher and a mother and thus establishes her *ethos* on the subject. Yuh uses a synthesis of personal anecdote, statements by credentialed authorities, and analysis to create an eloquent plea for multicultural education. In arguing his case against distance education, Barszcz dismantles the claims of the pro-tech position using appeals to logic as well as to emotion. With scathing examples, Twain counters the common assumption that humans are superior to other animals. The remaining essays are particularly helpful for illustrating different ways of dealing with opposing arguments. Citing compelling examples, Hentoff builds a case against those who would censor "politically incorrect" on-campus discussions of controversial issues. Paglia accuses feminists with spreading ignorance and falsehood regarding men and sex, and Jacoby directly refutes Paglia's position, charging her with being an apologist for rapists. On opposite sides of the debate about using torture against terrorism suspects, both Alter and Porter support their viewpoints by aggressively discrediting the opposition. Finally, Wilkins and Steele offer opposing arguments on the topic of affirmative action. Both use their own experiences to illustrate their points, but only Wilkins enlists emotionally charged language to dramatize his argument.

ANSWERS FOR PREWRITING ACTIVITIES

Below we provide possible responses to selected prewriting activities at the end of Chapter 11. Of course, your students will devise their own inventive approaches. (p. 508)

1. Listed below are some possible approaches to each of the topics. We recommend that you have students share their responses to this activity in groups or pairs. Seeing how others handled the assignments can provide inspiration for their own work.

    Topic: Defining hypocrisy
    Possible Audience: Employers
    Essay might argue the merit of these ways of behaving:

    Some employees react negatively to the hypocrisy of bosses not practicing what they preach. Employers should be careful to dispense advice that they themselves are willing to follow. For example, they shouldn't reprimand staff for taking office supplies if they also "borrow" such supplies; they shouldn't write memos outlawing personal phone calls if they themselves make such calls.

    Topic: The difference between license and freedom
    Possible Audience: College students
    Essay might argue the merit of these ways of behaving:

    While license involves nothing more than indulging one's every whim, freedom means acting with thoughtful regard for consequences. Students then, should think before going out to party before an exam, should reconsider substituting an easy course for a difficult one, and so on.

2. Below is an audience analysis for each thesis. Persuasive points for thesis will vary from group to group.

    a. College students: Hostile
        Parents: Wavering or hostile
        College officials: Wavering or supportive

    b. City officials: Hostile
        Low-income residents: Supportive
        General citizens: Wavering

    c. Environmentalists: Supportive
        Homeowners: Hostile
        Town council members: Wavering

    d. Alumni: Wavering or supportive
        College officials: Supportive
        Student journalists: Hostile

ANSWERS FOR REVISING ACTIVITIES

Below we provide possible responses to selected revising activities at the end of Chapter 11. Of course, your students will devise their own inventive approaches. (p. 508)

3. a. ***Begging the Question.*** The statement that "Grades are irrelevant to learning" requires proof, but this argument skips over this debatable premise. The second statement is also debatable; some students, those wishing to attend graduate school, for example, are in college to "get good grades."

    b. ***Over-generalization; Either/or; Begging the Question.*** Both statements are debatable; for example, that jail provides a "taste reality" is questionable, and that juvenile offenders will repeat crimes "over and over" unless jailed needs to be proven. Moreover, the argument presents only two alternatives: "either" a juvenile offender is jailed, "or" the offender will repeat crimes. It is possible to imagine other outcomes from not jailing juvenile offenders: with therapy, community service, job training, or suspended sentences, some may "go straight"; others may commit different crimes instead of "repeating" their initial crimes.

    c. ***Over-generalization; Begging the Question; Card-Stacking.***
        The first statement in this argument is an overly general description of the programs: they "do nothing to decrease the rate of teenage pregnancy." In addition, the argument begs the question of whether the programs truly do curtail teen pregnancies. The argument also fails to address whether there are other valuable accomplishments of the programs that might make them worth keeping. (For example, such programs most likely help reduce instances of sexually transmitted diseases.) Finally, the phrase "so-called sex education programs" is also a way of card-stacking; this term denigrates the programs without saying what's wrong with them.

    d. ***False Analogy; Non-Sequitur.*** By likening abortion to killing the homeless and pulling the plug on sick people, this argument commits a false analogy. In reality, these are all quite different situations with differing moral issues, motivations, and outcomes. Secondly, it is a non-sequitur to assume that if abortion is permitted that people "will think it's acceptable" to commit the other actions mentioned. There's actually no demonstrated causal connection between society's permitting abortion and its accepting the murder of unfortunate people.

    e. ***False Analogy.*** This argument compares two unlike things: locally imposed curfews on teenagers (often parentally supported) and curfews imposed by totalitarian governments on some or all of their population.

4. It's a good idea to set aside some time for students to see how others went about revising this paragraph. They may discover options they hadn't considered.
    Here are some of the problems with the introduction:

    —   Throughout the paragraph there's a hostile, confrontational tone that undercuts the impact of the position being advanced. Sarcastic descriptions of the administrators amount to an *ad hominem* attack: "acting like fascists" and "in their supposed wisdom" (both in sentence 2) and "somehow or another they got it into their heads" (sentence 5). These accusatory descriptions of the way the administration came to impose the dress code should be replaced with a more realistic explanation of why they made the decision they did. A more objective tone is called for.
    —   Inflammatory language used in the first two sentences *stacks the cards* in favor of the writer's point of view: "outrageously strong," "issued an edict," "preposterous dress code." Similar card-stacking occurs in the fourth sentence

when the writer refers to the administrators' "dictatorial prohibition." Such phrases need to be replaced by more neutral language.

— The writer's point that students will lose their "constitutional rights" (sentence 2) is not substantiated in any way. A brief explanation of this point would be appropriate.

— The statement (sentence 3) that "Perhaps the next thing they'll want to do is forbid students to play rock music at school dances," is a *non-sequitur*; instituting a dress code has no causal relationship to restricting music at school dances. This statement might also be considered a *red herring* because it brings in an unrelated issue about which the reader might have strong feelings. In any case, this unfounded prediction should be eliminated.

— There is no sound basis for the recommendation (sentence 6) that students and parents should protest all dress codes. Any such recommendation should be reserved for the end of the essay, after a logical, well-reasoned argument has been advanced. At that point, it would be appropriate to name specific actions parents could take, such as calling the principal or speaking out at a PTA meeting.

— The final statement that if dress codes are implemented, "we might as well throw out the Constitution" embodies at least two fallacies. It is an *either/or* statement, admitting of no lesser or even other consequences. It also is a *non-sequitur*, because no cause-effect relationship has been shown to exist between dress codes and the end of constitutional rights. This closing statement should be eliminated.

— Finally, the paragraph uses the cause-effect pattern but presents evidence for the causal relationship it claims. The writer discounts the *causes* of the administrators' decision (the current dress habits of the student body) and predicts extreme and unsubstantiated *effects* of the dress code. In revising, students might choose some of the following options: dispute the administration's claims that the lack of a dress code creates problems, discuss other possible ways of handling these problems, or analyze possible negative effects of a dress code. Of course, not all of these options could be pursued in the introductory paragraph, but they point the way to possible strategies for developing the rest of the essay in a thoughtful, logical manner.

IN PRAISE OF THE "F" WORD

Mary Sherry

Questions for Close Reading (p. 512)

1. Sherry's thesis, implied, is a combination of the assertions she makes in paragraphs 2 and 4. In paragraph 2, after describing what brings students to adult literacy programs, she tells us that the real reason they wind up there is that "they have been cheated by our education system." She rounds out this point in paragraph 4 when she asserts that poor academic skills are less a result of "drugs, divorce, and other impediments" than they are a result of teachers' unwillingness to use the threat of failure as a motivating tool. Bringing these two points together, one may state Sherry's thesis as follows: Students are cheated by an educational system that refuses to make the possibility of failure a reality.

2. Deliberately shocking, this statement gains our attention immediately. Most of us should be appalled that so many students—tens of thousands—will receive diplomas

that mean nothing. We wonder how such a thing could occur. But we also wonder what Sherry means by the term "meaningless." Later in the essay, this question is answered. Meaningless diplomas have no substance. They are useless slips of paper for those students who have been ushered through to graduation despite the fact that they have failed to achieve passing grades. Sherry concludes that passing students along in this manner cheats them in a sort of slippery-slope way. To begin, they feel increasingly inadequate as they move to higher levels without having mastered the material meant to prepare them for more advanced subject matter. Some continue on in this manner, realizing only later how little they really have learned—their lack of skill resulting, among other things, in limited job opportunities or disgruntled employers. For others, failure becomes a state of mind. Never imagining they have the power to learn and thus to move ahead, they abandon the idea of learning altogether.

3. According to Sherry, educators don't give reasons for passing students with poor achievement records; educators make excuses instead. For instance, they say "kids can't learn if they come from terrible environments" (8) or have experienced such things as "unemployment, chemical dependency, abusive relationships" (9). In other words, neither teacher nor student is responsible for achievement, or the lack thereof; the world at large is responsible.

    What excuses like this amount to is a "Why bother?" attitude, which is particularly destructive because it results in a kind of self-fulfilling prophecy: If little is expected from students, there is little incentive for either teachers or students to work hard. Such a cavalier view of students' ability to succeed falls short of addressing what Sherry sees as the real problem: the dearth of incentive in education today. She writes, "No one seems to stop to think that—no matter what environments they come from—most kids don't put school first on their list unless they perceive something is at stake. They'd rather be sailing" (8). It is not that students can't be educated, but that students are not encouraged to see education as necessary to their future success, something ultimately worth their time and energy.

4. Regardless of distractions, be they homelife- or peer-related, in order to get students to concentrate, teachers must gain students' attention. Most educators would agree that this is often easier said than done. And Sherry doesn't provide any specifics as to how this might be accomplished other than to say that teaching style has much to do with it (4). Since most instructors would rather not resort to turning cartwheels to keep students focused, Sherry gives another option when "style alone won't do it." She writes that "there is another way to show who holds the winning hand in the classroom. That is to reveal the trump card of failure." In other words, acrobatics are not necessary to move students to concentrate. What is needed is a clarification of the road to success: stay focused on schoolwork, or fail.

    Adult students, having the wisdom that comes with experience, understand the importance of education, Sherry tells us. Often their livelihood depends upon success in the classroom this time around. Thus, what lies at the heart of their motivation is "a healthy fear of failure" (9). And this—the understanding that something is at stake—can and must, Sherry believes, be instilled in all students.

5. *validity* (1): soundness, effectiveness
    semiliterate (1): partially educated
    equivalency (2): equal to in value
    impediments (4): hindrances, obstructions
    composure (6): calmness and self-possession
    radical (6): extreme, revolutionary
    priority (6): of utmost importance
    resentful (7): angry or bitter about

testimony (9): public declaration

motivate (10): stir to action

merit (11): value

conspiracy (11): plot

illiteracy (11): having little or no formal education, esp. the inability to read and write

Questions about the Writer's Craft (p. 512)

1. To convince readers that she knows of what she speaks, Sherry establishes her qualifications early on. She tells us in the first sentence of paragraph 2 that many of the students awarded meaningless diplomas eventually find their way into adult literacy programs such as the one where she teaches basic grammar and writing. In other words, as an adult-literacy teacher, she knows firsthand the type of student she refers to in the selection. Moreover, as we learn in paragraph 3, her experience as an educator has taught her "a lot about our schools." And what she has learned, as her examples make clear, directly relates to the issue of passing students through the system regardless of achievement. But Sherry doesn't stop there. To make sure her audience does not lose sight of her credibility, throughout the essay, she refers either to herself as a teacher or to her teaching experiences (paragraphs 4, 7, 9).

   Still, being a teacher is not the sum of Sherry's qualifications. Her home-life credentials her further. She is the parent of a student whose teacher used the "trump card of failure" to get him to succeed. Identifying herself at the outset and establishing her qualifications so often (and in more than one way) indicate that Sherry anticipates a possibly skeptical audience—one that requires a knowledgeable and credentialed voice if they are going to consider what she has to say, much less be led to her way of thinking.

2. The title probably makes some readers, perhaps most readers, think of a well-known scatological term. And Sherry probably hoped for this effect, for as outlandish as it seems, we might then assume she is going to argue the attributes of this term and its usage. This thought alone is likely to arouse readers' curiosity; they will want to read on to find out why Sherry applauds the "F" word. This is probably why Sherry chose this play on words for a title. Through it, she gets our attention.

3. Sherry quotes her students in paragraphs 3 and 7. By using these direct quotations, Sherry lets us experience directly how these students feel about their educational experiences and their own abilities. Through their words, Sherry demonstrates that the problem she sees is very real. She has come to understand the problem by listening to the statements she now shares with us. The students' direct testimony is her most valid proof that a problem exists. Although Sherry articulates the issue and argues the point, her students' comments illustrate that there is no one better than the students themselves to convey the reality of the problem.

4. Sherry's main proof that the threat of failure can work comes in the form of a personal example. We learn that although nothing could move Sherry's son before, he was motivated to succeed in his English class by the threat of flunking (5–6). Although Sherry concedes that one piece of proof is hardly enough—"I know one example doesn't make a case"(7)—this one example helps her support her position in a number of ways. To begin, using a personal example brings her readers closer to her and thus closer to her subject matter. In addition, this particular example has special power because it consists of a parent, a student, a teacher: There is someone in the example for almost any reader to identify with. Parents can imagine themselves in Sherry's shoes, having to accept that the threat of failure is the best way to motivate their child. Teachers can envision themselves as Mrs. Stifter,

adhering to a an unpopular policy because it brings about the hoped for results. And students can ally themselves with Sherry's son, a boy who chooses to succeed when the only alternative is to fail.

LET'S TELL THE STORY OF ALL AMERICA'S CULTURES

Yuh Ji-Yeon

Questions for Close Reading (p. 517)

1. Yuh states her thesis in paragraph 10, after a long and tantalizing introduction. She writes, "Educators around the country are finally realizing what I realized as teenager in the library. . . . America is a multicultural nation, composed of many people with varying histories and varying traditions who have little in common except their humanity, a belief in democracy and a desire for freedom." She restates it in paragraph 19: "The history of America is the story of how and why people from all over the world came to the United States, and how in struggling to make a better life for themselves, they changed each other, they changed the country, and they all came to call themselves Americans." The essay as a whole argues that students should receive information about the many streams of ethnicities that compose our country so that they can appreciate the contributions and struggles of all types of Americans.

2. The history books she was assigned in school portrayed America as formed by and developed through the efforts of white people such as "Lewis and Clark, Lincoln, Daniel Boone, Carnegie, presidents, explorers, and industrialists" (2). These portrayals are limited and place white European-descended people as the central players in our history. Her own research as a teenager determined that many other nonwhite groups had made contributions, but these were left out of the history. In the field of agriculture, she discovered that immigrants from Asia had cultivated California's deserts and worked the sugar cane fields in Hawaii; an Asian had developed the popular breed of cherry that now carries his name, Bing. Asians had also served in the U.S. armed forces in the first world war, but were denied citizenship nevertheless (4). In looking into history texts, she discovered that the only references to nonwhites were over-simplified and one-dimensional. African Americans were discussed only as slaves. Native Americans were portrayed as "scalpers" (2), as wild and violent. Her investigations thus led her to the conclusion that "the history books were wrong" (9). She has a special interest in righting the wrong because she herself is a nonwhite immigrant from Asia. Her evidence includes numerous examples of Native American (3, 15), Asian (4), African American (5, 15), and Hispanic (6) contributions to American life.

3. Yuh believes that history courses should teach about the various cultural groups that helped shape the nation (10, 14). More than this, however, students should "be taught that history is an ongoing process of discovery and interpretation of the past, and that there is more than one way of viewing the world" (14). What might look like a "heroic" achievement from one point of view, for example, could be considered barbarism from another, she notes, referring to the American domination of the Native American lands of the West (15). She believes all the various points of view about events in the American past should be presented.

4. Yuh believes that the truth about American history is multiple and that "there is more than one way of viewing the world" (14). But the most important reason for rewriting American history is that given by a New York State Department of

Education report: students should learn how to "assess critically the reasons for the inconsistencies between the ideals of the US and social realities." In addition, they should gain the knowledge and skills that can help them participate in "bringing reality closer to the ideals" (16).

5. *albeit* (1): even if or although
    tinged (1): with a slight trace of coloration
    galore (2): in plentiful amounts
    multicultural (10, 13, 18): drawing from many ethnic and cultural groups
    interdependence (12): reliance on connected groups
    indigenous (15): native or original
    dissenting (18): disagreeing with the majority
    ethnicity (18): membership in a cultural group based on ancestry
    bolster (19): prop up or support

Questions About the Writer's Craft (p. 517)

1. Yuh waits until paragraph 18 to mention that some people have concerns about multicultural education being divisive. By this time in the essay, she has expansively rendered her own position in concrete and convincing terms. Delaying the mention of opposing views allows her to develop her rather complex reasons for advocating multicultural curricula: that exposing the ethnic forces and achievements in our history is more accurate (10), that it presents history as interpretations rather than dogma (14), that it will help students understand the discrepancies between our great American ideals and our current social realities (16), and that it will give students the skills to help them improve our nation (16). Coming so late in the essay, the dissenting view of multiculturalism seems simplistic in comparison to Yuh's argued position, and so it is easier for Yuh to dispose of it as off the mark.

2. Yuh's examples demonstrate her point that schoolbook American history has restricted students' knowledge about what really happened in our past. She offers some specifics of traditional American history in paragraph 2: "Founding Fathers, Lewis and Clark, Lincoln, Daniel Boone, Carnegie, presidents . . ." and then contrasts this list with numerous more detailed examples of ethnic contributions to and viewpoints about America's past. Invoking images of Iroquois government, Asian agricultural talents, and Black initiatives toward freedom from slavery, the author shows concretely that there is more to the building of America than the heroic efforts of white men. Recalling the massacre of the indigenous tribes, the denial of citizenship to Asians despite their honorable World War I service, and the American overtaking of Mexican populations in California and New Mexico, Yuh dramatically pictures how our history plowed under nonwhite peoples. These specifics indicate that there are additional facts and alternative viewpoints to those traditionally taught as our history. These specifics also fill in knowledge gaps that readers may harbor and that may leave them poorly equipped to understand and appreciate her position. Placing them before the thesis renders the reader more aware of the complexity of our history and thus more open to her position. Hence, supplying these details is crucial to the success of her argument.

3. Much of the introduction consists of the author's personal recounting of what education she received (1–2) or failed to receive (3–6) regarding ethnic forces in our history. In paragraph 7, Yuh shocks us by revealing the degrading but inevitable taunts of her childhood peers ("So when other children called me a slant-eyed chink and told me to go back where I came from . . ."). This personal approach tells us what the educational and emotional consequences are of ignoring the diversity of people who have helped build America, and so sets the groundwork for Yuh's

argument in favor of multicultural curricula in history. She returns to the personal at the end of the essay. Here she affirms that focusing on ethnicity in our country's past is a way of demonstrating that "out of many" comes the "one" (20). She then underscores the link between her, a Korean immigrant, and her white-bred childhood "tormentors": the Americanness they have in common.

4. Yuh's stylistic repetitions begin immediately in the first paragraph, where she parallels two relative clauses: "I grew up . . . almost believing that America was white . . . and that white was best." The second paragraph uses this same device, paralleling the two last sentences and repeating the phrase "the only": "The only black people were slaves. The only Indians were scalpers." These short parallel clauses and sentences are emphatic and create a sense that "that was that," a sense of finality about the impressions she gained.

    The following four paragraphs open with the same repeated phrase: "I never learned one word about. . . . " And the sentences that follow within each paragraph begin, "Or that . . ." or repeat the words, "I never learned that. . . ." By using these repetitions, Yuh creates a catalog of her enforced ignorance. Each repeated opening signals the reader that more historical omissions are coming, and more, and even more. Through the repetitions, the reader understands that what has been left out of American history is not just one or two details, but whole vistas and vantage points from which our past looks very different.

    In paragraph 15, Yuh resumes the cataloging of omissions, again using repetitions. The first sentence sets the pattern: "the westward migration . . . *is not just* an heroic settling of an untamed wild, *but also* the conquest of indigenous peoples." The following two sentences use this "not just . . . but" structure, with small variations in wording, to convey the multiplicity inherent in our history.

CAN YOU BE EDUCATED FROM A DISTANCE?

James Barszcz

Questions for Close Reading (p. 522)

1. Barszcz doesn't state his thesis explicitly. In his final two sentences he indirectly expresses the thesis by quoting Robert Frost and interpreting the quotation in this way: "a college education requires" that a student be on campus (paragraph 9). Barszcz's thesis is a negative response to his title question "Can You Be Educated from a Distance?" and can be paraphrased simply as: "Despite the increasing popularity of distance learning in college curricula, several significant drawbacks accompany this means of education."
2. Students like the convenience of distance learning, of being able to do their work "in . . . pajamas" (3). Schools value the cost savings; while students pay tuition, they don't physically come to campus, resulting in reduced physical resource demands on the school—and, presumably, greater profits (4).
3. Barszcz says that proponents usually argue that distance learning makes education more *effective*—by giving students access to a "global virtual faculty" (5)—and more *meritocratic* (or democratic)—by potentially allowing students to shop around for quality courses rather than being tied to one institution (7).
4. Barszcz defines education as "cultivating intellectual and moral values" and as drawing out "from within a person qualities of intellect and character" (8), in contrast to merely imparting information.

141

Answers to the second question may vary. Some students may agree with Barszcz's noble vision of education. Others, however, may disagree, seeing education as more pragmatic. In addition, some might argue that his claim that education draws out qualities already within a person, rather than imparts qualities, is an example of the either-or fallacy. Education creates, as well as activates, intellectual and moral qualities. Otherwise, education would only draw out qualities already within us as infants.

5. *attrition* (3): dropping out
    virtual (5): created or carried on by means of a computer network
    facility (6): ease
    meritocracy (7): system that rewards ability and achievement
    mechanistic (8): simplistic with regard to cause and effect
    etymology (8): a word's origin and history
    dormant (8): not activated
    fidelity (9): accuracy of reproduction

Questions About the Writer's Craft (p. 522)

1. Barszcz seems to have written his essay for a wavering audience—an audience undecided on the topic but open to hearing arguments. The fact that he acknowledges and refutes opposing points of view demonstrates that he doesn't assume his audience is a supportive one. In addition, he doesn't rely on overly emotional appeals (*pathos*) in his essay, and he provides sound reasoning (*logos*), particularly in refuting opposing arguments. Nor is there any indication that Barszcz assumes his audience is hostile; his somewhat sentimental argument about education cultivating intellectual and moral values would likely be dismissed by a skeptical reader. Instead, Barszcz's combined use of *logos* and mild *pathos*—a middle-of-the-road approach—reveals he's likely writing for the general public, composed of individuals not necessarily decided on the topic of distance learning.

2. Barszcz uses division-classification here to categorize the different types of communication involved in distance learning: website postings, e-mail attachments, threaded messages, chat rooms, and minimal or no face-to-face communication. Barszcz uses emphatic order. By leaving face-to-face communication for last, he emphasizes its scant presence or total absence in distance learning.

3. Barszcz quotes literature from Fairleigh Dickinson University (FDU) in some detail (5) because FDU's statements come across as propaganda. Inflated language such as "premier learning tool," "life-long learning," "global," "world-class," and "around the world" are likely to make readers skeptical about distance learning's possible merits. In addition, the quote is an easy target for refutation in its unrealistic claims that students will have access to the caliber of experts being touted.

4. Barszcz's definition of distance learning (2) is specific and objective, involves no "definition by negation," and has an explanatory purpose. In contrast, Barszcz's definition of education (8) is general and subjective, uses definition by negation (education is *not* simply providing information), and has a persuasive purpose.

THE DAMNED HUMAN RACE

Mark Twain

Questions for Close Reading (p. 530)

1. Twain states his thesis in the first paragraph: "For it obliges me to renounce my allegiance to the Darwinian theory of the Ascent of Man from the Lower Animals; since it now seems plain to me that that theory ought to be vacated in favor of a new and truer one, this new and truer one to be named the Descent of Man from the Higher Animals." By this, Twain is humorously suggesting that humans beings' "traits and dispositions" are lower, not higher, than those of the other creatures.
2. Twain discovers humans have a long list of negative characteristics. He finds them cruel (4, 10), avaricious and miserly (5), vengeful (7), morally loose (7, 8), and indecent and vulgar (9). Humans are also the only animals to wage war (11), invade other countries (12), take slaves (13), and show patriotism (14). They are, somewhat paradoxically, both religious—hence intolerant of others with different beliefs (15)—and reasoning—though Twain prefers to think of them as maniacs (16). The overall defect that will forever prevent humans from ever beginning "to approach even the meanest of the Higher Animals" is what Twain terms the "moral sense" (19–20), "the ability to distinguish good from evil; and with it, necessarily, the ability to do evil" (21).
3. The earl and his party of sportsmen killed seventy-two buffalo, feasted on one, and left the seventy-one others to rot. The anaconda, in a scientific test conducted by Twain, killed only what he wanted to eat, and no more, although Twain provided him with seven calves in all. This "experiment" shows that the snake is less cruel and less wasteful than an earl, and therefore a superior creature.
4. Humans have "occasion to blush" because they feel shame about their bodies, and, having a "soiled mind," feel natural behavior to be indecent. Twain points out that people cover themselves, even their chests and backs, because they are horrified at the possibility of "indecent suggestion" (9). Also, humans consciously practice cruel and loose sexual behavior such as keeping harems, behavior about which they should blush. When animals are loose in their morals, Twain says, it is because they are totally innocent.
5. *confounded* (3): confused
   anaconda 4): a type of large snake
   wantonly (4): excessively, wastefully
   chicanery (5): trickery, deceit
   heretics (10): people who openly disagree with the church
   constitutionally (19): by nature, inherently
   ineradicable (19): not removable, unerasable
   smirchless (22): without a stain, without dishonor

Questions About the Writer's Craft (p. 530)

1. Twain humorously claims to have used the scientific method in order to put his credibility on a par with that of scientists. He pretends to have conducted experiments. By this device he satirizes not only human evil and cruelty but also our arrogance in presuming to be superior to all other creatures, a "superiority" we exercise by turning the other creatures into laboratory specimens. Ultimately, Twain shows that the standard the scientists, and people in general, use to decide what

constitutes a "higher" species is invalid. Using a moral yardstick, rather than an evolutionary one, Twain demonstrates that humans are really the lowest of creatures.

2. Many of Twain's examples of human inferiority are shocking, starting with his example of the hunting earl. In paragraph 10, Twain provides a list of atrocious cruelties from human history that most students will certainly find upsetting; he mentions mutilations, gougings, flaying, imprisonment, and burning as punishment for small offenses or religious disagreements, and, conversely, minor punishments, such as a ten-shilling fine, for incredible cruelties. Also, in paragraph 15, Twain uses very strong language to discuss human religious intolerance; some students will be shocked because they are used to hearing religion spoken of deferentially. For example, Twain writes that man "cuts his neighbor's throat if his theology isn't straight," and "has made a graveyard of the globe" in trying to spread his religions. Such shocking examples and language help Twain to convince us that his main point is valid—humans are cruel and inferior creatures.

3. One or two examples would be sufficient to support his idea that humans are inferior to animals, but Twain piles on examples to dramatize his point. He wants to show that such atrocities are not isolated and rare, but habitual and common among the human species. For example, he shows in paragraph 10 that all eras of history and all peoples of the world have engaged in vicious punishments and inhumane justice.

4. Absurdity appears in this essay in the form of Twain's "experiments," ridiculous studies confronting humans and animals with moral choices. It is certainly unlikely that he tested an anaconda's killer instinct with seven calves (4) or "furnished a hundred different kinds of wild and tame animals the opportunity to accumulate vast stores of food" (5). And his claim to have put a mixture of human races and religions in a cage to see if they could learn to get along is also far-fetched (18). Ironically, the morbid details of Twain's essay come from human history: they are not creations of the writer's mind, but examples of actual human violence (4, 10, 11). As Twain notes in paragraph 16, the human record "is the fantastic record of a maniac." So the essay does contain elements of black humor, and its conclusion, "And so I find we have descended and degenerated, from some far ancestor. . . . Below us—nothing," is dark indeed.

FREE SPEECH ON CAMPUS

Nat Hentoff

Questions for Close Reading (p. 537)

1. Hentoff's thesis is implied. We know his position because in paragraph 5, he so clearly opposes "preventing or punishing [offensive] speech," even if that speech contains "disgusting, inflammatory and rawly divisive" ideas (4). Hentoff introduces numerous supporting examples and points for his position, which might be stated, "Racist or cruel speech, no matter how much it offends, must be permitted because we have a free society." Another way of stating it might be, "The numerous recent attempts to forbid offensive speech or to punish those who commit it go against the grain of a free society." That he takes this position is also indicated by his endorsement of the quotation from Oliver Wendell Holmes that appears quite late in the article: "If there is any principle of the Constitution that more imperatively calls for attachment than any other, it is the principle of free thought—not free only for those who agree with us, but freedom for the thought we hate" (22).

2. Numerous events demonstrating intolerance and ignorance are presented in the article. A flier recommending that Blacks be lynched instead of permitted on the University of Michigan campus (1), swastikas and the phrases "White Power" painted on the Black cultural center at Yale (2), and the formation of a 130-member White Students Union at Temple University (2) are three examples Hentoff uses to begin the essay. He also mentions that swastikas appeared on the Jewish Student Union at Memphis State University and that "venomously sexist" letters were sent to women at the State University of New York at Buffalo (3). Another sign of bigotry's rise is the distribution of white supremacist hate literature at the University of Wisconsin (7).

3. At the University of Kansas, the student radio station was forbidden to interview a Ku Klux Klan official (6). At the Parkside branch of the University of Wisconsin, offensive white supremacist leaflets were collected by the administration and destroyed (7). At UCLA, the editor and art director of the student newspaper were suspended because they violated a publication policy forbidding "articles that perpetuate derogatory or cultural stereotypes." Their offense was that they published an editorial cartoon satirizing affirmative action (17). A student newspaper editor at a different campus of the University of California was also suspended when he wrote an opinion piece defending the editors at UCLA. The reasons for such punitive actions include the administrators' drive to curb unpopular or hurtful views and propaganda (7) and a policy against perpetuating "derogatory or cultural stereotypes" (17). For example, the University of Wisconsin president justified an order to destroy the white supremacist material by claiming the University was not "a lamppost standing on the street corner. It doesn't belong to everyone (7)."

4. Hentoff cites numerous reasons why free speech should be fully permitted on campuses. First of all, he believes, along with Professor Carol Tebben of the University of Wisconsin, that students do not need protecting from "bad ideas" (9); rather, he believes that students need to encounter such ideas in order to learn to recognize them and cope with them (10). In addition, he asserts that "sending such ideas underground simply makes them stronger" (10). He also complains that campus statements restricting free speech, such as the one at the University of Buffalo Law School, provide no process whereby an accused student might get a fair hearing ("no due-process procedures"). As a result, he is concerned that restrictions on what a student might say could trap the curious or innocent by guilt through "association" (13). Finally, there is a danger that students who speak out on any issue related to race, sex, or gender might be punished as holding intolerant views (16). Hentoff writes, "A student who opposes affirmative action, for instance, can be branded a racist." Also, students who hold unpopular positions might feel restricted or stifled, as one outspoken student did at New York University Law School (20).

5. *venomously* (3): poisonously

   knownothingism (4): an attitude of racial hatred and anti-intellectualism

   ukase (13): authoritative order or decree

   dissented (15): withheld approval; disagreed

   malignancies (15): terminal diseases

   sanctions (18): penalties

   pall (19): covering that darkens or obscures

   pariah (19): a social outcast

   pietistic (23): exaggeratedly holy

   distills (25): extracts or purifies

stocks (39): wooden frame used to immobilize criminals for public display and punishment
stigmatization (41): labeling as disgraceful

Questions About the Writer's Craft (p. 537)

1. Hentoff vigorously attacks the ideas of those who would suppress the free speech of extremists, racists, and bigots. In fact, he chooses to develop his argument largely by criticizing the actions of those university administrators who have presided over the banning of literature (7), the proclamation of speech restrictions (12–13), the censoring of student cartoons (17), and the punishment of outspoken instructors (39–40). In addition, he uses highly connotative language in describing the opposition's view in order to create negative associations in the reader's mind. For example, in paragraph 7 he compares the Chancellor of the University of Wisconsin to "the legendary Mayor Frank ('I am the law') Hague of Jersey City, who booted 'bad speech' out of town," and in paragraph 8 to King George III of Great Britain. He refers to "the wholesale cleansing of bad speech at Buffalo" (14). Later in the essay his language becomes sarcastic as he notes that Murray Dolfman of the University of Pennsylvania was punished "by—George Orwell would have loved this—the Committee on Academic Freedom and Responsibility" (38). Hentoff refers to Dolfman's punishment as going "to the stocks" (39) and then compares his forced attendance at a session on racial sensitivity to "a Vietnamese reeducation camp" (40). These descriptions appeal to our emotions and help to sway us to Hentoff's side.

2. Much of the article consists of examples, and the final one is a narrative extending from paragraphs 25–40. These numerous examples add interest to what might be a very dull article about constitutional law. At the very start, the series of five examples of bigotry and intolerance recently occurring on America's campuses creates a riveting introduction to the essay. We learn about an anti-Black flier distributed at the University of Michigan (1), swastikas and white power graffiti at Yale (2) and Memphis State (3), the formation of a White Students Union at Temple (2), anonymous sexist letters received by women at SUNY (3) and physical attacks on all types of minority and female students at colleges across the country (4). Hentoff then gives as examples two instances of the suppression of intolerant speech at the University of Kansas and at the University of Wisconsin's Parkside campus (6 and 7–10). These examples provide a vibrant and compelling demonstration of the significance of the free speech issue.

    The examples also serve to persuade us to accept Hentoff's position. Hentoff develops his argument by citing individual cases of free speech controversies, much the way lawyers use cases to develop their positions. The specificity of the details lends credibility to his allegation that free speech is being curtailed, and it also adds impact and interest. Many of the examples in the body of the essay focus on the human cost of attacking free speech; students who are merely exploring the work of far-out comedians such as Lenny Bruce, Richard Pryor, and Sam Kinison might be punished, for example (13). Hentoff also provides an example of student journalists punished because of their opinions on a racially sensitive policy (16–18). Finally, he uses the extended narrative (paragraphs 24–42) about Penn Law School instructor Murray Dolfman to argue that monitoring racial attitudes can lead to unwarranted punishment of controversial figures.

3. Hentoff appears angry and occasionally sarcastic toward those who support the curtailment of free speech. The staccato, emphatic style of paragraphs 1–3 and 5 clues us in to this attitude. Other signs of anger include the comparison of

Chancellor Kaplan of the University of Wisconsin to "the legendary Mayor Frank ('I am the law') Hague of Jersey City, who booted 'bad speech' out of town" (7) and to King George III. Hentoff also uses such critical phrases as "wholesale cleansing of bad speech" (14), "pall of orthodoxy" (19), "someone had to be sacrificed" (38), and the "stigmatization of Murray Dolfman" (41). He also uses sarcasm and irony to mock his opponents: "free speech . . . has become a decidedly minority view on campus" (11), "after all it was more important to go on record as vigorously opposing racism and sexism than to expose oneself to charges of insensitivity to these malignancies" (15), "highly unpopular with bigots, liberals, radicals, feminists, sexists, and college administrators" (22), and "who better than a part-time Jewish teacher with no contract and no union? He was sentenced by—George Orwell would have loved this—the Committee on Academic Freedom and Responsibility" (38).

Many of Hentoff's examples employ the same sentence structure. Five sentences begin with "at," including all three of the sentences in paragraph 2. Two sentences in paragraph 5 begin with "in." The similar sentence beginnings create the sense of a list of supporting points rather than just a series of examples. We get a kind of "here we go again" feeling as we move through the examples. This repetition and the numerous simple sentences, many of them somewhat short and staccato, create a style that is blunt and forceful. The style gives the impression that Hentoff is angry and wishes the reader to feel shock and indignation as well.

4. Both quotations are from sources who are credible commentators on the issue of free speech: Endick, a law student at a campus tainted by hostility to any nonliberal comments, and Holmes, the famous Supreme Court justice. In addition, Endick's style is direct and impassioned; he writes that his campus is marked by "a prevailing spirit of academic and social intolerance of . . . any idea which is not 'politically correct.'" Endick's sarcasm in the quotation in paragraph 21 is earthy and shocking. By speaking so vulgarly, Endick is using a "cut the crap" tone, cutting through the pretentiousness and self-righteousness of those who endorse limiting free speech to protect the feelings of various campus groups. Hentoff wholeheartedly endorses Endick's attitude, and he recommends that his statement "be posted on campus bulletin boards around the country." He also repeats the vulgar phrase in paragraph 22, supporting it by quoting the eminent jurist Holmes. Hentoff shocks us by stating that Holmes was referring to "racist assholes" when he wrote that speech must be free not only "for those who agree with us, but . . . for the thought we hate." Juxtaposing Endick's crass phrasing with that of Holmes and likening their ideas lends Endick increased credibility. Crudity aside, Endick is right, Hentoff believes.

RAPE: A BIGGER DANGER
THAN FEMINISTS KNOW

Camille Paglia

Questions for Close Reading (p. 544)

1. Paglia states the thesis clearly in her first paragraph: "feminism, which has waged a crusade for rape to be taken more seriously, has put young women in danger by hiding the truth about sex from them." In the rest of the essay, she explains what she means by the "truth" about sex and men.

2.   "Once," Paglia writes in paragraph 4, "fathers and brothers protected women from rape," but today people do not live in such close-knit clans and families. Also, rape was once punishable by death, but today the penalties are lighter. The author cites as evidence what she calls typical behavior in the "fierce Italian tradition": "a rapist would end up knifed, castrated and hung out to dry."

3.   According to Paglia, "feminism . . . keeps young women from seeing life as it is" (5). By this, she means that there are truths "we cannot change" (6) about the nature of men and sex, truths that should be told, not hidden. There are quite a few generalizations about sex and men in the article that appear to be the "truths" that she is speaking of. One is the commonness of "rape by an acquaintance" throughout history (3). Another is the "sexual differences that are based in biology" (6), which cause men to rape in order to create their masculine identity (7,14). "Masculinity," she says, "is aggressive, unstable, combustible" (18). Another "truth" for Paglia is the idea that women need protection, by the "clan" (3–4), by the "double standard" (11), and by their own self-awareness (19). Later, she talks about the truth embodied in the "sexual myths of literature, art, and religion" which "show us the turbulence, the mysteries and passions of sex. . . ." (14). She insists "there never was and never will be sexual harmony" (15).

4.   Paglia believes that women must be more vigilant and guard against male aggression. In paragraph 8, Paglia writes that women going to fraternity parties are putting themselves in danger; in her view, a women who goes alone, gets drunk, or goes upstairs is asking for trouble (8). In paragraph 15, she writes that "every woman must be prudent and cautious about where she goes and with whom." In her conclusion, Paglia explicitly states that date rape can only be solved by "female self-awareness and self-control." A woman must rely on her own resources to prevent rape and should involve the police if a rape does occur.

5.   *inquests* (2): judicial inquiries, often before a jury
     testosterone (8): male sex hormone
     constituted (13): set up or established
     grievance (15): complaint against an unjust or illegal act
     judiciary (19): the system of courts in a country

Questions About the Writer's Craft (p. 544)

1.   Both paragraphs begin with statements that seen incontestable; in using these ideas, Paglia is establishing common ground, an area of agreement between herself and the reader. In paragraph 6, most readers will fully accept the first statement, "we must remedy social injustice whenever we can." They would also agree with the next assertion, that "there are some things we cannot change," and with the third, "there are sexual differences that are based in biology." Many readers, however, would debate the nature of those differences; some would feel that biology ordains only the physiological distinctions, while Paglia obviously means that people's psychology and behavior are also determined by their sex (7–8, 14). Other statements in paragraph 6 are equally debatable: that feminism "believes we are totally the product of our environment" and that it is incorrect to believe that our environment can override biology. Paglia offers no proof for these assertions.

     Paragraph 8 also begins with some general assertions which most readers would accept: "College men are at their hormonal peak. They have just left their mothers. . . ." Many readers will also agree that college men "are questing for their male identity." (Of course, some readers will add that college women are likewise questing for their identities, sexual and otherwise.) After this point, however, Paglia draws some conclusions which many readers will contest and which are not

148

proven: that "in groups [college men] are dangerous," that fraternity parties are treacherous for women, that "a girl who lets herself get dead drunk at a fraternity party is a fool" (some readers would call anyone that drunk a fool), and that "a girl who goes upstairs alone with a brother . . . is an idiot." The latter two statements are judgments; as such, they are impossible to "prove," and Paglia offers no evidence regarding them.

2. Paglia uses numerous comparisons and contrasts in the essay. First, she describes the way acquaintance rape was handled in the past, in contrast with today's means of handling it (3–4). Throughout she contrasts the "feminist view" of sex with what she considers the accurate view. In paragraph 6, for example, she contrasts the position of "academic feminism" regarding sexual differences—that all but the biological are produced by society—with the correct view, her own. She concludes the paragraph with an analogy: "Leaving sex to the feminists is like letting your dog vacation at the taxidermist's." A few paragraphs later, she contrasts the "sugar-coated Shirley Temple nonsense" of the feminists (9) with the idea that "aggression and eroticism, in fact, are deeply intertwined" (10). Then she contrasts the "broken promises" of the 1960s view of women with the "cold reality" of rape (11). Paglia also develops a contrast between the feminist response to date rape and her own view of how to cope with it. The feminists show outrage and shock, according to her (2, 19; 15, 19). She contrasts male and female sexual appetite in paragraph 14, concluding that "it takes many men to deal with one woman." Then she compares the "high-energy confrontation" style of dealing with male vulgarity with the "dopey, immature, self-pitying women walking around like melting sticks of butter" (16). And in her conclusion, Paglia compares two ways of coping with date rape, calling the police or "complaining to college committees" (19).

3. This blunt style is found in paragraph 4, beginning with "Feminism has not prepared them for this." In paragraph 6, only the second sentence uses a transitional word ("but"). Paragraphs 7 and 8 also rely on a sequence of mostly short sentences without any transitional phrases. In paragraph 11, only the phrase "in short" introducing a summary statement provides any formal coherence. The first few sentences in paragraphs 15 and 16 (up to "In general") and most of paragraph 19 also lack transitions. Paglia's avoidance of transitions creates emphasis for what she has to say. She seems to pound her ideas into us, not wasting time with smoothing the way or being gradual. This style portrays the writer as extremely sure of her position, to the point of being aggressive, almost relentless.

4. There are numerous instances of highly connotative language in the essay. Paglia tends to emphasize or exaggerate the negative elements of feminism and men's behavior. For example, in her introduction she calls rape an "outrage," and asserts that feminism has "waged a crusade." In paragraph 3, she pronounces acquaintance rape "a horrible problem" and in the next paragraph calls young women "vulnerable and defenseless." She describes a fraternity party as "Testosterone Flats, full of prickly cacti and blazing guns" and says men are "dangerous." Later in the same paragraph, she labels girls who trust fraternity men "fools" and "idiots" (8). Her descriptions of feminism are particularly negative: she says its "sugar-coated Shirley Temple nonsense" (9) has brought "disaster" on young women.

Strongly worded absolute statements also occur frequently in relation to both men and feminism. Her very first sentence is an example: "Rape is an outrage that cannot be tolerated in civilized society." Other examples of extreme negative judgments include: "No, they can't" (4), "He was wrong" (6) and "There never was and never will be sexual harmony" (15), "Women will always be in sexual danger" (4), "The sexes are at war" (7), "When anything goes, it's women who lose" (11), "men and women misunderstand each other" (13), "feminism cut itself off from

149

sexual history" (14), "to understand rape, you must study the past" (15), "The only solution to date rape is female self-awareness and self-consciousness" (19). Paglia's use of *pathos* makes the essay exciting to read and adds electricity to her ideas, and some readers will find her stimulating and convincing. However, many readers will find her pitch to our emotions an offensive tactic which decreases her credibility in their eyes.

COMMON DECENCY

Susan Jacoby

Questions for Close Reading (p. 549)

1. Jacoby expresses her thesis in paragraph 3: "What seems clear to me is that those who place acquaintance rape in a different category from 'stranger rape'—those who excuse friendly social rapists on the grounds that they are too dumb to understand when 'no' means no—are being even more insulting to men than to women." In the rest of the essay, Jacoby shows the absurdity of the notions that men simply can't distinguish between "no" and "maybe" and that "mixed signals" cause date rape.

2. Gratitude is not necessary or appropriate, Jacoby feels, because her old boyfriend was acting in a normal responsible manner, as one does in "civilization" (6–7). In a parallel situation, if he had led her on, and she had restrained herself from stabbing him, she would not expect him to be grateful for her restraint. She would have simply been acting in a civilized and normal way. People don't need to be "grateful" when others treat them correctly instead of immorally.

3. For Jacoby, civilization is the condition in which men and women can understand each other, even though there may be mixed signals. She explains in paragraph 7 that her old boyfriend was civilized because he accepted what she said as her true meaning, that she did not want sexual intimacy, and left her apartment. He was angry, but he did not violate her. As civilized creatures, men and women are capable of understanding and respecting each other's wishes and relating to each other on more than just a physical level.

4. Jacoby believes that "even the most callow youth is capable of understanding the difference between resistance and genuine fear; between a halfhearted 'no, we shouldn't' and tears or screams; between a woman who is physically free to leave a room and one who is being physically restrained" (14). If men couldn't tell the difference, Jacoby implies, they would have to be pretty stupid creatures, and to insist they can't make these distinctions is therefore to insult their intelligence. As she points out in paragraph 4, those who insist that date rape is understandable or natural (the "apologists for date rape") (4) think "men are nasty and men are brutes." These are certainly insulting terms to apply to half of civilization. And if these apologists (such as Camille Paglia) were correct, women would have to "regard every man as a potential rapist" (10). As a result, a woman would have to decide very early in a relationship, perhaps before ever being alone with a man, whether to have a sexual relationship with him or not, because any slight hint of interest on her part might trigger the "rampaging male" to rape her (18). Such extreme suspicion and caution would also be insulting to a civilized person.

5. *apologists* (4): people who make a defense
    baser (4): morally lower
    deluded (10): believing something false to be true
    unsubtle (12): unintelligent; lacking in fine distinctions

implicit (16): implied; hinted at
benighted (18): intellectually ignorant
erotic (18): arousing sexual desire or love
rampaging (18): rushing furiously and violently
ambivalent (19): of two minds; unable to make a choice

Questions About the Writer's Craft (p. 549)

1. In paragraph 4, Jacoby interprets the belief of date rape "apologists" that men can't understand "no." She says this belief implies that men have no "impulse control" and are "nasty . . . brutes" at heart. If this is true, Jacoby says, then it logically follows that a woman would have to be "constantly on her guard" to prevent men from raping her. "If this view were accurate," Jacoby continues, "few women would manage to get through life without being raped, and few men would fail to commit rape." (5). In this sentence, Jacoby draws out the extreme logical consequence of the premise that men can't understand "no." Since it is obviously not true that practically all women are rape victims and practically all men rapists, the premise appears to be untrue. In paragraph 15, Jacoby uses *reductio* again; "the immorality and absurdity" of the mixed signals excuse for date rape is apparent, she says, when the phenomenon of gang rape is examined. If a woman gives a leading sexual signal to a fraternity brother, then how is that an excuse for a whole bunch of them to gang rape her? She concludes the paragraph by asking a question pointing to the absurdity of the premise: since the girl showed interest in one brother, "how could they have been expected to understand that she didn't wish to have sex with the whole group?"

2. Jacoby bases much of her argument on the premise that men and women are not so different (while Paglia's view is that men, with their uncontrollable passions, are very different from women). In paragraphs 5, 6, and 7, Jacoby compares the situations and behaviors of men and women and finds them similar: "all of us, men as well as women, send and receive innumerable mixed signals in the course of our sexual lives" (5), "men . . . manage to decode these signals . . . and most women manage to handle conflicting male signals" without resorting to violence (6), "I don't owe him excessive gratitude for his decent behavior—any more than he would have owed me special thanks for not stabbing him through the heart if our situations had been reversed" (7). Jacoby's thesis is, in fact, essentially a comparison-contrast statement; she believes date rape is the same as, that is, is comparable to, "stranger rape." She is critical of those who contrast them. She thus develops the contrast between the "apologists'" view of date rape and her own in the essay as a whole. Also implicit throughout the piece is the contrast between her ex-boyfriend, who left in a huff but who did not rape her even though she led him on, and those men who do rape women they are seeing socially. In the conclusion (19), this contrast appears as that between "real men," who "want an eager sexual partner," and men who prefer a "woman who is quaking with fear." Finally, there are two contrasting views of sex discussed in paragraphs 12–13 and 19: sex as "an expression of the will to power," as involving "domination" (12), and "sex as a source of pleasure" (12).

3. The introduction consists of an anecdote, described in the third person and presented very objectively and dramatically. The opening line could be that of a romantic short story: "She was deeply in love with a man who was treating her badly." Only after she explains the plot of this little story does she admit it is autobiographical: "I was the embarrassed female participant" (3). This anecdote vividly portrays the reality that is one of Jacoby's main points: that "mixed

signals" between males and females are common, and that if such confusions were the natural cause of rape, rape would be much more common than it is. That Jacoby herself has an example of a potential "date-rape" situation from her own life makes her credible on the subject of the usual course of male-female relations and also reveals her as an honest, thoughtful writer; that is, it contributes to a positive *ethos*.

4.   For the most part, Jacoby's tone is even and balanced, and this makes her a very credible commentator on her subject. Even her sentence style demonstrates a balance of phrasing in which sequential statements are expressed using similar sentence structure. For example, she writes that "those who place acquaintance rape in a different category from 'stranger rape'—those who excuse friendly social rapists . . . are being even more insulting to men than to women" (3); "men are nasty and men are brutes . . ." (4). Other parallel statements occur in paragraphs 5, 6, 7, 12, 13, 16, 18, and 19: "all of us, men as well as women, send and receive . . . and that is as true in marital beds at age 50 as in the back seats of cars at age 15" (5); "Most men somehow manage to decode these signals without using . . . . And most women manage to handle conflicting male signals without. . . ." (6); "I don't owe him excessive gratitude for his decent behavior—any more than he would have owed me special thanks for not stabbing him . . ."; "Most date rapes do not happen because a man honestly mistakes a woman's 'no' for a 'yes' or a 'maybe.' They occur because a minority of men . . . can't stand to take 'no' for an answer" (7); "no distinction between sex as an expression of the will to power and sex as a source of pleasure"; "the act of rape is defined not by a man's actions but by a woman's signals" (12); "It is true, of course, that some women (especially the young) . . . And it is true that many men (again, especially the young) . . ." (13); "the difference between resistance and genuine fear; between a halfhearted 'no, we shouldn't' and tears or screams; between a woman who is physically free to leave a room and one who is being physically restrained" (14); "a woman has the right to say no at any point in the process leading to sexual intercourse—and that a man who fails to respect her wishes should incur serious legal and social consequences" (16); "it would be impossible for a woman (and, let us not forget, for a man) . . ." (18); "neither the character of men nor the general quality of relations between the sexes is that crude" (19); "feminists insist on sex as a source of pure pleasure rather than as a means of social control" (19); "Real men want an eager sexual partner—not a woman who is quaking with fear or even one who is ambivalent. Real men don't rape" (19). These numerous balanced statements convey an impression of writing that is carefully crafted and of ideas that are well thought-out.

There are, however, a few places where Jacoby's word choice seems judgmental and almost mocking; this style predominates when she is discussing the position of the antifeminists. She speaks derogatorily of their views: "This is the line adopted by antifeminists like Camille Paglia" (10) (even her invented term, "antifeminists," is derogatory to her opposition). "According to this 'logic,'" she sneers in paragraph 11, calling Paglia's analysis "unsubtle" (12). In her view, "using mixed signals as an excuse for rape" is immoral and absurd (15). In addition, Jacoby's portrayal of the thought process of gang rapists is very satirical: "Why she [the victim] may have even displayed sexual interest in *one* of them. How could they have been expected to understand that she didn't wish to have sex with the whole group?" (15). Finally, she burlesques Paglia's point of view with a description of a "rampaging male misreading" a woman's intentions (18).

TIME TO THINK ABOUT TORTURE

Jonathan Alter

Questions for Close Reading (p. 553)

1. Alter essentially states the essay's thesis in paragraph 1: "In this autumn of anger, even a liberal can find his thoughts turning to . . . torture . . . to jump-start the stalled investigations of the greatest crime in American history." He more succinctly restates his main idea in the final paragraph where he asserts, "[W]e need to keep an open mind about certain measures to fight terrorism, like court-sanctioned psychological interrogation" (10).
2. The main form of torture that Alter champions is psychological torture, and he provides examples of what forms this kind of torture might take: "tapes of dying rabbits or high-decibel rap" (2), truth serum (2 and 8), the threat of deportation to nations like Saudi Arabia that punish convicts violently (2 and 9–10), and, most importantly, court-sanctioned interrogations (6–7, 10). In paragraph 5, he describes some of the tortures that Israel has inflicted on terror suspects. Oddly, it's not fully clear whether he supports these measures; he seems to, but he doesn't explicitly state as much. But in paragraph 9, he applauds a variety of psychological torture tactics that historically worked in various nations.

   What Alter appears to clearly oppose, on the other hand, is the legalization of physical torture, but even here his position is a bit murky. He never fully explains or exemplifies what he means by "physical torture" (apart from his flippant reference to "cattle prods or rubber hoses" in paragraph 1) but declares, "We can't legalize" it because "it's contrary to American values" (10). It's important also to note that Alter emphasizes that physical torture cannot be *legalized*, but he never says it shouldn't be *used*. In addition, he argues in favor of administering truth serum to terror suspects, but even this practice could be considered by some to have an inhumane physical element.
3. He implies that people are foolish if they don't realize that pre-9/11 methods of dealing with terrorism are now, since the tragedy, obsolete. Before the events of September 11th, he implies, we all were naïve and complacent to a degree, but to maintain such a frame of mind since then is foolish or, worse, dangerous.
4. The "strange moral position" that Alter identifies is how the legal community in Israel and the U.S. allow torture to occur but would never legalize it for fear of casting an ethical blemish on their legal systems. This is what he means when he says, "They prefer looking the other way to giving even mild torture techniques the patina of legality" (7). What he implies is that there is a degree of hypocrisy among these parties in their "don't ask, don't tell" policy regarding torture.
5. *stalled* (1): delayed
   decibel (2): unit used to measure intensity of sound
   serum (2): fluid, usually from blood or animal tissue
   deportation (2): expulsion of an undesirable alien from a country
   quibble (3): find fault or criticize for petty reasons
   provision (3): stipulation or qualification, especially in an official document
   tepid (3): lacking enthusiasm; lukewarm
   staunch (3): firm and steadfast; faithful
   anachronism (4): something out of its proper time period
   laundering (4): disguising the nature of funds by channeling through an intermediate agent

extracting (5): obtaining despite resistance
detainee (6): person held in custody or confinement
patina (7): change in appearance, usually due to corrosion
sanctioned (10): given official authorization or approval
squeamish (10): easily shocked or sickened

Questions About the Writer's Craft (p. 553)

1. The first instance in which Alter employs Rogerian strategy appears in paragraph 2, when he dismisses those who argue in favor of the old status quo and against the need for drastic new tactics: "Some people still argue that we needn't rethink any of our old assumptions about law enforcement, but they're hopelessly 'Sept. 10'." In paragraph 3, he posits that the Senate's antiterrorism bill has provoked only "tepid" opposition even from those who would normally decry such legislation—evidence, he implies, that dramatic measures being taken against terrorism are appropriate. Alter similarly uses to his advantage the seeming lack of outrage on the part of opponents when he discusses Alan Dershowitz's opinion in paragraph 6. Typically a vehement proponent of civil rights, even Dershowitz, observes Alter, allows room in his reasoning for a "torture warrant" whereby judges decide whether torture tactics are warranted on a case-by-case basis. In addition, after he has advocated Dershowitz's model for court-sanctioned torture, Alter essentially accuses of hypocrisy those in Israel and the U.S. who oppose such a notion while allowing torture to happen nonetheless (7). Alter's final use of Rogerian strategy appears in paragraph 8, when he acknowledges the drawbacks of sodium pentothal and of harsh torture but says that the former "deserves a chance" nevertheless.

   Regarding the second question, students' reactions may vary. Some students may find Alter's citation and refutation of the opposition satisfactory, while others might deem it inadequate.

2. In the first five sentences of the paragraph, he alternates between using questions and parenthetical statements. The function of the questions is to catch readers' attention and almost to beg for agreement. The parenthetical remarks, on the other hand, are a means for Alter to present information that reinforces the legitimacy of the questions he asks. Overall, this departure from normal sentence-writing allows Alter to catch readers' eye and to appeal to them on a more informal level.

3. Alter contrasts the views of Alan Dershowitz with the mindset of the legal communities in Israel and the United States. Dershowitz says that torture should be court-sanctioned, like search warrants, for individual cases. But, according to Alter, judges and lawyers in Israel and the U.S. would never agree to such a practice, as the court's tolerance of any type of torture would result in an ethical blemish on the legal system. Alter goes a step further, however, to suggest that these same legal communities would have no problem instead looking the other way when torture is, in fact, employed.

   This contrast functions to support Alter's argument in favor of reasonable and limited use of torture to fight terrorism. In fact, his entire concept seems to be based on Dershowitz's model. By contrasting Dershowitz's reasonability on the issue with the hypocrisy of the legal systems that refuse to adopt Dershowitz's model, Alter reinforces his own position.

4. Although he divides torture into psychological and physical categories, saying the former is acceptable while the latter is not, nowhere does he set forth a clear definition of what constitutes each. Of the two, the category of psychological torture is developed more fully. Alter provides numerous examples of actions that would fit in this category in paragraphs 2, 5, 8, and 9, yet nowhere does he set forth a concrete

definition of it. Worse still is his characterization of physical torture, which is neither defined nor exemplified except for his passing reference to "cattle prods or rubber hoses" (1). Rather, Alter leaves it to the assumptions and imagination of readers as to what constitutes this variety of torture.

While some readers might be satisfied with Alter's distinctions, others might find his lack of clarity to represent a general murkiness of logic that detracts from his argument. If the most basic terms of what is and is not acceptable in his ideology are not clearly set forth, then how can readers accept his logic? Therefore, it would be reasonable to argue that Alter should have more systematically defined and explained his ideas rather than leaving important aspects of them to the realm of readers' assumptions.

NOW THE TALK IS ABOUT BRINGING BACK TORTURE

Henry Porter

Questions for Close Reading (p. 558)

1. Porter implies his thesis throughout but states it explicitly toward the end of the essay, in paragraph 12: "Torture is an absolute evil and there can be no allowances, especially in a country which stands for liberty and spends a good deal of time distinguishing itself . . . on those grounds."
2. Porter is referring to what he perceives as the American populace's unified, unquestioning support of its government's policies and actions—a condition he finds dangerous because it opens the door to injustices such as torture of terrorist suspects. He implies that the devastation inflicted during the 9/11 attacks has rendered the public fearful and overly-willing to allow its government to do as it pleases in the name of national security. Answers to the second question will vary.
3. The topic he discusses is capital punishment. The way he connects the issue of capital punishment to that of torture is as follows: American commentators think torture is unthinkable in the U.S., but if Americans can tolerate "inflicting great pain and fear in the execution of convicted murderers," then why stop there? After all, he argues with irony, torture is less permanent and less barbaric than execution. As a result, Americans need to be vigilant to insure that torture does not become acceptable.

    Regarding the final question, answers will vary. Some students may agree with Porter's logic, while others may dismiss it as containing logical fallacies.
4. Answers will vary, but may include the following. Both authors are satisfied that readers have an appropriate idea of what *torture* means—the deliberate infliction of physical pain upon a prisoner. Or perhaps the authors didn't want to get bogged down in definitions but instead are seeking to make a larger point about whether the practice known as torture is legitimate in a post-9/11 world.
5. *cohesion* (1): act of forming a united and consistent whole
   overhaul (1): act of dismantling in order to make repairs
   vigorously (2): done with force and energy
   suppressed (2): curtailed or prohibited
   rhetorical (2): relating to the use of language
   modulation (2): ability to vary pitch, tone, or intensity of
   assets (3): useful or valuable possessions
   steel (5): make firm or strong

avert (5): prevent

speculations (6): reasonings based on inconclusive evidence

gurney (6): metal stretcher with wheeled legs used for transporting patients

reprieves (6): postponements or cancellations of punishment

inadvertent (7): marked by unintentional lack of care

routinely (8): done as a common or customary practice

insurgents (8): people rising in revolt against established authority

barbarity (9): savage cruelty in actions or conduct

clandestine (10): done in secret in order to conceal an illicit purpose

derogate (11): deviate from

consigned (12): set apart

concession (12): something that is yielded or granted

Questions About the Writer's Craft (p. 559)

1. A general thread throughout Porter's essay is that he expects more from a country as great as the U.S.; this sentiment works to soften the blow of the criticism he goes on to deliver. The first instance in which Porter employs Rogerian strategy is in the opening words of the essay, "For America's supporters"; he implicitly includes himself in that sympathetic group. This friendly gesture establishes common ground between Porter and those he's about to criticize. Porter concludes the essay in similar fashion; he compliments the U.S. in that it "stands for liberty and spends a good deal of time distinguishing itself . . . on those grounds" (12), and he refers to Americans' "very understandable fears" (13). This is to reiterate his general sympathy for the U.S. despite having some serious criticisms of it.

    Another aspect of Rogerian strategy Porter employs is his citation of "pro-torture" American commentators, such as Jonathan Alter and Jay Winick (3, 4). In acknowledging these opposing points of view, Porter helps his readers understand the larger context of the debate into which he's entering, while also using some points of view as a springboard for his own. He takes Winick's example of Abdul Hakim Murad and spins off a couple of ironic rhetorical questions about anything being justified in order to avert American deaths. Porter then cites a commentary in the *New York Times* positing that "the U.S. is still a long way off using torture" (6), only to then refute that claim by arguing that given the American tolerance of the death penalty, torture is not far off. Similarly, he plays devil's advocate in paragraph 10 in saying that if the U.S. government authorizes political assassinations, then torture, which can "perversely" be argued as less cruel, is not far behind. In ironically adopting this alternate point of view, Porter ultimately undermines it. Finally, Porter optimistically observes that some good that comes out of the "pro-torture" proposals is that at least this grave issue is being discussed in a public forum (12). After allowing for this benefit, however, he asserts his strong belief that more commentators need to declare the injustice of torture in this same public forum.

2. Porter's tone fluctuates throughout the selection. For much of the essay, he presents objective- and neutral-sounding logic regarding the precedents for torture being used by the U.S. government. In some places, however, he comes across as impassioned and subjective, such as in the phrases "blind cohesion" (1), "the institutions . . . which failed the people so drastically" (1), "fiercely uncritical mood" (3), and, most dramatically, in the final sentence of paragraph 12: "Torture is an absolute evil and there can be no allowances, especially in a country which stands for liberty and spends a good deal of time distinguishing itself . . . on those grounds." Apart from his overall objectiveness and occasional subjective outbursts, Porter adopts still another tone in a few instances: a condescending, patronizing manner, particularly

when discussing the U.S. government and populace. In paragraph 2, he begins, "If these things were discussed as vigorously [in the U.S.] as they are here [in England] . . ." (2) with at least a hint of superiority in his tone. And later in the same paragraph, he becomes clearly insulting when he asserts that the U.S. President "does seem to betray a pretty basic intellect—even to Americans" (2).

3. Porter implies differences in the intellect and demand for public discussion of government policies that characterizes each nation. In paragraph 2, he begins, "If these things were discussed as vigorously [in the U.S.] as they are here [in England] . . ." (2), suggesting that there is a lack of serious discussion of important policies in the U.S. when compared with England. Later in the same paragraph, he pulls no punches when he asserts that the U.S. President "does seem to betray a pretty basic intellect—even to Americans" (2), attacking not only the intellect of the President, but of the general populace as well. Though he doesn't explicitly mention England here, one might infer he does not regard his native country with the same condescension. And in paragraph 6, Porter subtly contrasts the two nations—again, to England's benefit, but students may not necessarily be aware of it: He decries the barbarity of the death penalty, which is legal in the U.S. but *not* in England.

    These contrasts Porter draws between England and the U.S. support his thesis: that Americans and their government need to forthrightly address the fearsome potential of using torture in the name of national security. Porter's implicit claim that such a state of affairs would be unacceptable in England enhances the persuasive force of his argument.

4. Porter first makes use of examples in paragraphs 3 and 4, when he cites commentators who have been arguing that torture may be warranted. These examples serve to establish context for Porter's opposing argument. The example of Abdul Hakim Murad in paragraphs 4 and 5 serves a different function; it is part of Porter's use of Rogerian strategy to understand the rationale of the opposition. He even poses some compelling rhetorical questions based on this example. Interestingly, Porter never fully refutes the power of this example, but rather switches gears to make an analogy between capital punishment and torture. In paragraph 6, he cites statistics to illustrate the frequency of executions in the U.S. and discusses the fact that only the U.S. and Somalia refused to sign a particular UN anti-execution convention. These facts work to illustrate Porter's idea that execution is a barbarous practice which makes the U.S. more likely to indulge in torture. In paragraphs 8 and 9, Porter discusses how the U.S. already is guilty of supporting regimes that "routinely practice torture" elsewhere in the world. The appalling examples he cites further illustrate his point that the U.S. is on the verge of using torture on its own soil, a possibility that the public needs to vehemently oppose.

RACISM HAS ITS PRIVILEGES

Roger Wilkins

Questions for Close Reading (p. 568)

1. Wilkins states his thesis most directly in paragraph 6: "Affirmative action has done wonderful things for the United States by enlarging opportunity and developing and utilizing a far broader array of the skills available in the American population than in the past. It has not outlived its usefulness." Wilkins feels it is necessary to continue affirmative action programs because "minorities and women are still disadvantaged in our highly competitive society and that affirmative action is absolutely necessary

to level the playing field" (13). He restates his thesis in the final paragraph: "If we want to continue making things better in this society, we'd better figure out ways to protect and defend affirmative action. . . ."

2. Wilkins defines *affirmative action* in paragraphs 4 and 5 as an "attempt to enlarge opportunity for *everybody*" by requiring "institutions to develop [hiring] plans enabling them to go beyond business as usual and search for qualified people in places where they did not ordinarily conduct their searches or their business." Affirmative action programs, according to Wilkins, "require . . . proof that there has been a good-faith attempt to follow the plan and numerical guidelines against which to judge the sincerity and the success of the effort." Otherwise, institutions will simply say they looked for qualified minority applicants but couldn't find any, "and then go out and hire the white man they wanted to hire in the first place" (5).

3. White people believe that the United States is superior to other countries and that Americans are superior as well; many of them think of the U.S. as a land of opportunity where people are rewarded for their abilities. Some whites even see America as a white country, one in which any problems that do exist were caused by Blacks (10). In addition, Wilkins quotes James Baldwin's observation that many whites still believe in certain myths about their history—that Americans are descended from freedom-loving heroes; that Americans are undefeated in battle; that Americans have always been heroic, honorable people who have dealt fairly with other cultures—myths that Black people, who "remember America differently," simply do not subscribe to (11–12). Believing in these myths blinds whites to the need for affirmative action. Finally, the implementation of affirmative action has given rise to a new "myth": that white males are now the victims of reverse discrimination (23, 25).

4. According to Wilkins, affirmative action benefits Americans in a number of ways. It increases the pool of qualified workers by finding such people in new and unexpected places (5); it takes greater advantage of the skills available in the American workplace by opening up the numbers and kinds of positions minority workers can compete to fill (6); it educates the white majority about the truth of racism in America (14, 20, 22, 25, 27–30); it helps America live up to its principles and actually make some of the "myths" about America come true (27–31).

5. *initiative* (1): question on a ballot requiring public approval by means of a majority vote
    adherence (1): sticking to, conforming to
    purported (2): pretended
    permutations (6): varieties
    bastardization (6): distortion
    inextricably (8): in a manner that is difficult to untangle
    disparate (9): separate
    invincible (11): unconquerable
    obliterate (15): blot out
    meritocratic (24): describing a society in which citizens are rewarded on the basis of their merit (talent; skills)
    perpetuates (25): prolongs
    vilify (32): speak evil of
    skew (33): tilt

Questions About the Writer's Craft (p. 568)

1. Wilkins acknowledges the views of the opponents of affirmative action throughout his argument. One opposing view he cites is the "reverse discrimination" argument

(2): "angry white men" insist that affirmative action has "stacked the deck against them." Wilkins quotes Washington Post columnist Richard Cohen's statement that "he had once missed out on a job . . . because [the prospective employer] 'needed a woman'" (2). This argument resurfaces later in the essay, when Wilkins describes an issue of *U.S. News & World Report* whose cover and lead story asked, "Does affirmative action mean NO WHITE MEN NEED APPLY?" (23) A second opposing view is Newt Gingrich's insistence that African Americans do not deserve special treatment because they were not the only victims of discrimination; in fact, Gingrich says that "virtually every American" has been so victimized (15). A third argument against affirmative action that Wilkins cites is the pre-1950 theory that African Americans did not deserve equal treatment because they were inferior (19); the current version of this argument is that the behavior of many Black people, specifically poor Black people, is inferior (19–20). A fourth argument Wilkins acknowledges states that since Blacks and other minorities are "victims," affirmative action is "a kind of zero-sum game in which only the 'victims' benefit" (22). Finally, by quoting Thomas Jefferson's 18th-century views on beauty, Wilkins acknowledges the most vicious opposing view of them all: "that skin color is destiny and that whiteness is to be revered" (32).

Wilkins's attitude towards these opposing views is one of vigorous disagreement, even contempt. He answers Richard Cohen's story with the story of his own appointment to an endowed chair at George Mason University, putting the lie to a white candidate's charge of "reverse discrimination"—said candidate having been eliminated early in the competition (3). Later, Wilkins asserts that "white men still control virtually everything in America" (25), countering the *U.S. News & World Report* argument. Gingrich's contention is disproved by statistics: "blacks have been on this North American continent for 375 years and . . . for 245 the country permitted slavery" (16). The plight of poor Blacks is the result of a "straight line of oppression" beginning with slavery (20); many poor Blacks have been "brutalized by our culture"—forced to live in "isolated pockets of urban poverty," weakened by crack cocaine, afflicted with double-digit unemployment rates even for those looking for work (20), and being repeatedly shown as dangerous or unqualified by politicians and the media (22). Wilkins's story of his student in paragraphs 27–30 shows that affirmative action can benefit white males as well. Finally, Wilkins argues that any society that agrees with Jefferson "abandons its soul and its economic strength, and will remain mired in ugliness and moral squalor because so many people are excluded from the possibility of decent lives" (32).

Wilkins considers all of these opposing viewpoints racist, "myths," or "denials"—and even compares the denials to addictions to drugs, alcohol, and gambling (18). The vehemence with which he denounces the opposition strongly reinforces his thesis.

2. The anecdote establishes Wilkins's *ethos* by narrating his firsthand experience with both affirmative action and racism. It reveals that he is Black; that he is a highly competent professional; that he won his prestigious position at George Mason University, at least in part, through affirmative action (Mason "was under a court order to desegregate"—presumably this is why he was encouraged to apply); and that later a white candidate stated that he had lost the job to an "unqualified black," using the "reverse discrimination" myth that Wilkins will later cite as one of the forms of denial practiced by the opponents of affirmative action. Wilkins's career, then, serves as a paradigm of the process he advocates. The fact that the white historian lied about his chances for the job—he had "not even passed the first threshold" in the application and review process—further underscores Wilkins's point that the

supporters of affirmative action must find ways to protect and defend it against "the confused, the frightened, the manipulators, and, yes, the liars" in all professions.

3. Paragraphs 8–13 compare and contrast whites' and Blacks' perceptions and experiences of life in America, both past and present. Wilkins states that there are some areas for example, "rooting for the local football team"—where Blacks and whites share experiences and views; however, other arenas—work, school, the affirmative action debate, even a knowledge of their own history—reveal vastly differing attitudes and opportunities for the two races. In paragraph 14, Wilkins uses an analogy to compare racism and the Mississippi River, pointing out that they share several attributes: both carry cargo (the assault on affirmative action "flows on a river of racism"), both are broad and powerful, both can be violent and deadly, and both are American. But, Wilkins points out, while no sane person denies the Mississippi exists, millions of Americans deny the existence of racism (14). Wilkins then contrasts the forms of "denial" practiced by opponents of affirmative action with the realities of racism in America (14–17, 19–20, 22–30). Finally, Wilkins draws upon other analogies in paragraph 18 when he likens racism to the denials accompanying other addictions—to alcohol, drugs, and gambling. All these comparisons-contrasts help Wilkins establish his thesis firmly in the minds of his readers: Affirmative action is still desperately needed in this country, precisely because so many people either deny or are unaware of the insidious persistence of racism.

4. Feeling passionate about his subject, Wilkins at times draws upon highly emotional language. Examples of loaded words include "nightriding terrorists" (16), "slough" (17), "lying" (17), "addictions" (18), "cultivated ignorance" (20), "slammed" (20), "deadly" (20), "whiners" (27), and "manipulators and . . . liars" (30). Wilkins may be assuming that most readers would not share his views and is trying to shock—or shame—them into seeing things his way. Yet Wilkins doesn't bombard readers with an unrelieved stream of charged language. (That would turn off most readers.) Overall, he presents his case in a well-reasoned, moderate fashion, which doesn't risk alienating his audience.

AFFIRMATIVE ACTION: THE PRICE OF PREFERENCE

Shelby Steele

Questions for Close Reading (p. 575)

1. Steele states his main idea at the end of paragraph 4: "But after 20 years of implementation I think that affirmative action has shown itself to be more bad than good and that blacks . . . now stand to lose more from it than they gain." The rest of the essay shows in what ways affirmative action deprives African Americans of real, lasting power.

2. Steele tells us that his own (presumably middle-class) children, who will be applying to college in a few years, have never experienced racial discrimination of the sort that would keep them from achieving a goal (1); yet they have been told that if they state on college applications that they are Black, they will receive preferential treatment (1). Because Steele feels that affirmative action harms Black people more than it helps them, both demoralizing them (9) and forcing them to see themselves as victims (11), he feels that having his children declare their race when applying to college would be "a Faustian bargain"—i.e., similar to selling one's soul to the

devil. He goes on to say that "the unkindest cut is to bestow on children like my own an undeserved advantage while neglecting the development of those disadvantaged children in the poorer sections of my city . . ." (14). Instead of preferential treatment based on race, Steele says, "Give my children fairness" and give less advantaged minority children better education and financial assistance (14).

3. According to Steele, under affirmative action, Blacks are given preferential treatment based on "an implied inferiority" resulting from centuries of deprivation. Steele feels that any hint of inferiority is demoralizing because of the self-doubt it triggers (9), the result of the Black person's awareness of "a mindless . . . reflex that responds to the color black with negative stereotypes" (10). Eventually, this self-doubt can become an unrecognized preoccupation that undermines a Black person's ability to perform well at the job that affirmative action has provided (10). Affirmative action, in Steele's opinion, also leads to a victim mentality among Blacks (11–12) and an illusion of entitlement (13).

4. Steele would prefer social policies whose goals were as follows: first, educational and economic development of disadvantaged people of any race, and second, the disappearance of racial, ethnic, and gender discrimination from our society (14). Even with affirmative action, fewer Black high school graduates are entering college, and more Black males are in prison than in college (14). What is wrong with affirmative action, Steele concludes, is that both Blacks and whites focused more on its goals than on the means to the goals. Preferential treatment for minorities alone will not do the job.

5. *malevolence* (1): evil
    sanctimoniously (2): in a holier-than-thou manner
    meagerest (2): smallest
    recompense (2): repayment
    residual (2): leftover
    symmetry (3) evenness
    diversity (5): all-inclusiveness, variety
    absolution (6): release from guilt
    mandates (6): orders
    eradicate (8): get rid of
    demoralization (9): loss of self-confidence
    myriad (9): many
    ineptness (10): lack of ability
    debilitating (10): weakening
    reparation (13): repayment
    residues (13): remaining parts

Questions About the Writer's Craft (p. 576)

1. Steele uses the first refutation strategy. He cites opposing viewpoints in paragraphs 2 and 3 (affirmative action is compensation for centuries of oppression; affirmative action is moral in intent) and refutes them in paragraphs 8–13 (despite its good intentions, affirmative action has deleterious psychological effects on Black people; suffering cannot be compensated). The evidence Steele presents is primarily anecdotal, consisting of personal experience—for example, "talking with affirmative-action administrators and with Blacks and whites in general" (5), along with the specific anecdotes in paragraphs 12 and 13—and generalizations about large historical movements (6–8), rather than statistics, studies, etc. The closest he comes to statistical evidence is his statement that "A smaller percentage of Black high school graduates go to college today than 15 years ago; more black males are in

prison, jail or in some other way under the control of the criminal-justice system than in college. This despite racial preferences" (14). Some readers may find the support thin.

2. By mentioning his children in the opening paragraph, Steele establishes his *ethos* and also reveals his personal stake in the affirmative-action debate. Learning that Steele's children are nearly of college age, the reader might assume that Steele would be delighted to use any strategy that would help them get into a good college. By rejecting affirmative action for his own children, Steele immediately focuses the reader's attention on its possible hazards for *everybody's* children.

3. Steele prefaces his statements with "I think" or "I believe" in paragraphs 1, 4, 5, 6, 8 ("I don't think"), 9, 10, 11, 13, and 14. Steele's reliance on "I think" has several effects. It creates goodwill by not sounding too authoritarian or judgmental; it clearly labels the views in the essay as Steele's personal views; finally, it suggests that he assumes a wavering audience and is depending on *ethos* and *logos*, rather than *pathos*, to prove his points.

4. The two words Steele repeats—each appears three times in the paragraph—are *inferiority* and *fact*. Steele uses repetition to stress the point that affirmative action only *seems* to put Blacks in a better position; in reality, affirmative action reinforces the belief that Black people's status (and, by extension, their abilities) are lower than those of whites. Inferiority is the reality underlying the appearance of preference; this is the fact that Steele wants us to realize.

COMBINING
THE PATTERNS

The brief discussions which follow provide insight into the dominant or organizing patterns of development and the blend of patterns in the essays in this section.

PROFESSIONS FOR WOMEN (p. 594)

Virginia Woolf

Woolf's speech to the Women's Service League relies primarily upon narrative to convey that a woman must overcome two obstacles before she can devote herself to her profession, whether it be writing or some other work. Woolf launches her narrative with little hint of where she is leading; her thesis is revealed only gradually as she recounts the narrative of her beginnings as a writer and the two inner struggles she endured in order to be a success. One struggle is narrated as a battle against "the Angel in the House," the tendency to fulfill the traditional role of woman as supporter, flatterer, and caretaker of men. The second is recounted as the woman writer's discovery of an explosive and hidden subject: the passions and truth of the body. The narrative format allows Woolf to deliver her experiences in a dramatic, even electrifying way, rather than discursively or analytically. Within the narrative, Woolf makes use of description in paragraph 3, where she helps us to understand what the "Angel in the House" represents by describing her demeanor and behavior, and in paragraph 5, where she describes the writer as a fisherman. Also within the narrative, Woolf conveys the process by which a person might begin as a writer (paragraph 2) and succeed in writing novels (paragraph 5: "He [the novelist] has to induce in himself a state of perpetual lethargy . . . ").

Near the end of the essay, Woolf compares her professional experiences to those of the women in the audience, suggesting that although the listeners are not writers, their way is obstructed by inner "phantoms and obstacles" like her own (7). If women writers, she notes, occupied in "the freest of professions for women," must tussle with "ghosts," "prejudices," and "rocks," then "how is it in the new professions which you [the listeners] are now for the first time entering?"

WHERE DO WE GO FROM HERE:
COMMUNITY OR CHAOS? (p. 599)

Martin Luther King, Jr.

King argues eloquently for a change in the mindset of world leaders and its citizens, a change away from militarism as the major means of problem-solving to the use of peaceful methods of conflict resolution. He supports his argument largely with reasoning, but also relies upon cause-effect, exemplification, definition and comparison to examine and validate his viewpoint. The thesis is introduced in the first sentence of the essay and supported by invoking the increasing military technology that dominates the international scene. In paragraph 2, King shows that there is no valid cause for international squabbling over resources, since modern science assures enough resources and transportation of them to support all nations.

King then compares the words and deeds of "large power blocs," finding that they often promote peace verbally but indulge in arms stockpiling and development all the while (paragraph 4). He cites historical examples of conquerors who killed in the name of peace (5), and then uses a contemporary war—Vietnam—to deplore the same tendencies in our nations today (6), before restating the need to reconcile the gap between our words and deeds. In cautioning that we "read the warning on history's signposts," he again implies that the effect of our military buildup will be disastrous. In paragraph 8, King asserts that not only is peace the desired effect or result of international dealings, but it is the "means," or cause, of that achievement. "We must pursue peaceful ends through peaceful means." Paragraph 9 continues the argument that the effects of war, particularly of modern war, are too calamitous to entertain. Paragraph 10 begins with a plea for the study of peace, implying the positive effects this will have on our world community, and paragraph 11 discusses the negative "ancient habits" that have caused violence in the past. Paragraph 12 provides a definition of non-violence, differentiating it from the mere absence of violence. In moving towards conclusion, King argues in paragraph 13 that only "a mental and spiritual re-evaluation" will bring about the effects he seeks, "a new world" where peace reigns. He uses the example of Ulysses and the Siren to explain further what he means by affirming peace (14), and in the final paragraph, he closes his argument with the contrast of "world power struggle" with what he terms "a peace race." Throughout the essay, he uses many persuasive tactics, ranging from eloquently balanced phrasing and repeated phrases (2, 3, 4, 6, 14, and others), to the use of descriptive detail, metaphor, and highly connotative words (5, 6, 14).

THE WORLD HOUSE (p. 603)

Martin Luther King, Jr.

In "The World House," Martin Luther King, Jr., argues that the people of the world must learn to live together and ensure justice and freedom for all people everywhere. In support of this position, strands from numerous patterns of development interlock, creating a complex texture of imagery, logical reasoning, and eloquence. In supporting his assertion that humans now live in "a world house," he contrasts the modern world of speed and technology to the recent past (3–4). Within this contrast, he uses several examples (3) and much descriptive detail (4). The technology he invokes is identified as the cause of the interrelatedness that underlies the "world house" (4). He compares our present to the future effects likely to result from continued scientific research (5), again using descriptive details. In paragraph 6, he points out that the revolution in technology parallels, that is, is similar to the revolution of the spirit that is also occurring throughout the world; and in 7, he uses descriptive imagery to present the process of liberation he sees spreading worldwide. The cause of this clamor for freedom is identified in paragraph 8: the inevitable yearning of the downtrodden for release. He uses the metaphor of "chapters" in the "continuing story" of humans' struggle to be free, citing the Moses story in the Bible and the civil rights struggle in the U.S. as only two examples of the liberatory impulse. He argues then that some people always ignore or deny liberation, using as an example Rip Van Winkle, who slept through the American Revolution (9–10). He returns to comparison-contrast in paragraphs 11–15, indicating through analysis, imagery and quotation that our technological progress has not been matched by spiritual progress, that our external and internal realms are out of sync. At the end of 15 through 16, he returns to cause-effect, predicting that if we "minimize the internal of our lives and maximize the external, we sign the warrant for our own day of doom."

THE SANTA ANA (p. 607)

Joan Didion

In this essay, Didion blends several patterns to achieve two distinct ends: a definition of the Santa Ana phenomenon and a causal analysis of its impact on the people and things that lie in its path. The thesis, that "the violence and the unpredictability of the Santa Ana affect the quality of life in Los Angeles" (6), is not stated until the final paragraph, but Didion develops this idea over the course of the essay as she explains what the Santa Ana is and how it influences atmosphere and behavior. In the opening paragraph, she describes the "unnatural stillness" of her surroundings as a Santa Ana approaches, saying that the Los Angeles air is charged with tension and unease (1). At this point, she provides an initial definition of the Santa Ana as "a hot wind from the northeast . . . drying the hills and the nerves to a flash point" and begins to demonstrate some of its effects. She provides a string of brief examples illustrating that everyone feels its onset without explicitly knowing of its arrival: the baby frets, the maid sulks, Didion, herself, has a worthless argument, then lies down, "given over to whatever is in the air." A personal anecdote structures the second paragraph, as Didion recalls Santa Ana lore and her first encounters with Santa Ana-related behaviors. Having observed and felt the effects of the hot wind, Didion says she can empathize with those Indians who, as folklore had it, "would throw themselves into the sea when the bad wind blew" (2).

She goes on to describe in vivid detail the ominous tranquillity of her Pacific coastal surroundings during a Santa Ana, which results in bizarre, off-kilter human behavior, such as that of her neighbors who would either remain indoors with the lights out or roam the place with a machete, claiming to have heard a trespasser or a rattlesnake. Didion continues exemplifying the Santa Ana's impact in the third paragraph, where she quotes Raymond Chandler's observations about the hot wind's idiosyncratic effects on people. For the remainder of the paragraph, Didion provides scientific evidence to bear out the folk wisdom about the Santa Ana. Using definition and division-classification strategies, Didion identifies the Santa Ana in meteorological terms as being of the *foehn* category of winds, which are known to have unpleasant and inevitable consequences wherever they occur. She goes on to provide examples of the scientifically-observed effects around the world of these "persistent malevolent winds" (3). Paragraph 3 ends with further scientific definition of the Santa Ana and its electromagnetic characteristics, which Didion suggests explain this wind's "mechanistic," negative impact on human beings.

In paragraph 4, Didion draws a brief contrast between the misconception about California weather as "numbingly bland" and the reality of its "violent extremes" caused in part by the Santa Ana. Here Didion goes on to offer data demonstrating the harrowing, fiery aftermath of four different Santa Ana periods. This presentation of factual evidence continues through paragraph 5, where she chronicles in numeric detail the havoc wreaked in 1957 by the longest running Santa Ana in recent history. And paragraph 6, Didion piles on further examples of the destructive toll (human and environmental) taken by this ostensibly harmless, but ultimately malignant phenomenon. In a final attempt to convey the Santa Ana's overwhelming influence on the psyche of Southern Californians, Didion employs a comparison: just as the permanence of New England life is tied to winter's reliability, the impermanence of Los Angeles life results from the Santa Ana's unpredictability. Didion forcefully concludes her analysis by saying that the Santa Ana's effects demonstrate "how close to the edge we are" (6).

MARRYING ABSURD (p. 610)

Joan Didion

The title of "Marrying Absurd" conveys its thesis, which is stated at the beginning of paragraph 2: "What people who get married in Las Vegas actually do expect . . . strikes one as a curious and self-contradictory business." In other words, rapid Las Vegas weddings are absurd. They're incongruous, too quick—both comical and grotesque, idealistic and clichéd. Blending different patterns of development, Joan Didion shows the absurdity and sadness of these makeshift marriages. While pink champagne bubbles float at their surface, an undercurrent of urgency and desperation flows below.

In paragraph 1, Didion immediately launches into the process by which couples marry in Las Vegas. The bride and groom attest either that they have parental permission to marry or that they're old enough to marry without it. Someone pays $5 or $15 for a marriage license. That's it. Absurdly brief. Hardly a process at all.

Didion then moves into contrast for the rest of paragraph 1. Unlike marriages in all other states, Nevada marriages require no blood test or waiting period. Primarily through description, Didion juxtaposes the natural and artificial, traditional and offbeat, bringing out the incongruities that make Las Vegas marriages fragile and absurd. Across the silent desert, electric signs shout advertisements for wedding services. From a flat highway, people view signs eighty feet tall. Las Vegas is a city of contradictions: call girls and brides. Words signify their opposite: a crassly mercenary chapel advertises "sincere and dignified" weddings; a wedding organist plays "When I Fall in Love, It Will Be Forever" in a state as well-known for quickie divorces as quickie weddings. Paper windows mimic stained glass. A bride wears an orange mini-dress rather than a white floor-length gown. The father of a bride jokes about wedding-night loss of virginity, but his daughter is visibly pregnant. Already a mother, another bride drunkenly attempts to carry out motherly duties: "I gotta get the kids. I gotta pick up the sitter."

Didion also uses examples to convey the absurdity of Las Vegas weddings, especially their ludicrous rapidity. She includes a couple of brief narrative anecdotes in paragraphs 4 and 5 to illustrate the "curious, self-contradictory business" (2) of Vegas weddings. A battery of other examples serve the same purpose. On August 26, 1965, she tells us, 171 couples married in Las Vegas. A justice of the peace who performed 67 of the ceremonies reached a speed of three minutes per wedding (1). Advertisements, too, illustrate speed. Their wording is abbreviated: "Witnesses Available," "Ample Parking" (3). Couples quickly move from motel, to courthouse, to chapel, and back: "Free Transportation from Your Motel to Courthouse to Chapel and Return to Motel." The honeymoon occurs in the same place as the wedding ("Honeymoon Accommodations" a sign advertises). Wedding organists play "only a few bars" of the traditional wedding march (4). The sign indicating a wedding in progress states, "One moment please."

"One moment" in which to declare a potentially lifelong commitment? Not good enough, Didion indicates. And herein lies Didion's implied causal analysis: Giving heavy commitments lightweight treatment—the hallmark of Vegas-style weddings—leaves them vulnerable to breakage.